HOW TO UNLEASH EMAIL MARKETING *with* MAILCHIMP

Going from contacts to repeat customers without spending the big bucks

By
TRAVIS L. HOLT

Copyright © 2017 H-Impact LLC, All Rights Reserved.

How to Unleash Email Marketing with MailChimp

Published by:
H-Impact LLC
PO Box 620696
Charlotte, NC 28262

www.h-impact.com

Copyright © 2017 H-Impact LLC, All Rights Reserved.

ISBN-13: 978-0-9995315-0-1

ISBN-10: 0-9995315-0-6

Library of Congress Control Number: 2017919787

No part of this publication may be reproduced in any form without the express written consent by the publisher or author.

With the exception of the referenced publisher, example organizations or companies should be implied as fictitious. Other fictitious example content includes events, places, logos, e-mail addresses, products, domain names, and people.

Limitation of Liability/Disclaimer of Warranty: This publication expresses the author's opinions and views. The publication is made available to you on an "as-is" basis. The publisher and author make no warranties, representations, or conditions of any kind, express, statutory or implied as to the accuracy, integrity, completeness, quality, legality, and usefulness of the publication.

In no case shall the publisher or author or any affiliate entity responsible for drafting this publication be liable for any direct, indirect, incidental, punitive, special, or consequential damages arising from or related to the use of this publication's content or of any of any of the products or services referred to, including, but not limited to, any errors or omissions in any content, or any loss or damage of any kind incurred as a result of the use of this publication's content if advised of the possibility of such damages.

What Readers Say

"Impact Orthopedics is a cutting edge orthotic and prosthetic practice that prides itself in effectively communicating with patients and healthcare providers. The **How to Unleash Email Marketing with MailChimp** book by Travis Holt and published by H-Impact was easy to follow and has helped my office gain more business by showing us how to get our message out to key people. As a result of purchasing the book and taking the course, my practice is able to quickly and easily communicate the good news about Impact Orthopedics and upcoming events to hundreds of patients, therapists, nurses, and physicians. The book has also improved our ability to reach potential patients and referral sources."
— **Rondell Richardson**, Impact Orthopedics, Co-Owner and Clinical Director

"In the book **How to Unleash Email Marketing with MailChimp**, the author Travis Holt gives a detailed, hands-on training for the development of a marketing and analytics tool which every business should have. The book was enlightening. The processes, as taught, demonstrate an effective means to increase the scale of marketing efforts- with minimal headache! MailChimp offers an array of what I think of as 'tethers' to social networking platforms, by connecting to LinkedIn, Facebook, etc. ...Monies once spent in mailings, labor, and archaic data collection, have given way to a streamlined, progressive, and well implemented strategy based upon real time data. Moreover, the ability to tailor the email campaigns is crucial for maximizing results. This is truly bang for the buck marketing. After all, time is money. Thanks to the lessons in **How to Unleash Email Marketing with MailChimp,** we are welcomed to the digital age."
—**Rico Phronebarger**, Impact Orthopedics, Co-Owner/Director of Technical Services

"Qunique Creations is a pioneer in the new wave of apparel companies. We design to fit your style. Staying connected with our customers is very important. Over the years we've collected plenty of business cards by networking within the community. We were in need of a more efficient and effective process to communicate with our customers and vendors. Purchasing the **How to Unleash Email Marketing with Mailchimp** book by H-Impact's Travis Holt was the easiest and best thing we have done to advance our advertising. With just a few clicks of a mouse I can compile a list to send an email with our newest product, promotions and offer discounts."

—**Quantella Victor**, Qunique Creations, Founder and CEO

"As the owner of a budding cake design company, I quickly discovered it was hard to reach clients to let them know what we had to offer. Our business was just word of mouth and referrals. Purchasing the **How to Unleash Email Marketing with MailChimp** book by H-Impact, has improved our ability to reach new and potential customers. As a novice in email marketing, I thought the book was very easy to follow. This book is now helping me grow my business with cutting edge marketing techniques."

—**Danette Yard**, Romeo's Delights, Owner and Lead Cake Designer

Dedication

To **Alphonso Holt, Jr**, my father who spent his life being the example of a man of many amazing God-given talents of which countless respected and were inspired by while having limited resources in his younger life, overcame impossible odds to provide a world of opportunity for my mother, brother and I.

To **Ruby N. Holt**, my mother and phenomenal woman with an unmatched creative talent and spirit who consistently exemplifies all the qualities of a professor of unconditional love. Mom, you poured into our family your unbelievable care, faith, trust, and love that is directly responsible for us positively impacting and inspiring others, just as you inspired us.

About the Author

Travis L. Holt graduated from the University of North Carolina at Charlotte with a degree in Economics. After college, Travis began his career in the banking industry where he worked as a Performance Analyst & Technical Analyst for the bank's sales and service teams. After obtaining programming certifications using Microsoft VB, C# and ASP.NET, he transitioned from the business area into the IT Department.

In 2004, Travis started H-Impact with Dr. Howard L. Beatty – Technology Professional, close friend and former college roommate. He left the bank in 2005 and has been working in a full-time capacity as H-Impact's CEO. Travis is a big advocate of education and loves to share his knowledge and experiences to help others learn and develop.

Travis currently resides in Charlotte, North Carolina where he strives each day to live out H-Impact's mission by using technology and education as vehicles of advancement for students and professionals of all industries. With the help of his team, he runs H-Impact and frequently consults and conducts trainings for various organizations and companies.

Courses by the Author

Students can register for our **How to Unleash Email Marketing with MailChimp** course taught by the author Travis L. Holt, as well as other courses by creating a Free account and registering on our site.

www.h-impact.com/all-upcoming-events

Articles by the Author

Visit H-Impact today to read articles by Travis L. Holt on topics like Employment, Business, and Healthcare.

www.h-impact.com/article-search

Acknowledgements

As the Co-Founder and CEO of H-Impact, I, Travis L. Holt, would be remiss if I didn't acknowledge the overwhelming amount of support that we have received for this project, as well as H-Impact as a whole. I am so grateful for the individuals that have contributed their expertise directly or indirectly to ensure this book has been delivered to completion in the form in which you are reading. As a token of my appreciation, I have listed a few of our greatest supporters along with their contributions below:

Ruby N. Holt – Mom, thank you for every ounce of energy you and my father exhausted to get me to be the man I am today. As you invested your time and energy in the things you felt would lead to success for my brother and I, but without 100% certainty, I hope that the completion of this work and future works help to bring full circle the excellent choices you made which highlights the importance of your uniquely irreplaceable contributions as my loving mother. Without you in my life and the unconditional love and support you've provided, none of this would be possible. Thank you for everything.

Howard and Angela Beatty – Dr. Howard L. Beatty, without you, H-Impact would not exist. Many years before helping me to form this company, we met on the campus of UNC-Charlotte to form something much more significant – a life time brotherhood. Thank you for always thinking outside the box and constantly challenging me to think bigger and better. Angela, your support as Howard's loving wife, mother of three, while possessing your own entrepreneurial spirit, has been a blessing to Howard and consequentially to me. He could not have married a more selfless and beautiful person

from the inside out. Thank you for your support. It has not gone without notice and is very much appreciated.

Andrew and Tammie Holt – Drew, it is impossible for me to thank you for all the support you have provided me through the years by just simply being my older and only brother. The many challenges that I would've had to face alone, I didn't have to because you had been there and done that and was always ready and available to help me along the way. As a result, your direct and indirect guidance and support have ultimately allowed me to become the business owner I am today. It is because of your introduction to your dear and close friend, Howard L. Beatty, Jr, the future Co-Founder of H-Impact on the campus of UNC-Charlotte, that H-Impact was even established. From the platform H-Impact has provided, I have been able to take on new and exciting projects and services like providing IT consulting to businesses, performing online or instructor led training, writing and publishing articles, and writing and publishing this book. Tammie, as my sister-n-law, you have been an inspiration in your continuous ascent in the corporate world, while being a wonderful mother to my niece and nephew. Your passion around education and reading has been an inspiration over the years and played a huge part in my decision to write this book. You are a gem to the family and I am blessed to have you in my life. Thank you both for all you have done to support H-Impact and all we have to offer.

Alina L. Miller – After acquiring multiple generations of Microsoft Master's certifications, performing essential inner office functions including countless online video training tutorials, data analysis, business analysis, programming, web design, marketing, brand management and more…we end up here – providing marketing materials to show others how to effectively get their word out just as we did for H-Impact. You are a blessing to me, my family and H-Impact and I whole heartedly appreciate the support you've provided to get us to where we are today. Thank you for playing a critical role in my life which has contributed greatly to the success of this project and H-Impact.

Travis and Sheleea Leonard – Trav, I can't count the number of times I have done things in the name of H-Impact that needed to go out to the public and after little to no communication with you, I look around, and there you are, lock and step already informing our social media base, email subscribers, colleagues, family and friends about what *we* just did. You're "I've got your back" mentality, beyond our brotherhood, is a God send and I cannot thank you enough for it. The Microsoft certifications you've acquired, online video tutorials you've recorded, and articles you've written make your contribution to the success of this organization irreplaceable. Thank you for all you do and have done to make this project and all projects possible. Sheleea, our days date back to your undergraduate days in college as Travis and I traveled to visit you -his future wife. Through the years you two have created a beautiful bond, family, and life together. As a result of enhancing Travis's life, you also made mine better. My conversations with you as a passionate educator have helped me to understand how technology has become instrumental in the learning process. This book which focuses on an online web application can be used as a technical training guide, and in essence is a by-product of those conversations. Thank you for being the amazing wife you are to Travis, being a model mother and standout educator, while sharing your knowledge to inspire training enthusiasts such as myself.

Bryan A. Withers – Brother Bryan, together as children we explored the world as it was presented to us. Now that we are older, we now are able to shape the world we see. Thank you for standing in the gap through the years and encouraging me throughout it all, to continue to reach for the vision God put in my heart. Without the deep discussions around family, athletics, education, and life as a whole, this project would be missing a critical part about what even made it possible in the first place. Your support has been instrumental to this project's success and the success of H-Impact and for that I simply say, *"Thank you"*.

Ervin L. Fortune – From preschool to grade school into college and beyond, you have been a brother to me like no other. In our early years we teamed up to slay all the beasts of the world from English journals to Term Papers, from the wrestling mat to the football field, from Geometry Proofs to Physics Labs, from SAT's to College Applications and from College Orientation to College Graduation. Facing the world together lock and step has created the bond we have today that is responsible for the unspoken support and admiration we have for one another regardless of what we face. Thank you for continuously supporting me, my family, H-Impact and particularly this project. Along with your preliminary reviews and drafts of this book, it is those fundamental lessons we learned together early in our lives in English and computer courses that has allowed this project to even be possible.

Tim Kenny – Based on my experience and our faith, I truly believe, that certain people are put in our lives in order to help each other accomplish something that could not

have been possible without the collaboration of individuals with their own unique backgrounds and talents. Whether it is to get through a challenging time or accomplish something that is unimaginable, we are destined to encounter individuals that if allowed can change our lives forever. Tim, you are one of those persons to me. We started on the same day years ago at an organization that saves lives on a daily basis. At that organization, I was able to witness first hand your tremendous leadership skills coupled with your extraordinary people skills, in your role as the Director of the department. The time spent under your leadership, enabled me as an IT consultant, whose primary role was to right computer code, to perfect my leadership and people skills to prepare me and H-Impact for what we are doing today. On top of all of this, as a result of your extensive background in journalism, being a published author, and director of the writers in our department, I was able to gain a better understanding of writing as a profession. With your help, unbelievable support and encouragement, I have been able to launch my writing career by opening up H-Impact's online article section and to write and publish the very book you are reading. Tim, thank you for your continued support. May my experiences with you, be as impactful and life changing as your experiences have been to me.

Rafael Santos – As a marketing wiz, photographer and graphic designer, I have to take my hat off to you for what the world sees when they see H-Impact. From initial sessions on the design of our logo, the look and feel of our website, designing H-Impact print media including business cards, post cards and brochures, to the cover of this book, you have been amazingly valuable, helpful, and supportive. I can honestly say that what the world sees when they see an H-Impact product or service accompanied by the branding that goes with it, has been filtered through your creative guise to form something special that I alone could never have conceived. Thank you for helping to create the visual experience which I hope resonates in the minds of many and leaves a lasting positive impression for all.

Dane Johnson – I can't say enough how appreciative I am from working with you on various projects. Not only are you a good person who sincerely cares about the people you work with, but you are exceptional when it comes to doing what you do. Your attention to detail has proven to be freakish, to say the least, and as a result has prevented many GO-LIVES from failing due to unforeseen errors. As teammates in our original roles as computer programmers, I as well as many of our colleagues quickly began to appreciate the extensive review process that you undertake in our normal day to day tasks or during large implementations. Thank you for applying those same rigorous processes to this book and other works here at H-Impact. Your willingness to help regardless of the size or complexity of the project makes my job a lot easier knowing that I can count on a resource like yourself to follow-up, review, test, and try to break what is supposedly unbreakable in efforts to ensure what we produce is free of any errors – minor or catastrophic.

Jonathan Garrett – From PC Maintenance to Network Configuration, your IT consultation has proven in many cases to be a life line. Your extensive wealth of knowledge has been a blessing to H-Impact, our clients, family and friends. You've provided valuable consultation in launching major legs of our business like our online training where you led the effort in imaging our computers for the production of training videos available at H-Impact.com. More specifically to this book project and its subsequent instructor-led training, you've provided a blueprint on the ideal training room configuration which we have adopted as a standard at H-Impact. Thank you for your excellent support and willingness to share all you know to keep H-Impact afloat and ready for our next big thing.

Donald Rice – Along with brotherly love, your words of encouragement have never been lacking. I have taken on many things in my personal as well as professional life, and when it comes to you, I can honestly say, one of your most valuable contributions, has been your innate ability to encourage me when I need it the most. Regardless of where I am in my life, your encouragement has found me. I so much appreciate that considering the array of familiar and unfamiliar things that I have encountered. From graduating from college, entering Corporate America, acquiring computer certifications, establishing H-Impact, writing computer programming code, embarking on video production services, training, consulting, and now writing articles and books like this one, you have delivered the consistent and timeless message of encouragement. Thank you for always being in my corner "from the windows to the walls".

Honorable mentions also go to **Mr and Mrs Howard and Barbara Beatty, Mike and Nikki Boyd, Sonyia Richardson, Michael Breedlove, Jennifer Hall, Dean Sterling, Terry Lowery, Russell Bacon, Zynythia Garrett, Angela Thomas, A. Kyra Jones, Egypt Drew, Keenan Tarpley, Eric Erickson, Catasha Riché, Cathy Davis, Adam Boyd, Shawn Alexander, Avery Wilkerson, Sr., Ossie Knox, Jean Victor, Andrew Rice, Edward Concepcion, Steve Cook, Rance Aaron, Kristy Etheridge,** and **Tiffany Jothen.**

To all supporters (listed or not) – I owe you a tremendous amount of gratitude as you have played instrumental roles in your unique ways in the success of this book, H-Impact and other services we provide. Thank you so much for all you've done.

Table of Contents

What Readers Say 1
Dedication 3
About the Author 4
    Courses by the Author 4
    Articles by the Author 5
Acknowledgements 6
Table of Contents 12
Introduction 16
Chapter 1: Getting Started 18
    Available Plans 18
        New Business (Forever Free) 18
        Growing Business (Starting at $10 a Month) 18
        Pro Marketer (Additional $199 a Month) 19
    Picking a Plan 20
    Create Your MailChimp Account 20
    Welcome or Home Screen 21
Chapter 2: Campaigns 24
    Review Existing Campaigns 25
        Activity 25

- Opens vs Clicks 26
- Top Links Clicked 28
- Subscribers With Most Opens 28
- Social Performance 29
- Top Locations by Opens 29
- *Chapter 3*: Templates 31
  - Defining Links with Source Codes (Optional) 32
    - Source Code 32
    - Query Strings 33
    - Benefits 34
  - Creating a Template 34
    - Drag and Drop Templates 35
    - Code Your Own Template 37
    - Save Your Template 38
  - Create Drag and Drop Template - Step by Step 39
    - Step 1: Choose a Layout 39
    - Step 2: Remove Unnecessary Default Content Blocks 39
    - Step 3: Insert Content Blocks 40
    - Step 4: Save Your Template 71
  - Editing a Template 72
    - Code Your Own Template 72
    - Drag and Drop Template 73
    - Save Your Template 75
  - List Management 76
  - Creating Lists Overview 76
    - Creating Lists Process Configuration 78
    - Collect Email Addresses 81
    - Define List Fields and MERGE Tags 82

MERGE Field Tags 84
Add New Fields 84
Required and Visible Field Properties 85
Save List Changes.. 85
Remove Fields 86
Add Subscribers.. 86
Add Subscribers Form.. 86
Import Subscribers 88
Chapter 4: Creating Campaigns 95
Old Versus New Campaign Builder Process 96
Old Campaign Builder Process 101
Recipients 101
Setup 102
Templates 114
Design 115
Confirm 121
New Campaign Builder Process... 130
To 131
From 132
Subject 135
Content 136
Social Media Connection 148
Settings and Tracking... 153
Confirm 158
Send Campaign... 160
Resulting Emails & Posts 165
Email Example A 165
Post Example A 166

Email Example B 168

Chapter 5: Summary 170

About H-Impact 172

    Contact H-Impact 173

    Connect On Social Media 173

Introduction

For many companies, their product or service may be superior to their competitors and their customer service may be unmatched. But they still have one problem that can truly be a show stopper and in many cases lead to an early exit causing them to slap up a "Going Out Of Business" sign and launch a liquidation sale of which there is no coming back. For these companies and many others they have all the right pieces but fall short in one critical area – marketing. Companies that have done a poor job at marketing often struggle because they have not put the adequate amount of time and planning into this critical part of their business.

With all the many forms of marketing that are available including: *Word of Mouth*, *Social Media*, *Websites*, *Hard-Copy Print Material*, or *Email Marketing*, in order to be successful, businesses have to be flexible, very knowledgeable of their market, know their product or service, and know their current and potential customer's tendencies well enough to understand the most effective marketing strategies to engage them.

There is one form of marketing that has been here for ages, extremely dependable, and if implemented correctly can easily serve as a business's lifeline. I am speaking specifically about **Email Marketing**. Everyday businesses perform analysis of their ideal customer, look at their services or product they have to offer, thoughtfully craft emails with special promotions and send them out to the masses. You see it all the time. There is a reason you are still getting emails from your favorite stores, or your not so favorite stores, on their latest promotions or deals. This method of marketing must be working. Right? Think of it this way. Why would you still be receiving these types of emails if this form of marketing wasn't working?

In **How to Unleash Email Marketing with MailChimp**, we take a tour *in full color and illustration*, of the Email Marketing features available online for free under **MailChimp's Forever Free** plan. After creating an account on MailChimp, we jump right in and familiarize ourselves with some of the main features including:

- Email Templates,
- Performance Reports, and
- List Management tools

Then we take a stab at setting up our own Email Campaign using an Email Template to merge and send to a Mailing/Subscriber list. We use Microsoft Excel and MailChimp's online web forms to collect email addresses for our Mailing list. By the end of this book, you will have the skills needed to create, send and monitor your own Email Campaigns or eBlasts using the powerful free service services provided by MailChimp. **Let's get started!**

Chapter 1: Getting Started

Available Plans

MailChimp offers three versions or plans for companies or organizations. We recommend starting with the plan that best meets your needs as a business owner. Although all three are described below, the focus of this book is on the first of the three plans named the **New Business or Forever Free** plan.

New Business (Forever Free)

With the **New Business or Forever Free plan**, a Business can start today at no cost. This plan is designed for businesses with 2,000 or Fewer subscribers. The **Forever Free plan** allows users to send up to 12,000 emails a month for free. This plan doesn't expire. There is no contract and credit card information is not required.

The **Forever Free plan** offers:

- **Building Lists** using tools like out-of-the-box **Sign up Forms**,
- Ability to create **Email Templates** with customizable **Merge Fields**,
- **Customize Lists** with **Segmentation** abilities to target subscribers based on data collected,
- Monitoring Email Campaigns using **Real-time Reporting Tools**, and
- **Automation** options.

Growing Business (Starting at $10 a Month)

The **Growing Business plan** is designed for businesses that need an email marketing system which grows along with their company. The monthly cost starts at $10.00 and

is dependent on the number of subscribers in the company's subscriber list. For the alternative billing type with a one-time payment option, the cost will depend on the number of emails the user needs to purchase at one time.

The **Growing Business plan** offers:

- **Database Integration** with CRM systems plus integration with Ecommerce systems for sales reports,
- Ability to monitor **reporting** in conjuction with **Google Analytics** to analyze **ROI** complete with mobile app accessibility,
- Target audiences using **Segmentation** that is prebuilt or custom with API integration,
- **Collaboration Platform for Teams** that allows teams to comment on campaigns and provide feedback with user permission level configurations,
- **Delivery tools** that enhance the effectiveness of emails using **Send Time Optimization** and **TimeWarp** with TimeZone considerations**,** and
- **Automation** options.

Pro Marketer (Additional $199 a Month)

The **Pro Marketer plan** is designed for businesses that need a marketing system to grow along with their company. The monthly cost starts at $10.00 + $199 monthly payment and is dependent on the number of subscribers in the company's subscriber list. Similar to the Growing Business plan, for the alternative billing type with a one-time payment option, the cost will depend on the number of emails the user needs to purchase at one time.

The **Pro Marketer plan** offers:

- **API Integration** for tracking and targeting of Ecommerce data with integration with common shopping carts like Magento and Shopify,
- **Test Variations** that allow testing of campaign effectiveness using variations on fields like subject, from name and the email content,
- **Comparative Reports** which allow the business to view patterns or trends in subscriber engagement which may support adjustments that improve campaign effectiveness,
- **Transactional Emails** with the **Mandrill** API which enable a one to one email communication for ecommerce and personalized messages, and

- **Automation** that built on triggers allows the delivery of more timely and targeted emails based on subscriber interests and behaviors.

Picking a Plan

If you are unsure of which plan to choose, it is a safe bet to start with the **New Business Forever Free plan**. By doing so, you avoid any risks related to cost and are given time to immediately start using your new **MailChimp** marketing platform.

You can rest easy as well knowing that this book's focus on the **New Business or Forever Free** plans will allow you to learn the fundamentals of using **MailChimp**. The skills taught and lessons learned are transferable to the alternative paid plans for **Growing Business** or **Pro Marketer**. When the time is right, and when the you as the business owner is ready, it is relatively easy to upgrade to the next plan level. Upgrades are possible by choosing the desired plan and simply providing the necessary account and verifiable billing info.

Create Your MailChimp Account

The first thing you need to do is to create a **MailChimp** account. If you already have an existing verified active account, sign-in and skip to **Welcome Or Home Screen**. Otherwise, to obtain a **MailChimp** account simply go to:

www.mailchimp.com

As described earlier there are three **MailChimp** plans - one Free and 2 that require payment. The New Business or Forever Free plan is the default when signing up for a **MailChimp** account. For the scope of this book we will sign-up and use the **New Business or Forever Free** plan. For more information on the **Growing Business** and **Pro Marketer** plans visit www.mailchimp.com.

Sign-up for the **New Business or Forever Free plan** by clicking the **Sign-up** button. Complete the fields including your **Email**, **Username** and **Password**. Click **Get Started** and proceed to complete **Company Info**, **Address Info** and any **Contact Info** required. You'll also be asked to fill out a blurb that your subscribers will receive that describes why they are receiving the email from your **Company**.

Complete all verification steps required by **MailChimp** which should include an email verification step.

Sign back in to **MailChimp,** if required, upon receiving the email verification, to ensure you can access the system.

Welcome or Home Screen

Now that you are logged into **MailChimp** you can take a look around at what **MailChimp** has to offer. The **Home Page** (ie **Dashboard**) which is the first page that you see, is accessible anytime by clicking the MailChimp logo in the upper left corner. The **Home Page** (ie **Dashboard**) is designed to provide a high level **Overview** of your **Campaign** performance as a whole. It will be empty at first due to the fact that you have yet to send out any email **Campaigns** or loaded **Contacts** into the system. This page will show more activity once you start using **MailChimp**.

*A **Campaign** can best be defined as the entire process of configuring, designing and sending an **eBlast**.*

Once you have sent a **Campaign** you will see this page broken down into 3 sections.

1. Explore MailChimp

This section describes features of **MailChimp** and **Email Marketing** concepts. Usually the topics of discussion are in the knowledge base or **MailChimp's** blog. Some topics that you may see include the features like **A/B Testing** which allows a user to send the same **eBlast** to different recipients in efforts to be configured with different identifying factors that seem to play a role in increasing **Open**, **Click** and **Conversion** rates. Other topics may be about the benefits of upgrading to the **Paid Plans** vs the **New Business Forever Free plan** for **MailChimp**. Somedays there may be info about a new release of the **MailChimp** platform. This section changes daily based on what **MailChimp** sees as valuable topics, which may lead to an increase in the user's **MailChimp** proficiency level.

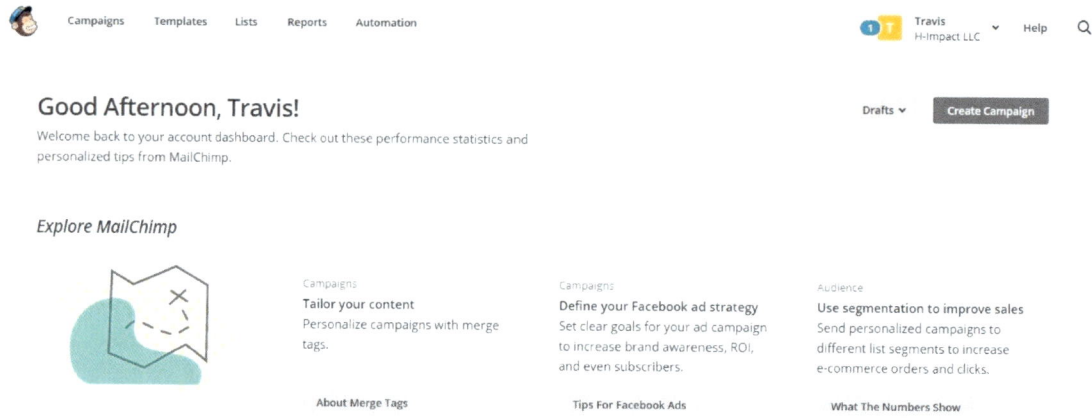

2. Audience Change

Audience Change can be used to provide an overall view of the changes in your **Contacts/Subscribers**. Whether you have a website that uses **MailChimp's** backend process to add or remove **Subscribers** or you use the built-in forms that are readily available under the **Lists** section in **MailChimp**, the **Audience** section provides a real time count of the change in your overall audience within a certain timeframe. Note the drop down that allows you to change the number of days in the rears that it reports. **7 days** is the default.

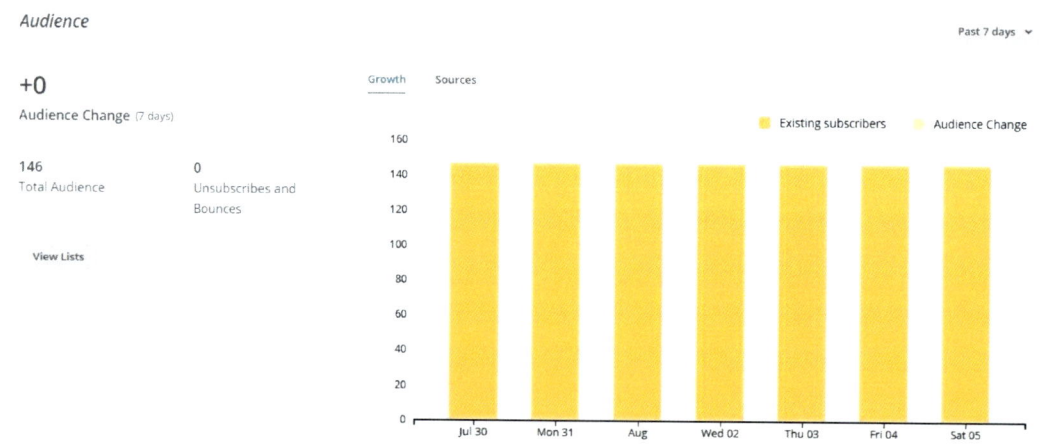

3. Campaign Engagement.

This section gives the you a quick peek at the high level **Opens** with **Delivered** and of those that are the number of **Clicked** that were **Opened**. As a reminder **Email**

Marketing has certain metrics that determine the effectiveness of the **Email Campaigns**. At the top of the List are **Deliveries**, **Opens**, and **Clicks**. Note the drop down that allows you to change the number of days in the rears that it reports. **7 days** is the default.

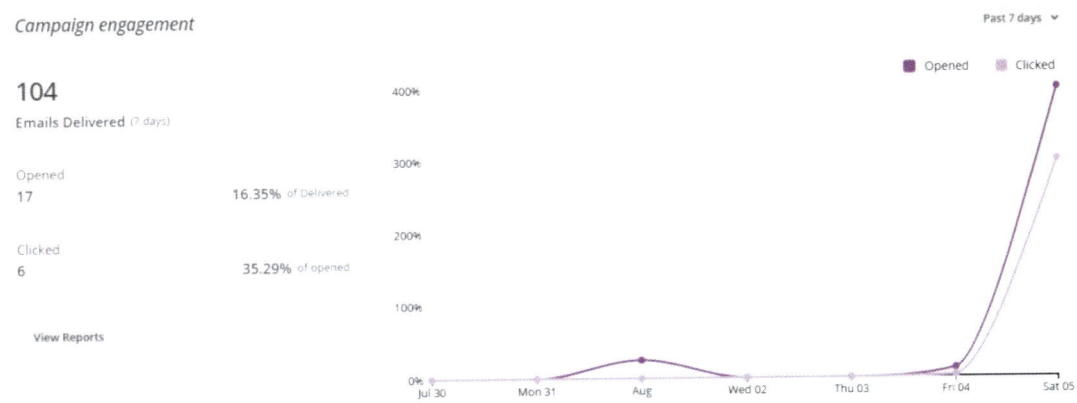

Chapter 2: Campaigns

Navigate to the **Campaign** listing page by clicking the link at the upper left top corner of the screen. As described earlier:

A **Campaign** *can best be defined as the entire process of configuring, designing and sending an eBlast.*

The Campaign page is designed to list **Campaigns** that are classified as **Recent**, **Ongoing**, **Draft** and **Completed** campaigns. Note the menu on the left that defines these different categories of **Campaigns**. This menu can be used to easily display your **Campaigns** according to their categories.

Note once you do have **Campaigns** listed, each **Campaign** will include the **Name**, **Recipient List used**, **Date Sent**, **Status**, and **Open** and **Click** percentages. Notice the gray **View Report** button on each row appears once the respective campaign is hovered over. This drop down allows you to **View Email**, **Rename**, **Replicate** or **Social Share**.

To create a new **Campaign**, click the **Create Campaign** button at the top right of the page.

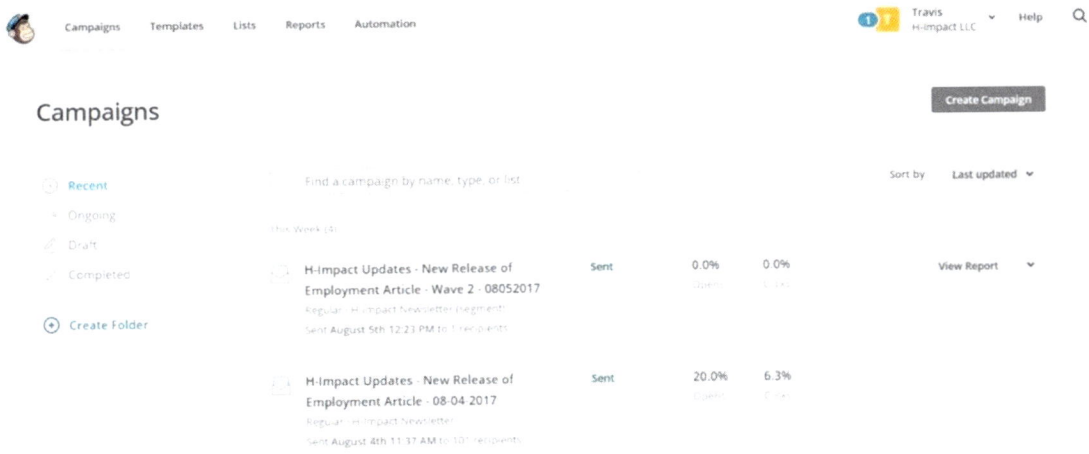

Review Existing Campaigns

Review Existing Campaigns by clicking the **View Report** button or the **Campaign's** name link. **Campaign Drafts** will show an **Edit** button instead of the **View Report** button. Each Campaign will display on a Report as detailed by the **Campaign** menu that breaks down the **Overview, Activity, Links, Social, Ecommerce, Conversations** and **Analytics360**. For the purposes of this book we will focus on **Activity** and **Links**.

Activity

The top most title of the **Campaign** page is the **Name** of the **Campaign** followed by a **Switch Report** Drop down that allows the user to navigate between **Campaigns** and displays the respective **Campaign** results info.

Followed by the **Campaign** menu that breaks down the **Overview, Activity, Links, Social, Ecommerce, Conversations** and **Analytics360** for each **Campaign**, the number of recipients is display. In **MailChimp**, just like the number before "recipient(s)" all blue formatted links are clickable. You'll notice them throughout the reports and other pages. These links will allow you to drill down into the content deeper. For instance this will allow you to view all recipients of this **Campaign**.

The high level configurations include the **List with Segment if applicable**, **Subject**, **Delivery Date** along with a **View Email**, **Download**, **Print** and **Share** options.

For **Ecommerce** dependent **Email Campaigns** notice the breakdown of

- Orders
- Average Order Revenue
- and Total Revenue.

This book will not cover the **Ecommerce Conversion Tracking**. For more information on **Ecommerce Conversion Tracking** visit www.mailchimp.com.

Opens vs Clicks

Below this you'll notice a side-by-side section comparing **Opens** to **Clicks** starting with **Open**, **List Average**, and **Industry Average** rates. This is one of the most important sections on the report because it will allow you to review **Industry** rate comparisons and **Cross Campaign** comparisons base of the various **Campaigns** sent using similar or different recipient list.

Below this header rate info, you'll notice a section that breaks down the

- Opens (unique),
- Clicks (unique),

- Bounces, and
- Unsubscribes.

This area that follows displays another side-by-side comparison on the left side of **successful deliveries** with a count and rate, **Total Opens**, **Last Opens**, and **Forwards**. The comparison section to the right includes **Clicks Per Unique Opens**, **Total Clicks**, **Last Click**, and **Abuse Reports**. Note the **Opens** and **Clicks** in this section are not unique and may display one user opening the **eBlasts** multiple times. It also may display one user clicking a link multiple times.

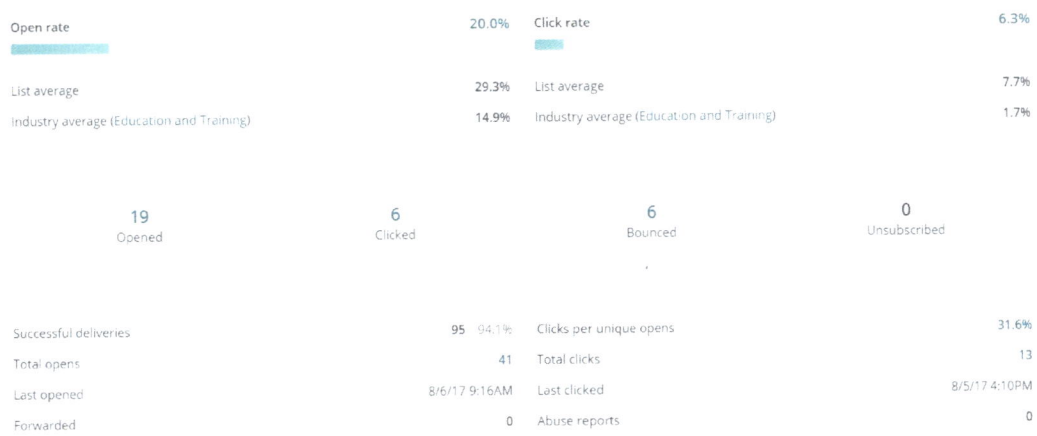

The next section is titled **24-hour Performance** which entails a chart that shows the **24-hour Performance** of the **Campaign** using **Opens** and **Clicks** against a timeline. This chart could be used to show the most advantageous times to send out particular **eBlasts** to certain **Recipient Lists**, or **Groups/Segments** of the **Recipient Lists**.

H-Impact Tip: As a rule of thumb and from our experiences it is better to send emails out in the early morning during the early part of the week. Mondays and Tuesdays seem to work the best, before 7:00 am.

Top Links Clicked

As you already know emails that are sent often come with clickable links. These clickable links may come in the form of images or HTML buttons. Without a doubt, one the main purposes of sending emails using an **Email Marketing** platform is to encourage users to click on the links to get to the content you are marketing. **MailChimp** provides a quick preview of the **Top Links Clicked** with the ability to drill down further, if the number of links exceeds the 5 links displayed in the quick preview.

Subscribers With Most Opens

Another important statistic once emails are sent is trying to identify which recipients opened the content. **MailChimp** provides a quick preview of the **Subscribers** with the **Most Opens** with the ability to drill down further if the number of links exceeds the 5 users displayed in the quick preview.

Social Performance

MailChimp also provides a quick preview section that can assist users with **eBlasts** that integrate with **Social Media**. As you will see **MailChimp** allows users the ability to easily synchronize **Email Campaigns** with various **Social Media Platforms**.

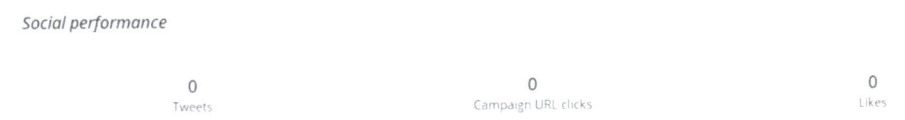

Top Locations by Opens

MailChimp provides a map that is interactive that allows you to click on a country and drill down to state or province with real-time counts of how many emails were opened in that state or province. As you can imagine, this can be helpful if you have you contacts in your **Recipient List** defined by state/province or region. This can allow **Email Marketing Specialists** to send emails to particular locations based on **Corporate Sales Initiatives** and **Market Expansion Initiatives**.

Top locations by opens

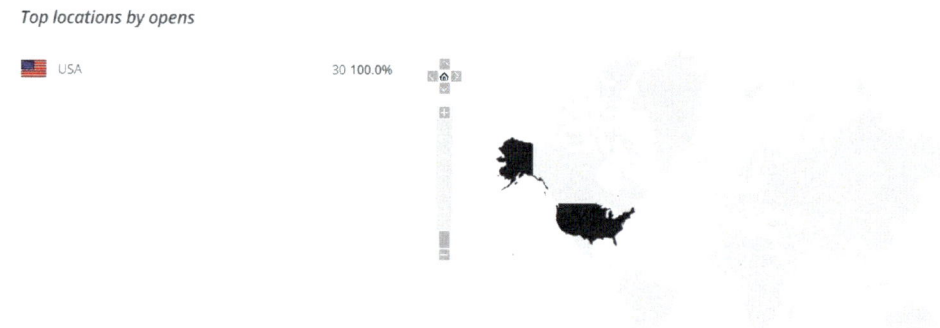

Chapter 3: **Templates**

The **Templates** section is accessible via the **Template** link in the top menu.

A **Template** *can best be defined as the email framework with content that can be designed by a HTML expert or* **MailChimp** *user without any HTML experience.*

A seasoned web designer can write their own code or a novice user can use pre-built **MailChimp** templates with **What You See Is What You Get (WYSIWYG)** tools to design/edit their own Email Template. Normally before creating an **eBlast Campaign** the user has already created and saved an **Email Template** to select during the process. These templates allow uploading, saving and referencing images from the **Content Manager**. They also allow the user to format text with color, bold and italic emphasis within the body of the email.

By clicking the **Templates** link at the top of the page, a list of all **Templates** will displays. You may edit the Template by clicking the name of each. You may also **Edit** the Template by using the gray button in the Template row. **Replicate** is also an option if you use the gray button. The type of Template is listed below the name and date created. The two options are **Code Your Own** or **Drag and Drop**. The **Code Your Own** type is for the more advanced user, while the **Drag and Drop** type is suitable for the **Beginner** with little to no HTML experience.

From the **Templates** page, you will notice the **Content Manager, MailChimp's** asset repository, which allows you to access a control panel that provides the ability to upload images, files for download, videos and other assets that can be referenced from **Email Templates**. The **Create Template** button is also available at the top right corner of the page.

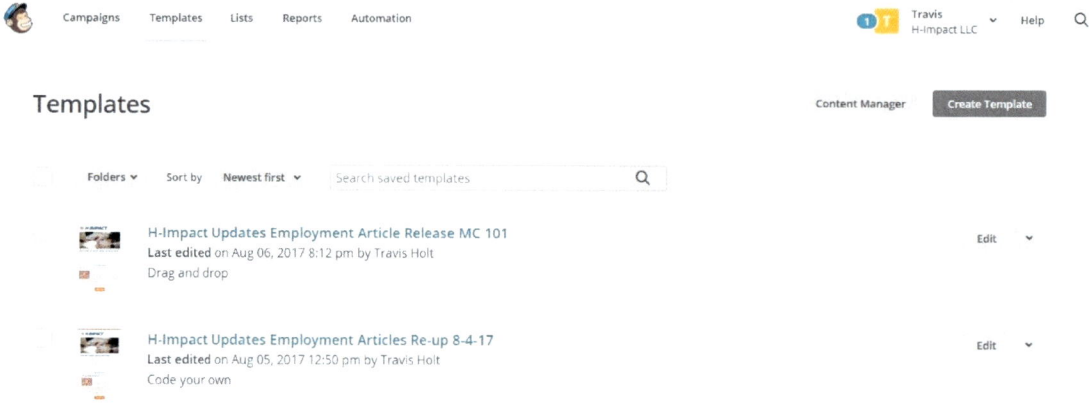

Defining Links with Source Codes (Optional)

Many times companies need to track where their website traffic is coming from. In many cases this data is used to determine the effectiveness of their marketing efforts. This is something you may want to consider when creating your email marketing campaigns and associated **Templates**.

In the web world, a common practice is to use a source code along with a query string to identify where web traffic originates. Although using source codes along with query strings is completely *optional* when defining website links, you may find that there are some added advantages to using this technique to improve targeting and marketing of your email campaigns.

Source Code

A **source code** is a text value consisting of letters, numbers and/or symbols that is internally defined by companies. **Source codes** provide information about website traffic sources.

As long as the target website has tracking or analytics support built-in (either custom or more notable applications like **Google Analytics**), using a **source code** is a very effective means to determine where your website traffic originates. Some information used in **source codes** may be media type information, date information, and company, website or agency the traffic is sent from.

For example, a **source code** may be:

EMLNEWSXYZ030518

More specifically this code may be further defined as:

- Media Type: EML (for Email)
- Topic/Purpose: NEWS
- Company: XYZ
- Date (Day Month Year): 030518

Here is another example of a **source code**:

BLOGPOSTABC121018

This can be better defined as:

- Media Type: BLOG
- Topic/Purpose: POST
- Company: ABC
- Date (Day Month Year): 121018

These are just a few examples of **source codes**. The element order as well as the elements themselves are limitless and are up to the agency or company that creates the **source codes**.

Query Strings

Now that you understand some basics of the use of **source codes**, let's look at how they can be added to your **Campaign Emails** which are derived from your **Email Templates**. As a part of linking to websites from emails, a **URL** (**Web address**) will need to be defined. When creating a link to a website, a **query string** which is appended to the **URL** can be used to pass data to the target website. A **query string** is comprised of a list of **query string** parameters and their associated values. By adding the **source code** in a data element or **query parameter** of the **query string**, the **source code** can easily be supplied to the target website and processed and tracked accordingly. *Note: Multiple query parameters in a key value pair format(ie. http://www.company.com?z=abc45&x=def74) can be passed to the target website using an "&" to concatenate additional query parameters.*

Here is an example a **URL** with a **query string**:
http://www.h-impact.com?hisrccd=EMLNEWSXYZ030518

Here is another example:
http://www.h-impact.com?hisrccd=BLOGPOSTABC121018

As a rule of thumb, the query string begins with the "**?**" and continues to the end of the **URL**.

Benefits

If you choose to define your email links with **query strings** and **source codes**, upon logging into external tracking software like Google Analytics connected to your website, you will easily be able to identify the traffic you received from your **Web address** email links considering they should include the **query parameters** along with **source codes**.

In several places in this chapter and beyond you will need to define a **Web address URL**. For this reason, you may want to use a **query string** along with a **source code** to define links to your website. Alternatively, you may simply want to define the **Web address URL** without the **query string** or **source code**.

For example:

http://www.h-impact.com

This is completely up to you and your company's direction. Defining your website links depends on your goals and envisioned outcomes around email marketing and website referral tracking.

Note: For the purposes of this book, to simplify defining **Web address URL's** for learning purposes, we *will not* define our **Web address URL's** with **query strings** with **source codes** while building **Email Templates** for our **Email Campaigns**.

Creating a Template

To **Create a Template**, use the **Create Template** button at the top right corner of the page. You will first need to make a decision on the layout based on the **Featured** or **Basic Layouts** available. Choose the layout based on the purpose of the **eBlast** you are sending.

Drag and Drop Templates

Featured Layouts include:

- Sell Products
- Make an Announcement
- Tell a Story
- Follow-up
- Educate

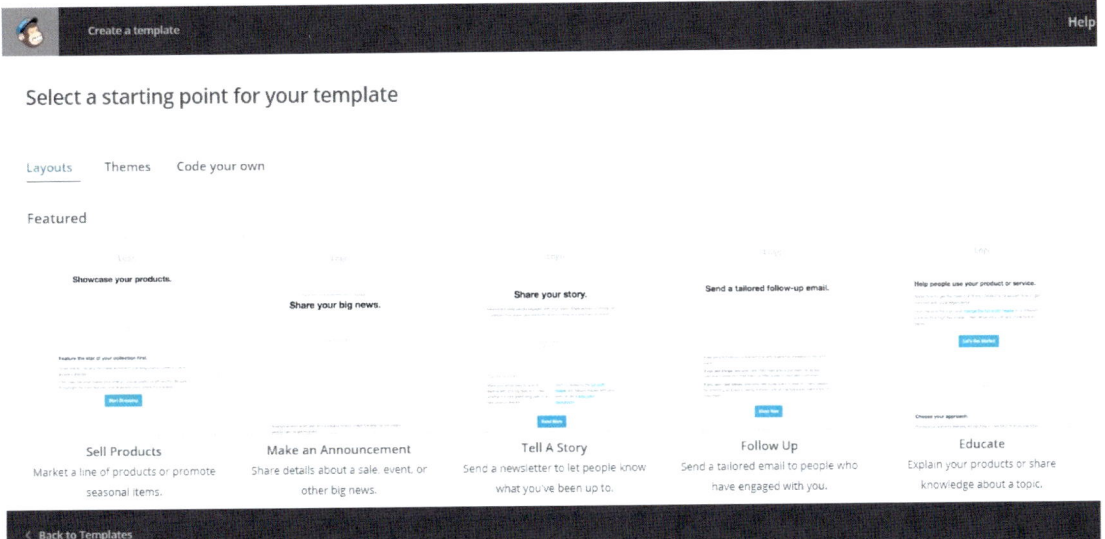

Basic Layouts include layouts based on **Columns and Widths**.

With these **Drag and Drop** Layouts **MailChimp** has built in resize styles that are responsive to various device sizes in which the layout will display. From a large display to a small display, emails will maintain their proportions to fit all sizes. It is important that the **MailChimp Template** layout accounts for this level of flexibility because emails that are not well formatted statistically result in lower opens and clicks reducing the effectiveness of the **Campaign** overall.

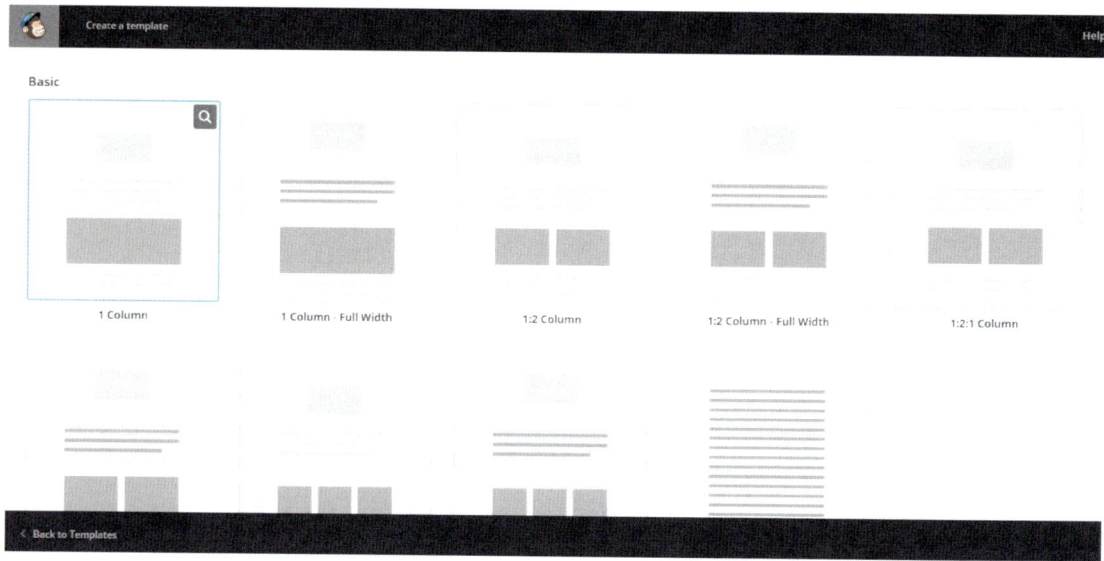

Double click the **Preferred Layout** to display the dual window screen with one side with the formatted layout and the other with the **Drag and Drop Content Blocks**.

Update the **Content Blocks** as needed replacing default text, images, rearranging or replacing the **Drag and Drop Content Blocks** as desired. Reposition the **Content Blocks** by using the checkered box visible when hovering over the pre-existing **Content Blocks**.

To begin the editing process, make sure the **Content Block** is in edit mode. To update the **Content Blocks** on the left, use your mouse to hover over the **Content Block**, until you see a transparent black border around the **Content Block** with icons in the upper right corner resembling a

- Checkered Square to Reposition
- Pencil to Edit
- Trash to Remove
- A Window with a + Symbol to Duplicate

To **Edit a Template** you must follow the steps below defined in the **Edit a Template** section.

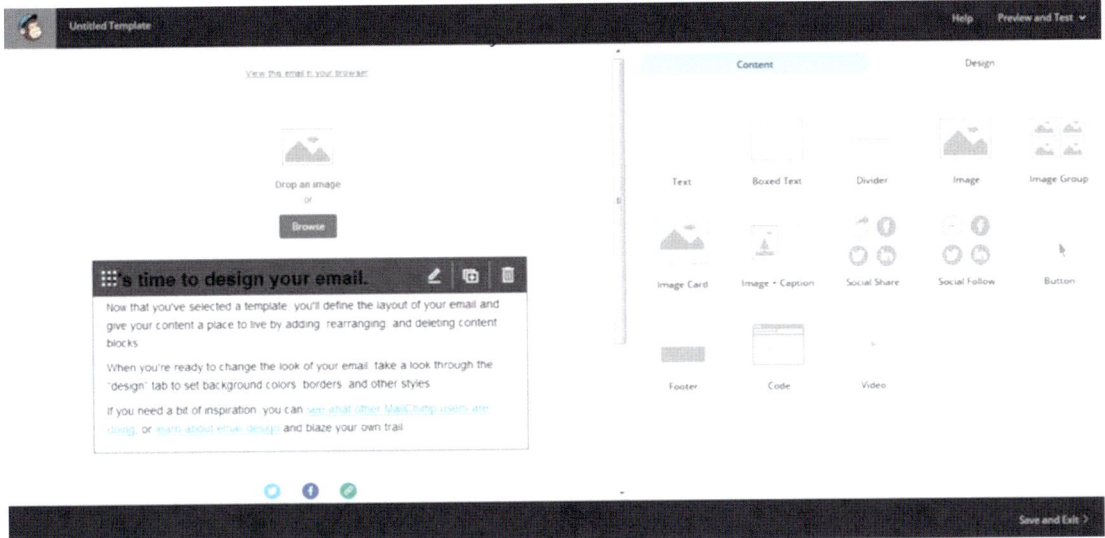

Code Your Own Template

By creating a **Code Your Own** template a page will display with the well-formed email layout on the left but an HTML panel on the right that allows you to edit the HTML directly. Note any edits performed on in the **Edit Window** will auto-save within seconds after each update. This is something to keep in mind considering it is possible to lose the original HTML based on how quickly the auto save occurs. It is highly recommended that **Beginners** use the **Drag and Drop** type Templates and avoid using the **Code Your Own** Templates. **Code Your Own Templates** require an advanced level of understanding of web design and HTML.

To completely **Create a Template** the same rules apply when editing. See Editing a Template.

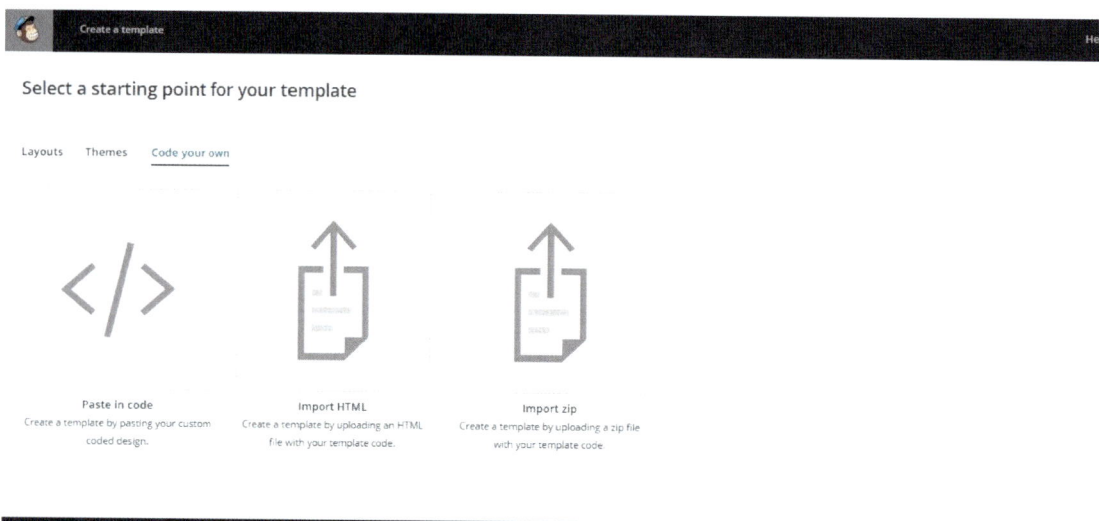

Save Your Template

Once your **Template** has been edited, including replacing default text and other content, you must click **Save and Close** to finish editing the **Content Blocks**. Click **Save and Exit** to **Save the Template**. Enter the name of the new **Template** understanding it may be sent multiple times to various recipients. Unlike a **Campaign** name, the **Template** name should be less specific.

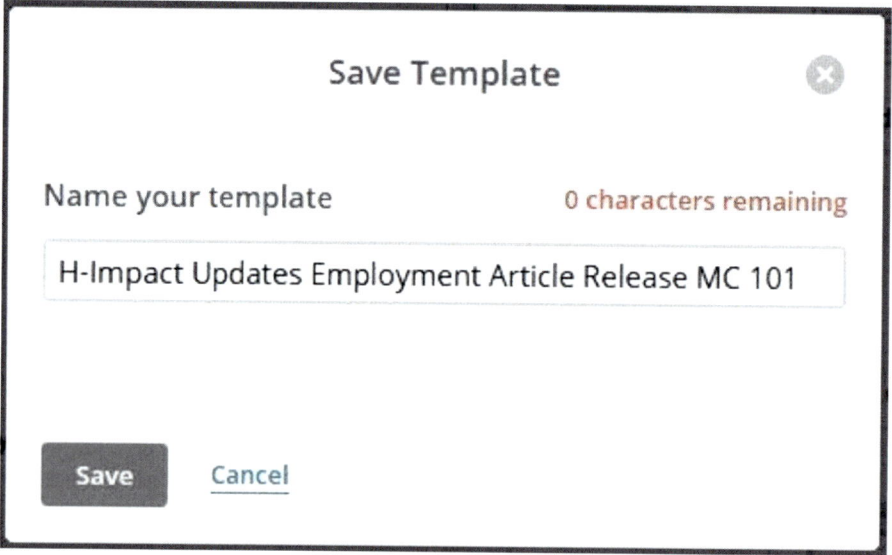

Create Drag and Drop Template - Step by Step

In this section we will create a **Template** from scratch. This **Template** will be used later in the **Creating Campaigns** chapter to generate an actual email to be sent to subscribers. An example of the resulting email can be viewed in the **Creating Campaigns** chapter. It is titled **Example A** within the **Resulting Emails** section.

Step 1: Choose a Layout

For this example we will use a **Basic** Template layout to create the **Email Template**. With **Templates** from the main menu:

- Click the **Create Template** button in the upper right of the screen.
- Scroll to the **Basic** Template Section.
- Choose **1 Column**

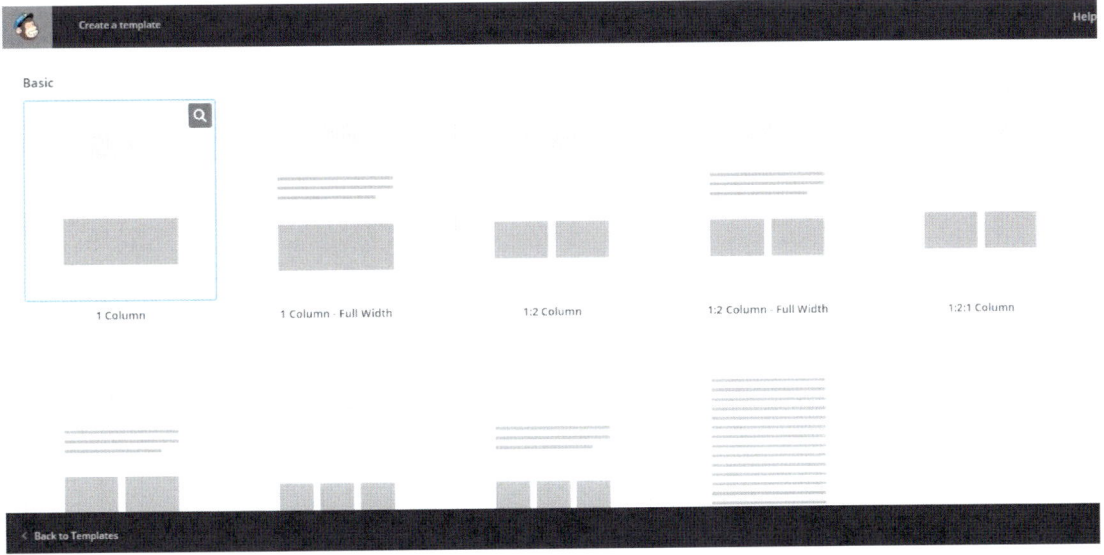

Step 2: Remove Unnecessary Default Content Blocks

- Use the mouse to highlight the first **Text Content Block** with the link: **View this email in your browser**
- When the black transparent border appears click the **Trash Can Icon**.

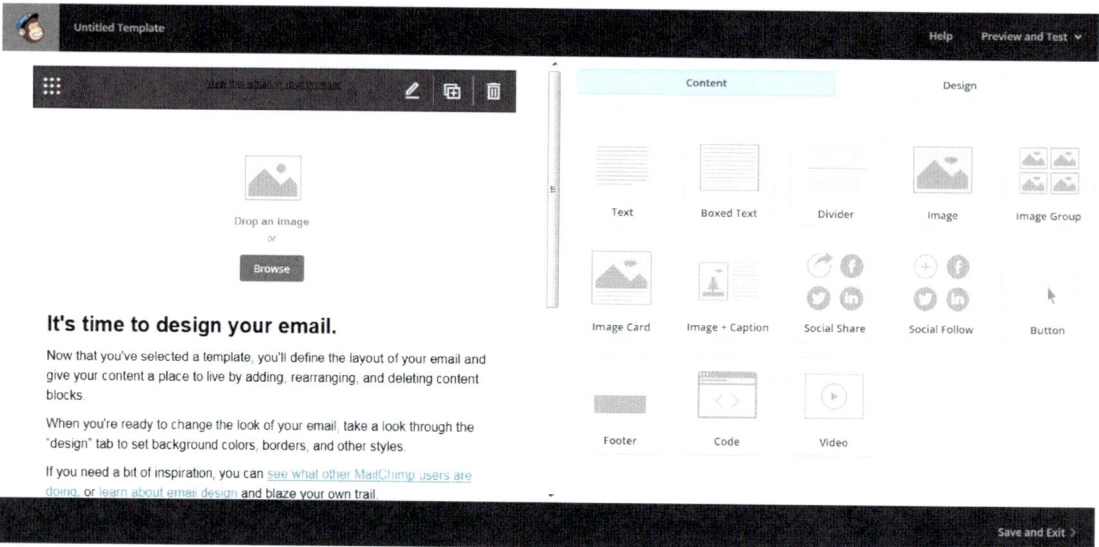

- Click the **Delete** button on the **Confirm** dialogue to delete the **Text Content Block**.

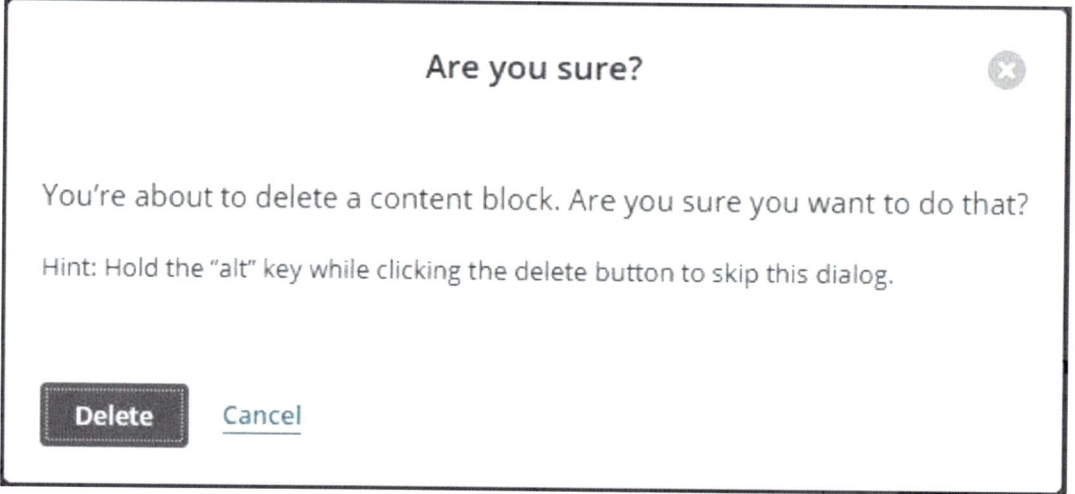

Step 3: Insert Content Blocks

Adding Image Content Block for the Logo

Now we need an image at the top of our email that helps to identify the company from which the email is being sent. To do this we need another **Image Content Block** to be placed above the existing **Image Content Block**. To add another **Image Content Block** we can drag the **Image Content Block** from the right pane and place it where we want to in the left pane.

- Use the mouse to **Click** to **Select** the **Image Content Block** in the right pane.

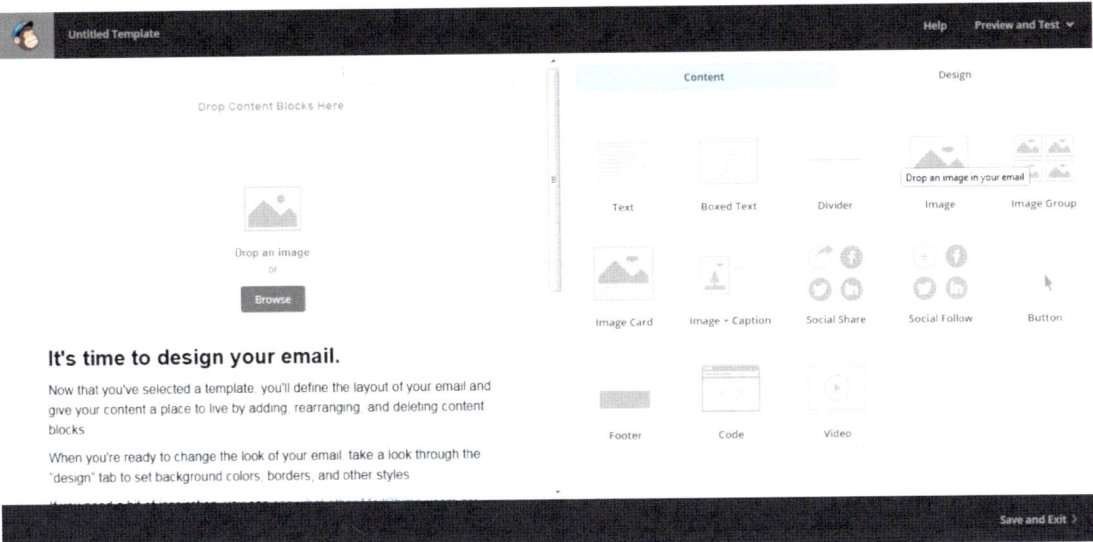

- **Click** and **hold** the **Image Content Block** and **drag it** to the left pane to place it above the existing **Image Content Block**.

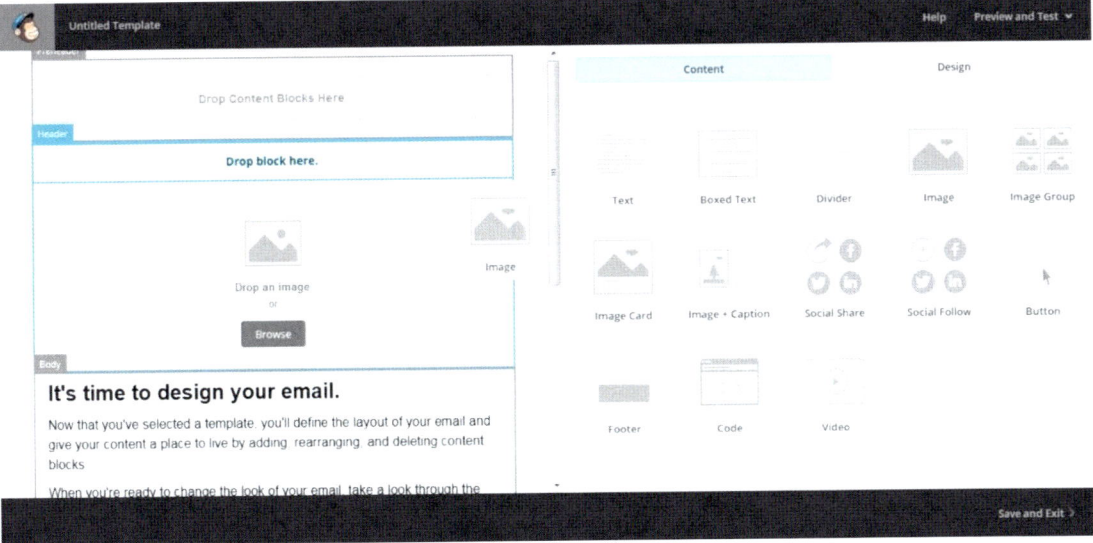

- When the right pane displays the **Drop block here** message release the mouse to place the **Image Content Block** above the original **Image Content Block**.

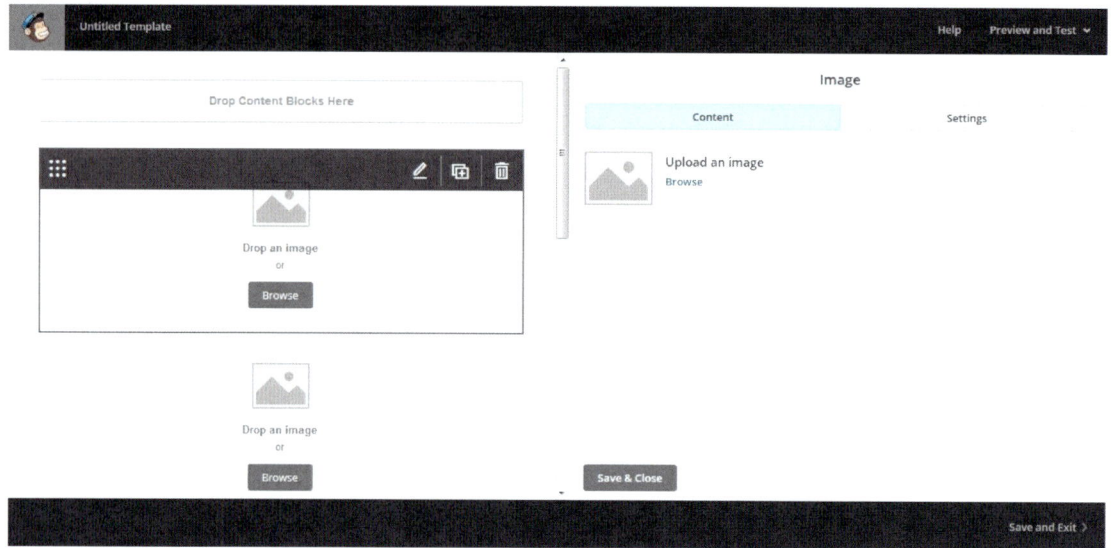

Configure Logo Image Content Block

- The right pane should now be in edit mode. To upload an image, you can either drag one from your computer and drop it inside the **Image Content Block** or use the **Browse** button or **Link** to upload an image from **MailChimp's** central asset repository location - **Content Manager**. Click the **Browse** link in the right pane to **upload** the company's **Logo** image.
- The **Content Manager** displays. Notice the **Search** bar at the top of the page along with the **Upload** and **X** (Close) buttons to the far right. To the far left there is a menu, under the **Content Manager Page** title, with **My Files**, **Products**, and **Giphy** links. Also, notice the **Filter**, **Folder**, **Sort by**, and **Toggle View buttons**.

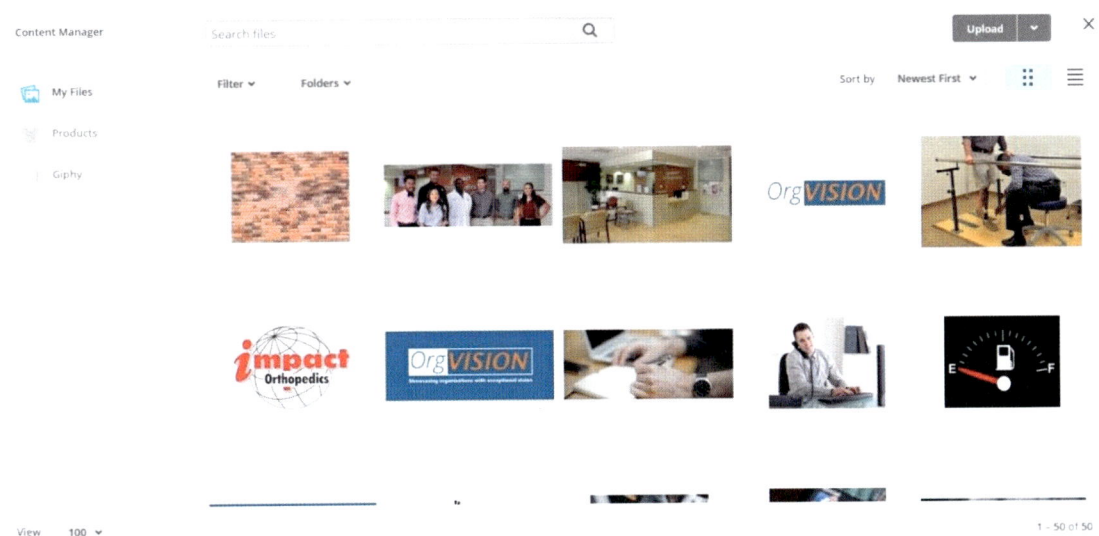

Define Logo Image Using Content Manager
- Locate the image you would like to insert into the **Image Content Block**. Use the scroll bar on the right if available to locate the image.
- Click to select the **logo** image you wish to insert. *Note: If the image is not available you will need to use the Upload button at the top of the page to upload the logo image into the Content Manager prior to selecting it from the list of items. For directions on how to upload an image, refer to the next section titled:* **Upload Main Image Using Content Manager**. With the exception of the differences of the filenames and dimensions, the process to upload the image using the **Upload** button then navigating to the location of the logo should be the same. *The logo's image filename may vary. Our filename is* **logo.png** *with a width of 400px and a 70px height. Once uploaded using similar steps to the* **Upload Main Image Using Content Manager** *be sure to return to this section to update the link as directed below to the home page of the company's website, as well as left justifying to the logo image.*

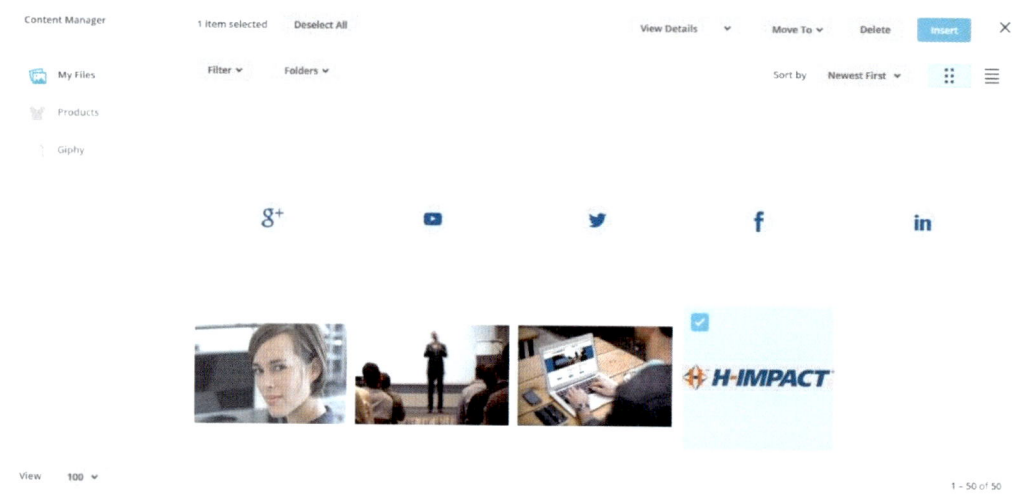

A new label and set of buttons appear which allows actions to be performed on the selected image. From left to right note the label **1 item selected**, and buttons – **Deselect All**, **View Details**, **Move To**, **Delete**, **Insert** and the **X** (Close) button.

- Click the **Insert** button to insert the selected **logo** image. The image should now be positioned in the proper place at the top of the **Email Template**.

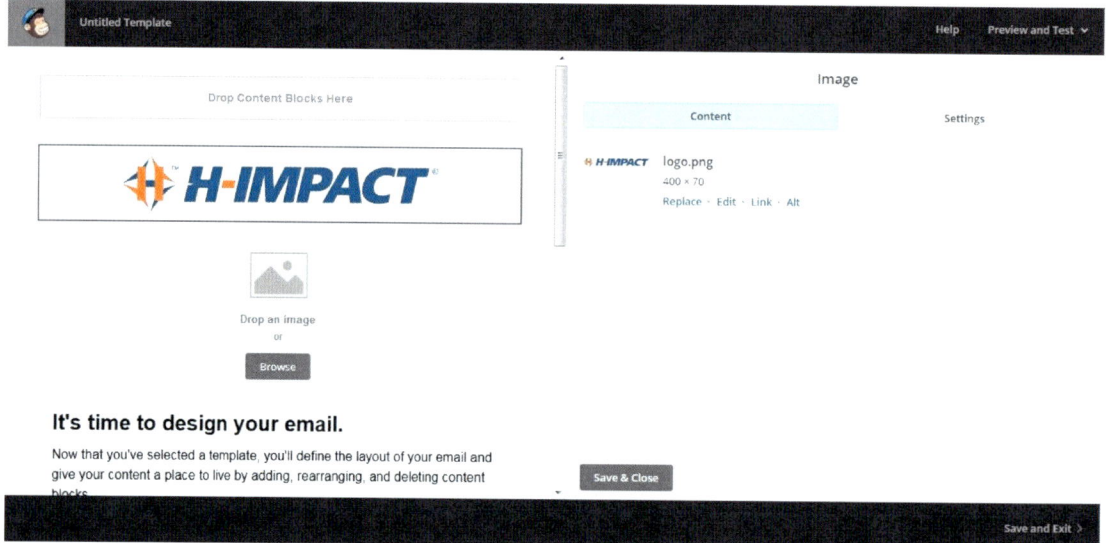

Update the Logo Image's Link to Web address

- Update the **logo** image so that it links to the Home Page of the company's website. Click the blue **Link** in the right pane. The dialogue box displays.

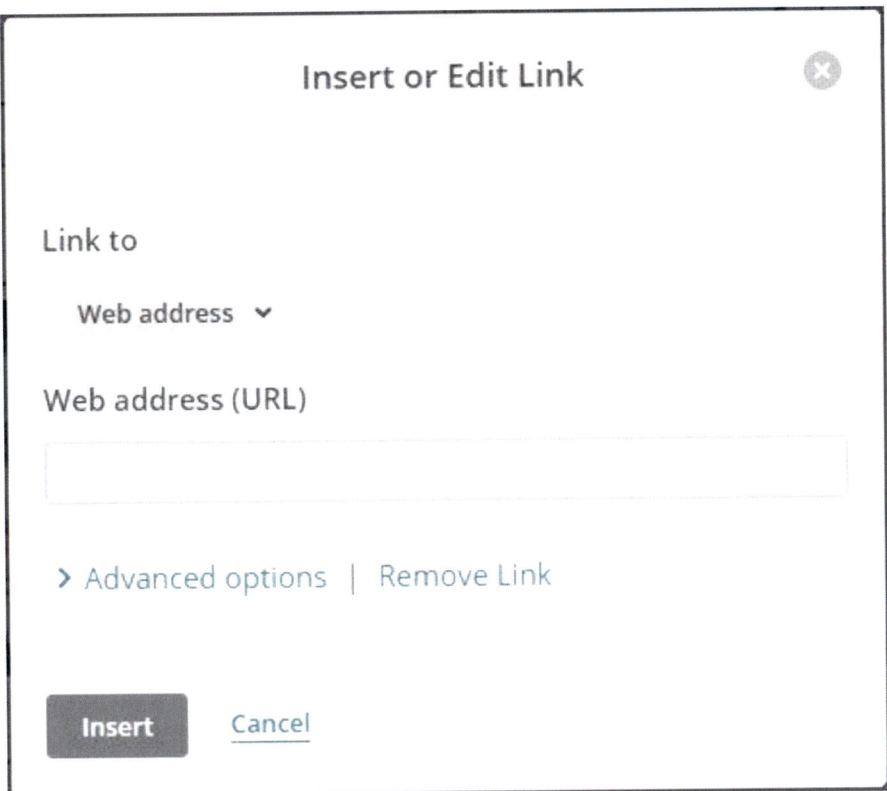

- When the dialogue box displays, enter the following to point to the company's home page: http://www.h-impact.com/home
Note: Alternatively, you may want to define your link with a query string and source code as mentioned previously in the **Defining Links with Source Codes** section.

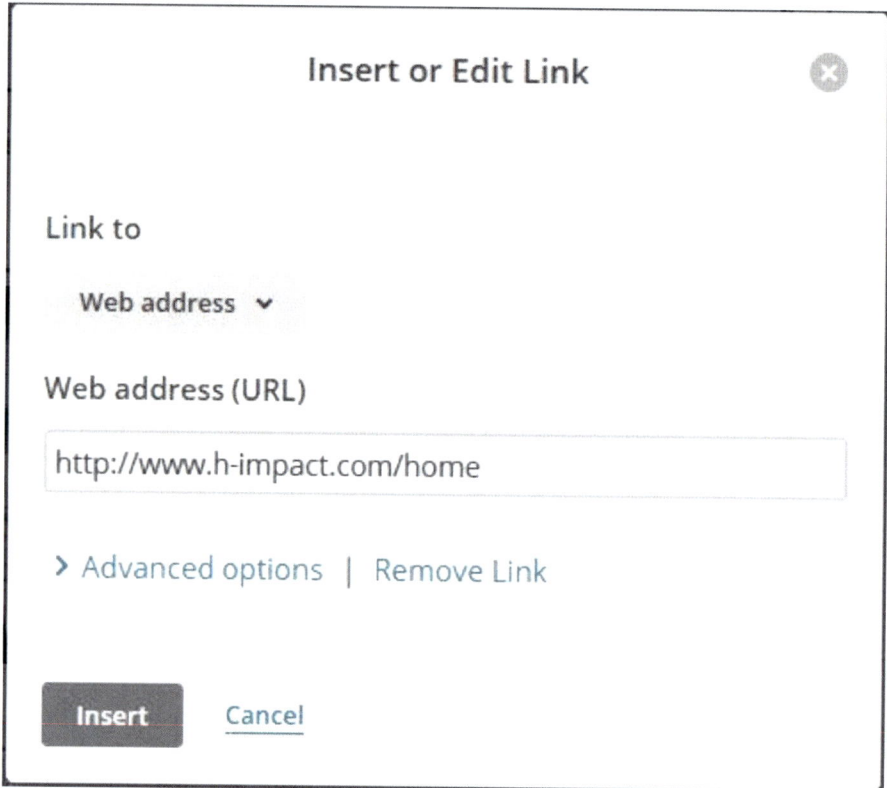

- Click **Insert**.

Now we need to align the logo to the left.

- Click the **Settings** tab in the right pane.

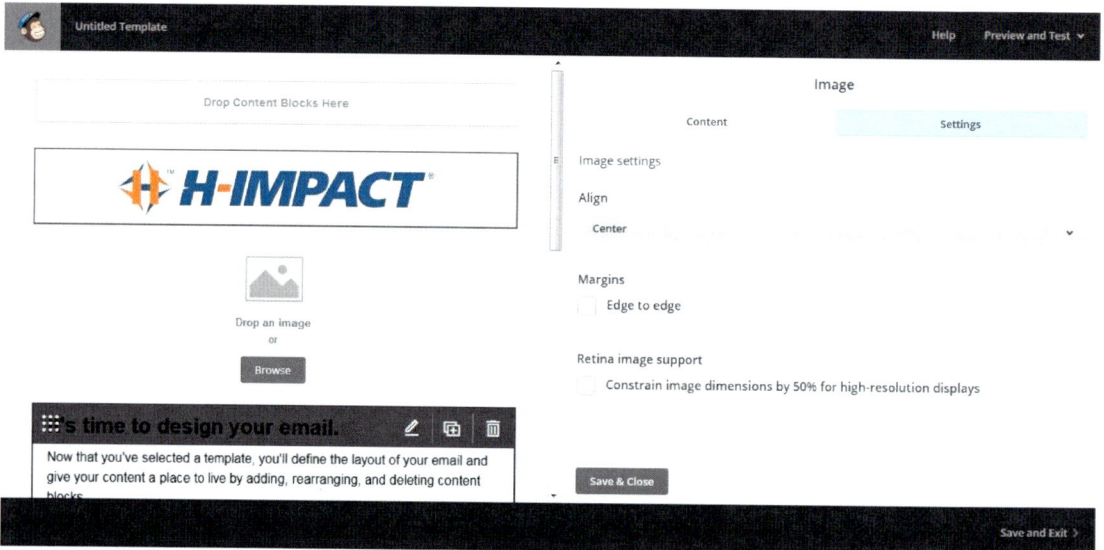

- Now use the **Align** drop down to change from **Center** to **Left**.

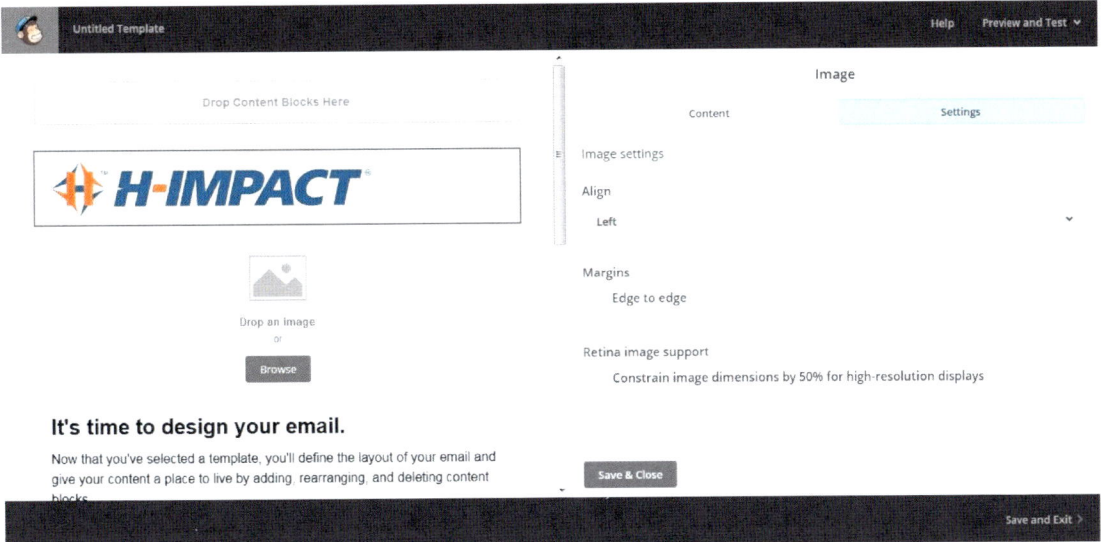

- Click **Save & Close**.

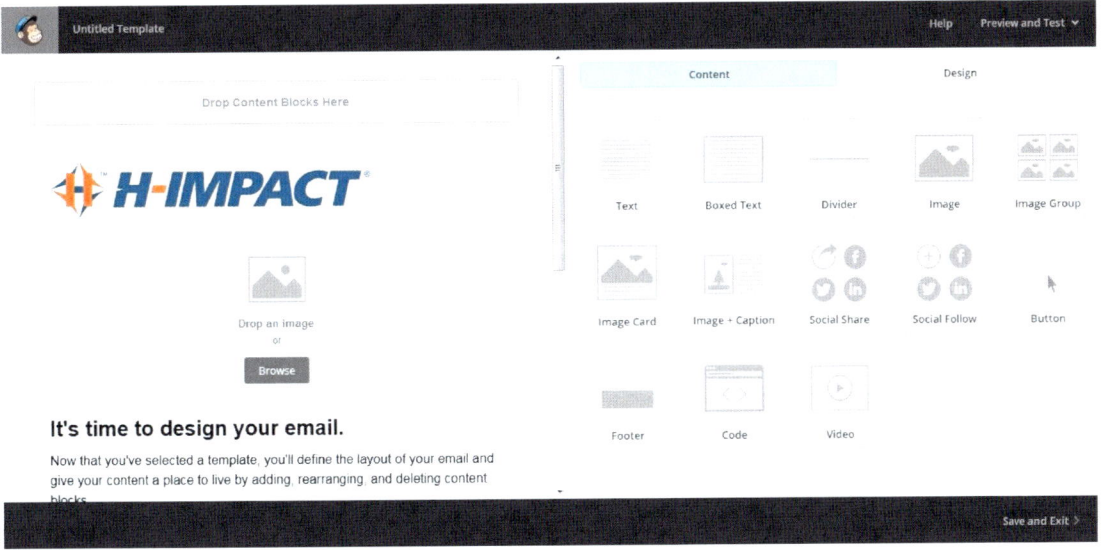

Configure Main Image Content Block

Now we need a header image that helps to describe the email message. We will use the original **Image Content Block** to insert this image.

- Use the mouse to **Click** and **Select** the original **Image Content Block** in the left pane.

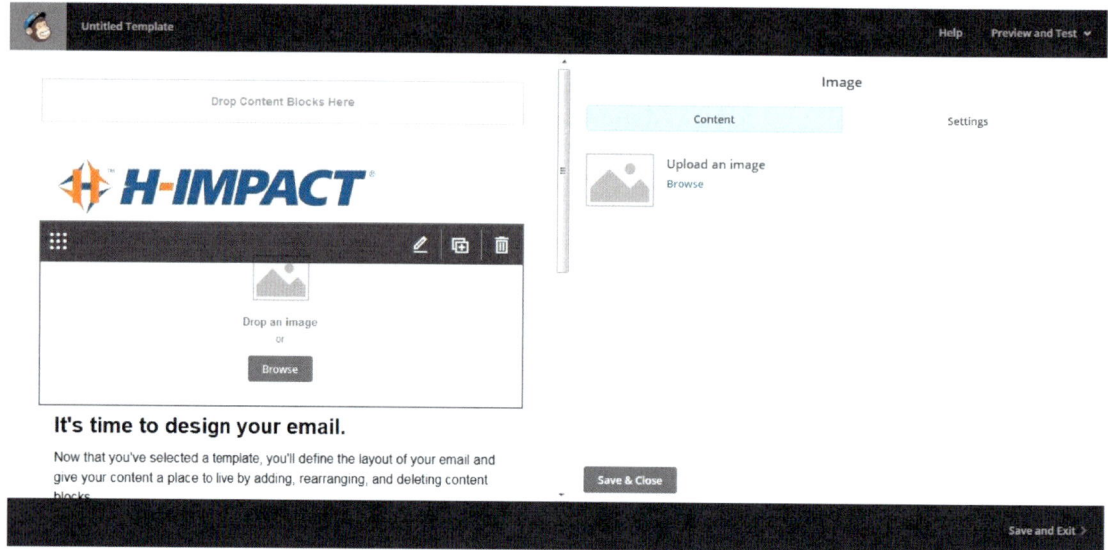

Click the **Browse** link in the right pane to upload the **Template's Main Header Image**.

Upload Main Image Using Content Manager

The **Content Manager** displays. Unlike the **Logo** Image, we need to upload into the **Content Manager** the **Main Header Image** from our local drive or folder source.

- Click the **Upload** button in the upper right hand corner of the screen.

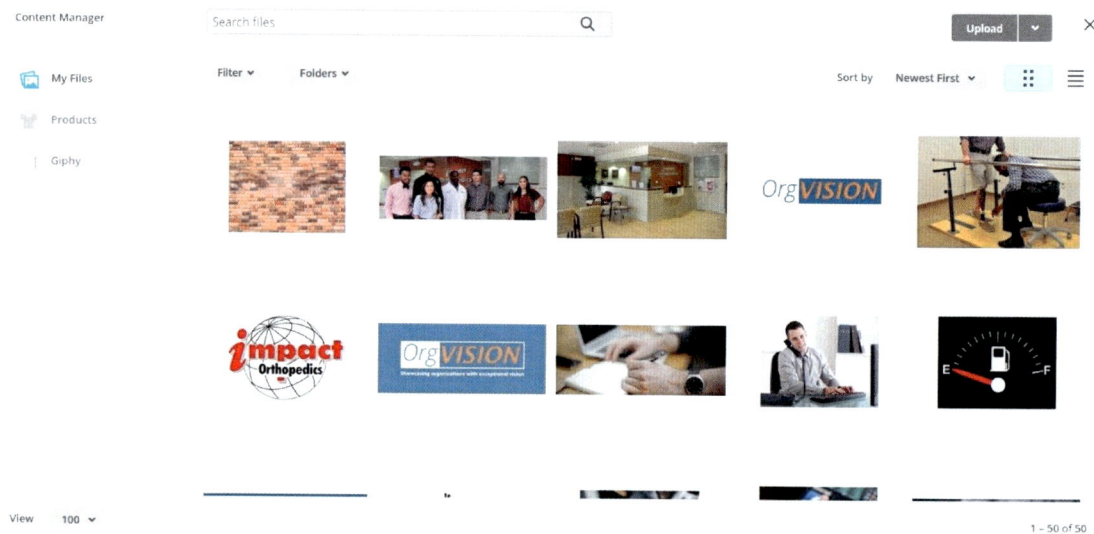

- The **Open Dialogue Box** displays. **Navigate** to the source folder that contains the **Main Header Image**.

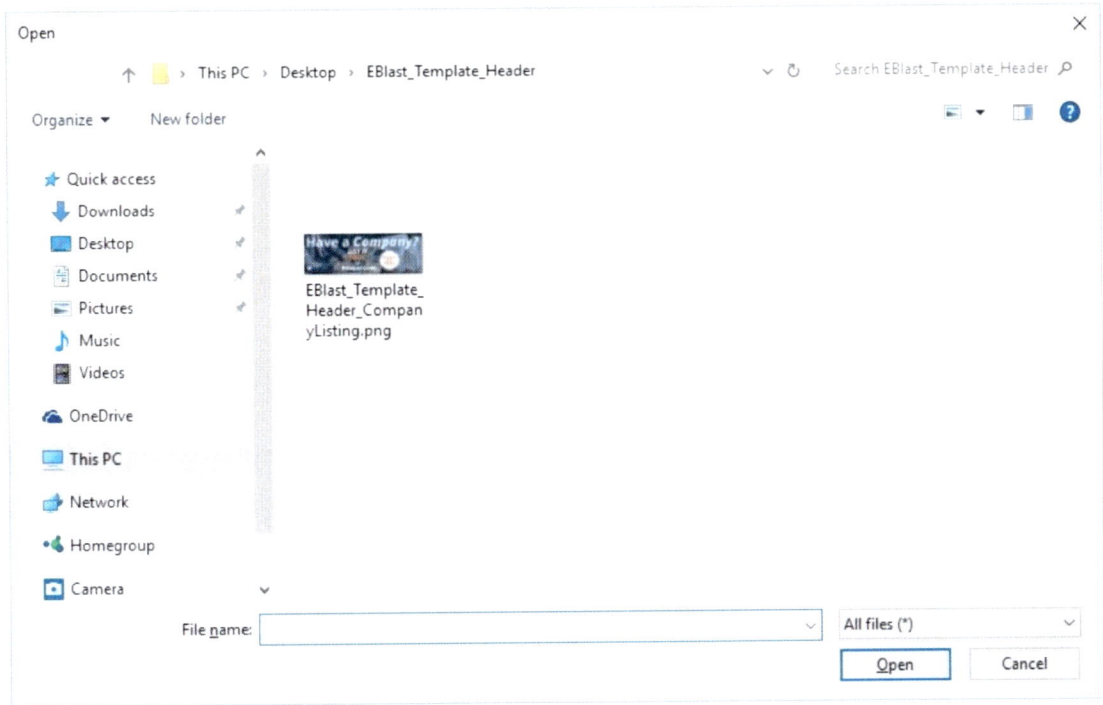

- Click the **Main Header Image**. In our case the image file is named **EBlast_Template_Header_CompanyListing.png**. *Note: Our image is a PNG. JPEGS and other image types are acceptable. Also, our image has overlaid text with some other colorization effects which was created in a photo editing or graphics program prior to this upload. The image does not have to have text or have any colorization effects. It can simply be an image without text that gives the user an idea about the content of the email. Also, the image that we have chosen has a width of 600px and a height of 200px. Once uploaded,* **MailChimp** *will give you a warning if the image doesn't meet their dimension recommendations for the image's best possible display.* **MailChimp** *may autocorrect your images dimensions or require you correct the image and then upload a corrected version of the image. The image we've currently selected does meet the recommendations.*

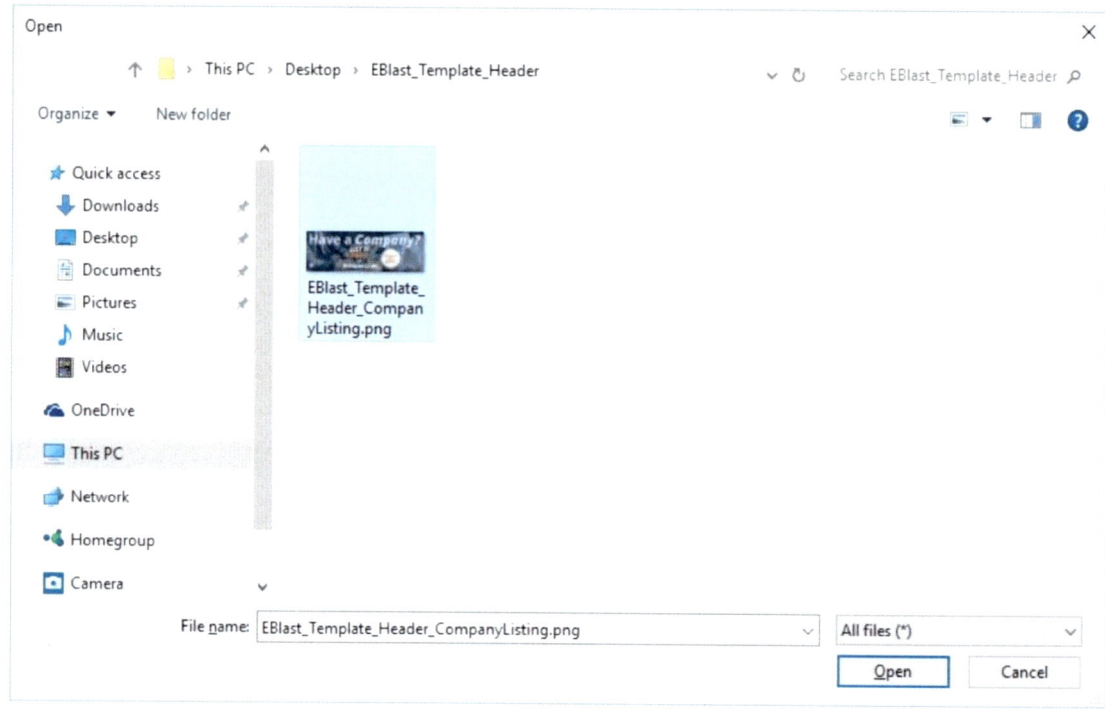

- The image should now be positioned in the proper place beneath the logo in the header of the **Email Template**.

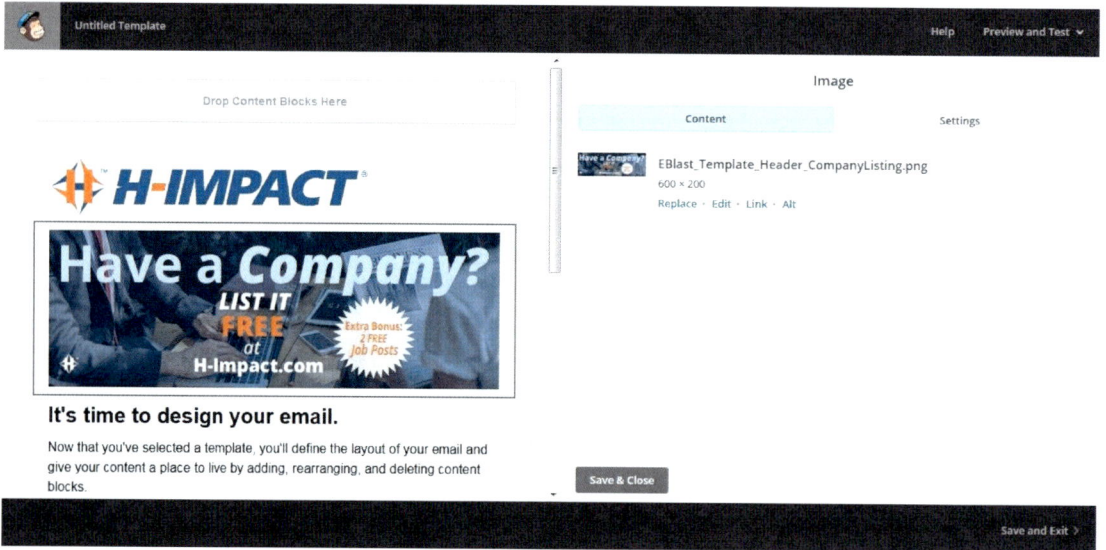

- Click **Save & Close** to save the changes.

Update the Main Image's Link to Web address

- Update the **Main** Image so that it links to the company's web page with the content that best describes the email's content. Click **Link** in the right pane. The dialogue box displays.

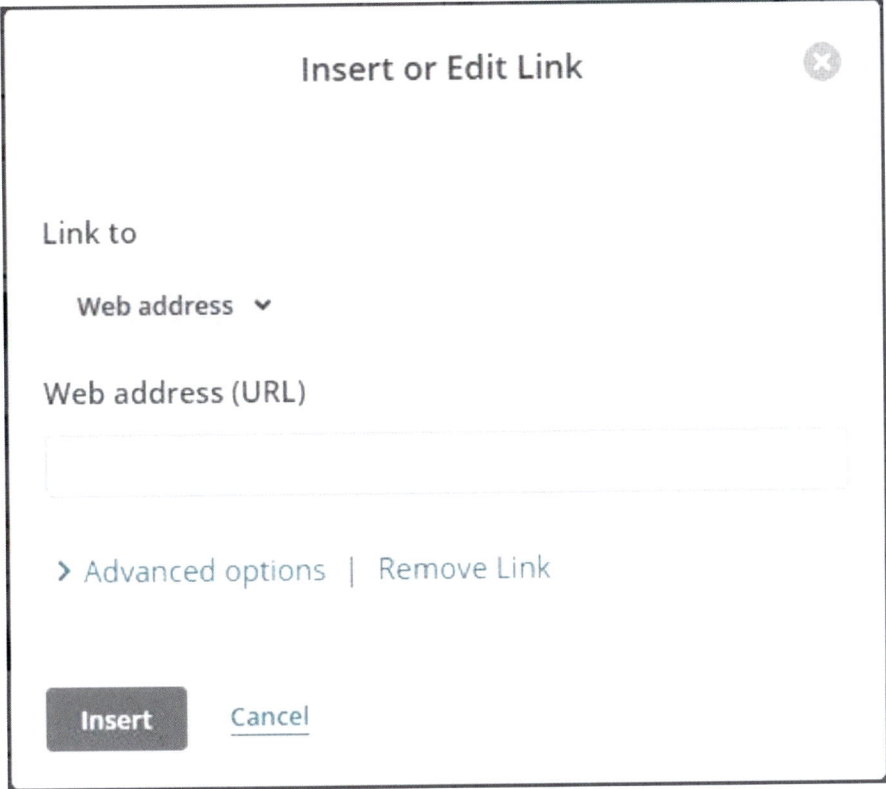

- When the dialogue box displays, enter the following Web address to point to the company's web page that best describes the email's content:
https://www.h-impact.com/organization-benefits
*Note: Alternatively, you may want to define your link with a query string and source code as mentioned previously in the **Defining Links with Source Codes** section.*

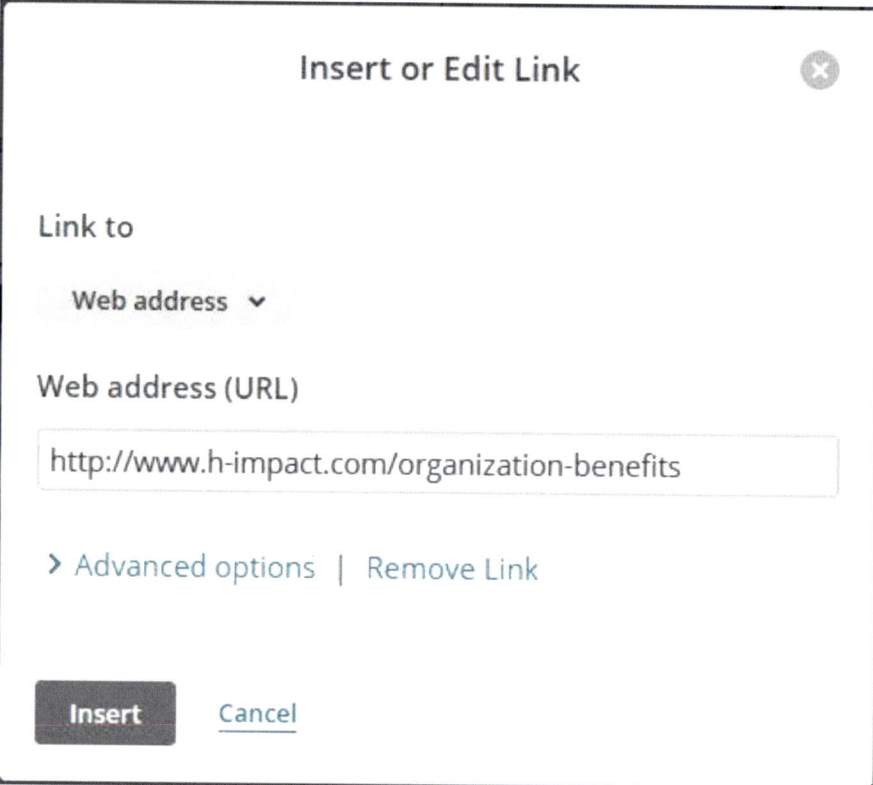

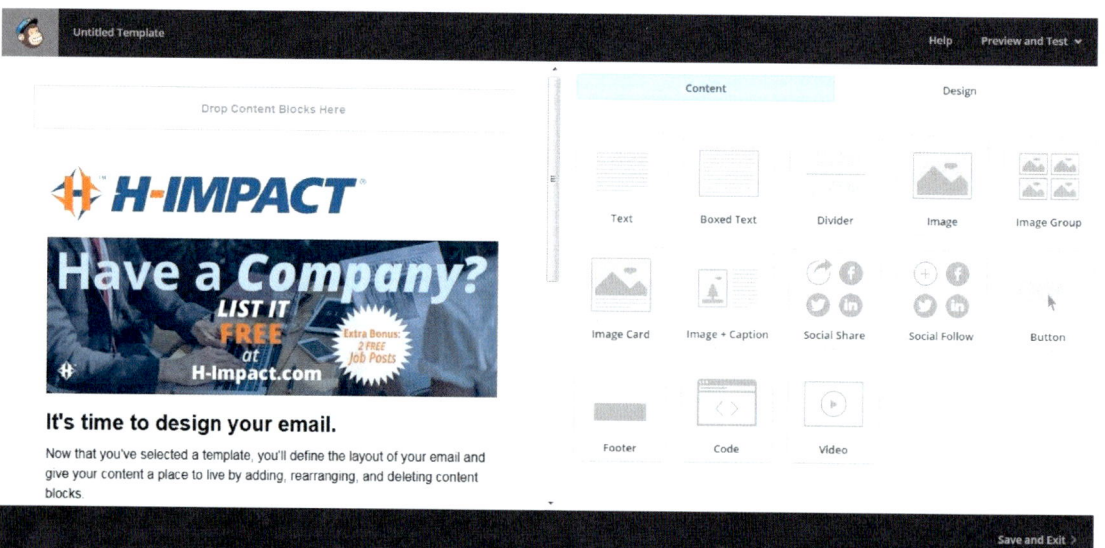

Update Main Body with Text Content Block

Now let's begin composing the body of the email.

- Use the mouse to **Click** and **Select** the original **Text Content Block** located in the body of the template in the left pane. An editable **WYSIWYG (What You See Is What You Get) Text Content Block** appears in the right pane which is used to update the text in the email.
- Use the middle scroll bar to fully display the formatted text in the left pane as the text is entered in the right pane.

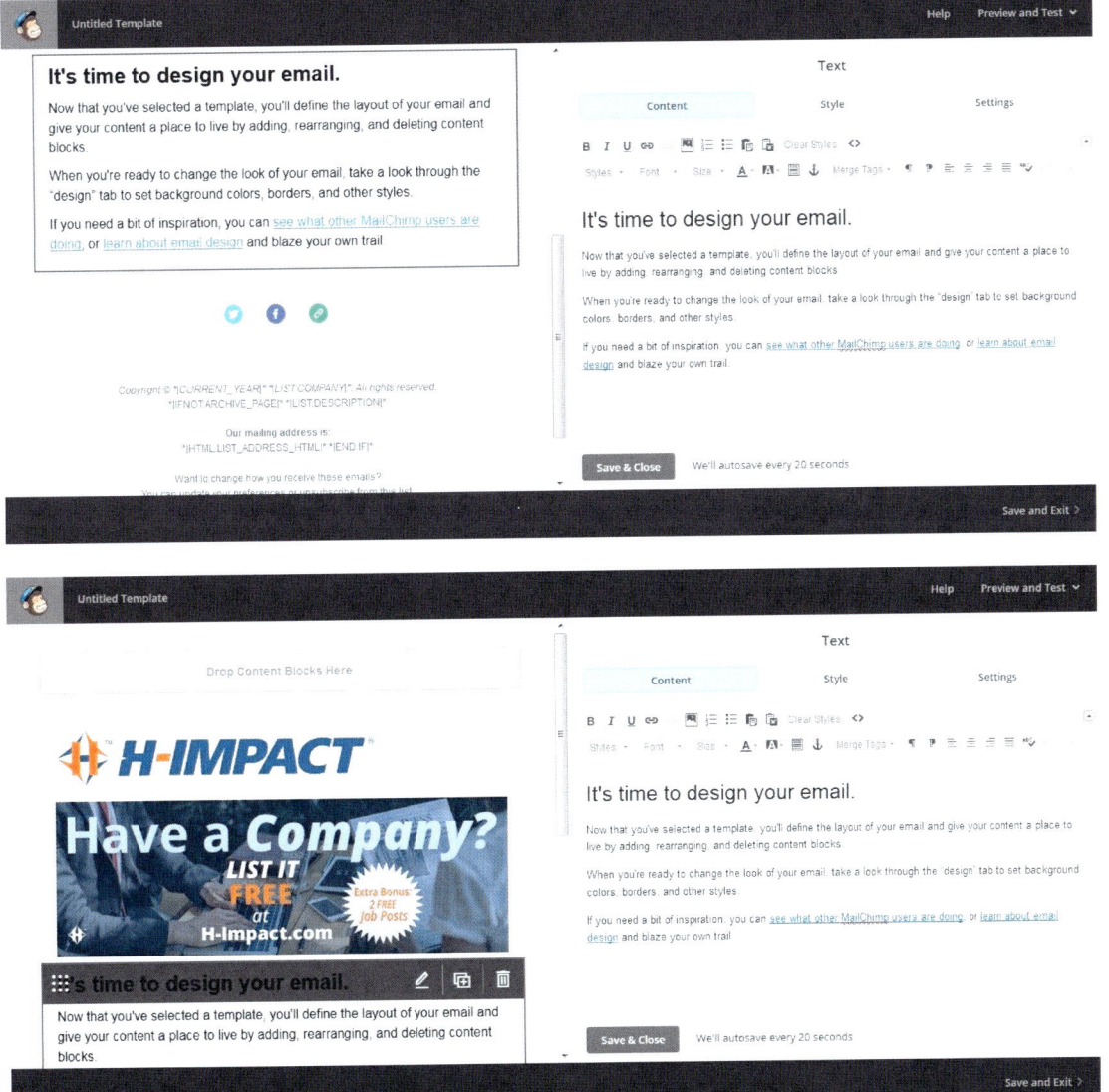

Now let's update the header text using the text editor.

- In the right pane, highlight the default text and replace it with a heading more suitable for our email. Enter **List Today and Increase Your Exposure** for our heading.

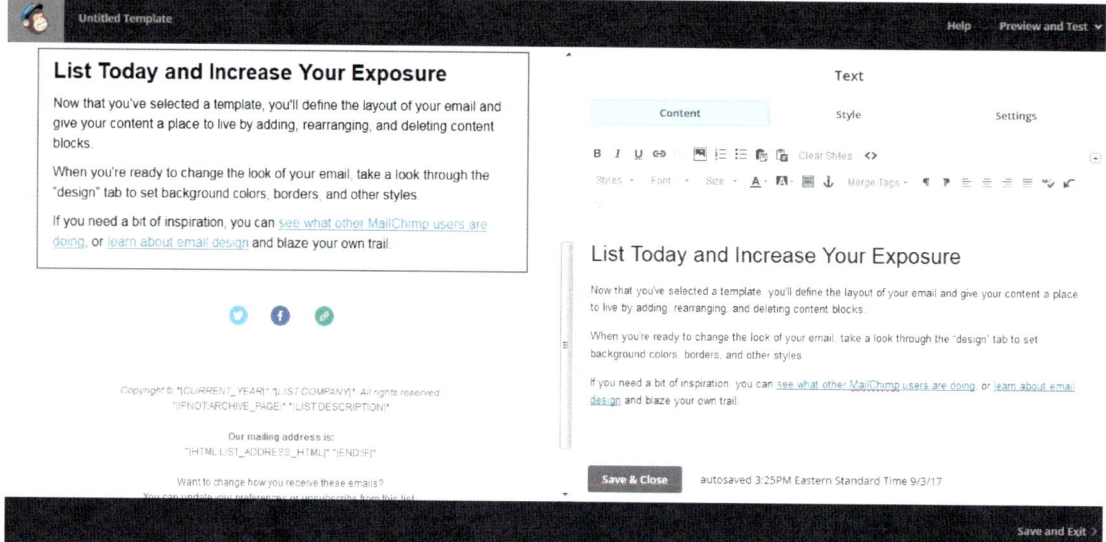

Now let's include a salutation to make this email more personable which studies have shown results in more **Opens** and recipient engagements overall. We need to use **Merge Field Indicators** to take advantage of the field names (ie Column Names) in our **Subscriber Lists**. We will discuss **Merge Field Indicators** and **Tags** later on in this book.

For now, simply enter the following line, with the exception of the bullet symbol of course, below the bolded heading:

- Hello *|IF:FNAME|* *|FNAME|*, *|ELSE:|* Friend, *|END:IF|*

This line of code will either generate a salutation that will address the recipient by their **First Name** or by **Friend** if the **First Name** is not included in the **Subscriber List**. Again this will be explained in more detail later in the sections titled **Creating Lists Overview** and **Add Subscribers**. For now simply enter this line *exactly* as it is written above.

- After entering the salutation, enter the following text to complete the main body text in the email (without the double quotes):

"Do you own a company or organization and want more online exposure?

At H-Impact, you can list your company/organization for FREE. At no charge, your organization is provided a custom page to update with your logo, organization's contact info with description, phone, web address, map of your location, and more. Sign-up FREE and get listed today to appear in our online publicly searchable Organization directory.

Need to post jobs as well? Enjoy the extra bonus of 2 FREE Job Posts."

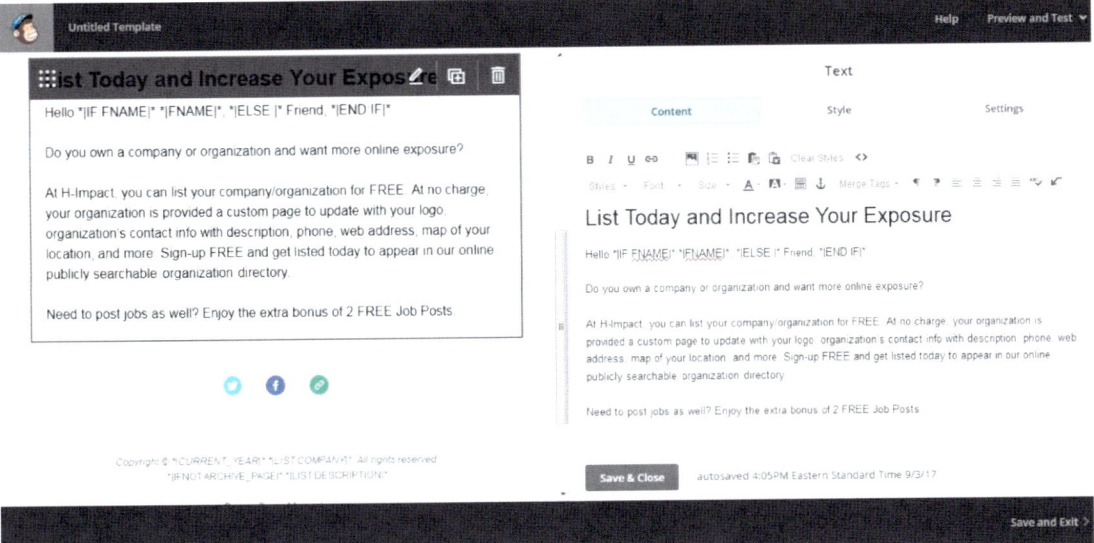

- Click **Save & Close**.

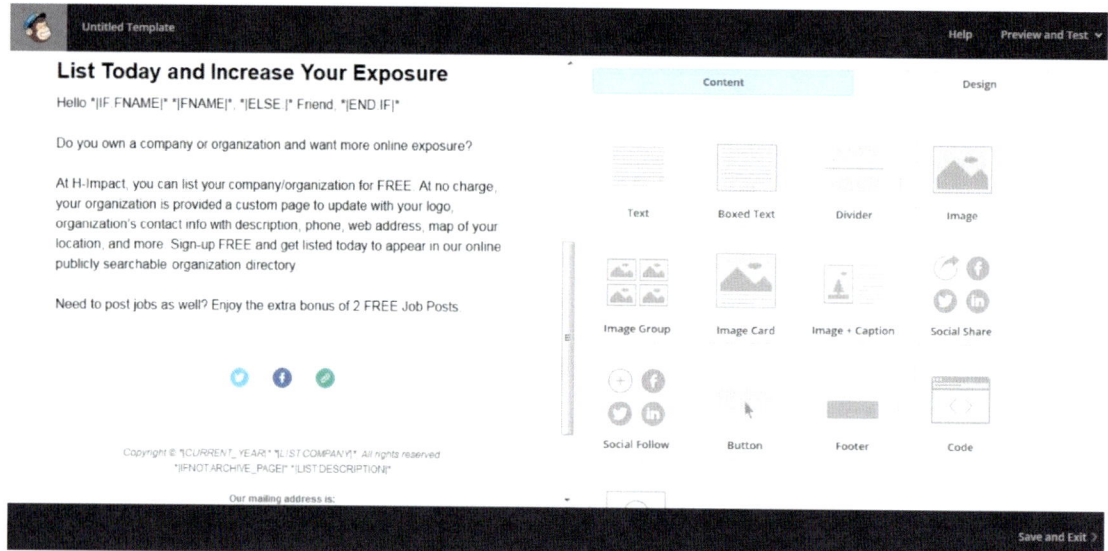

Adding Button Content Block

Now we need to add a **Button** as a **Call-to-Action** to visit the company's website from our **Email Template**. To add the **Button Content Block** we can drag the **Button Content Block** from the right pane and place it where we want to in the left pane.

- Click and hold the **Button Content Block** and **Drag it** to the left pane to place it right below the **Body Text Content Block**. Make sure you place the **Button Content Block** in the body with the white background on the inside of the gray line right beneath the text. The message **Drop block here** should appear to help you place the **Button Content Block**.

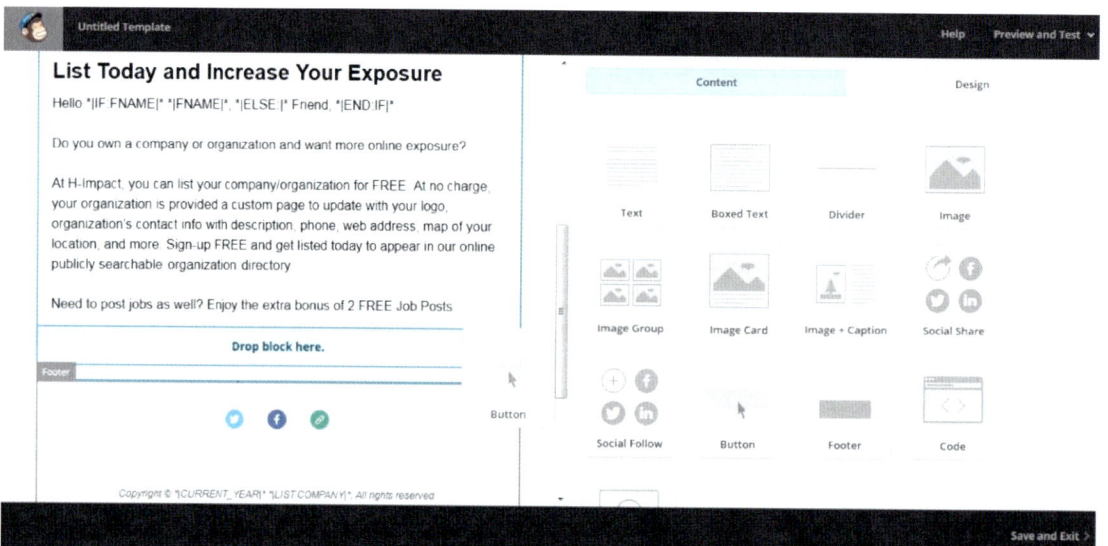

- Release the mouse to place the **Button** beneath the **Body Text**.

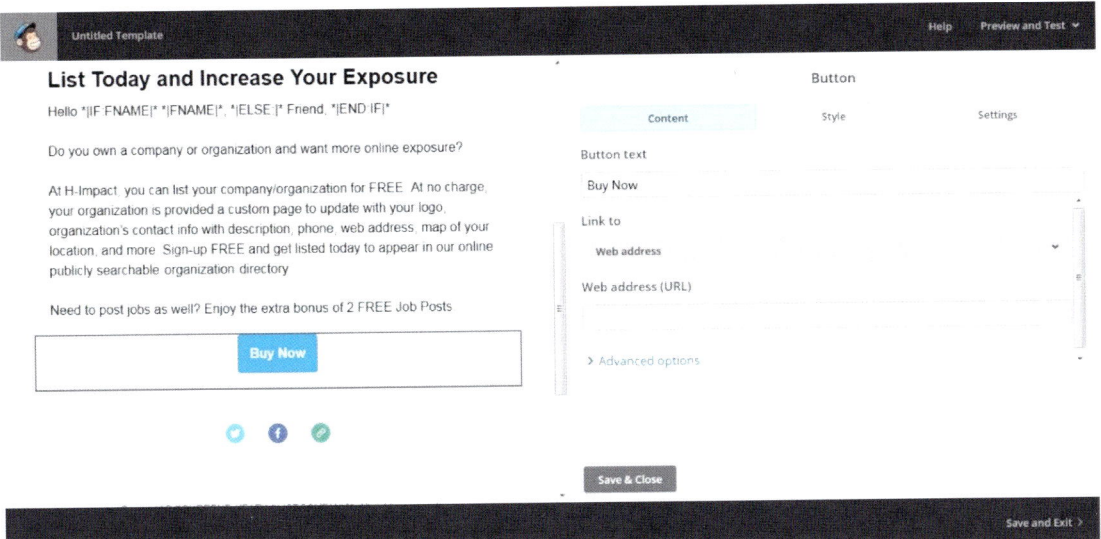

Update Button Content and Style

Now let's update the **Button's Content** and **Style**. We need to customize the **Button** to match our company's branding and colors. This, as well as all content within the email, will vary depending on the purpose of the eBlast.

In the right pane with the **Content** tab selected:

- Change **Buy Now** to **List Today**.
- Enter the following for the **Web address (URL)**: https://www.h-impact.com/organization-benefits
  *Note: Alternatively, you may want to define your link with a query string and source code as mentioned previously in the **Defining Links with Source Codes** section.*

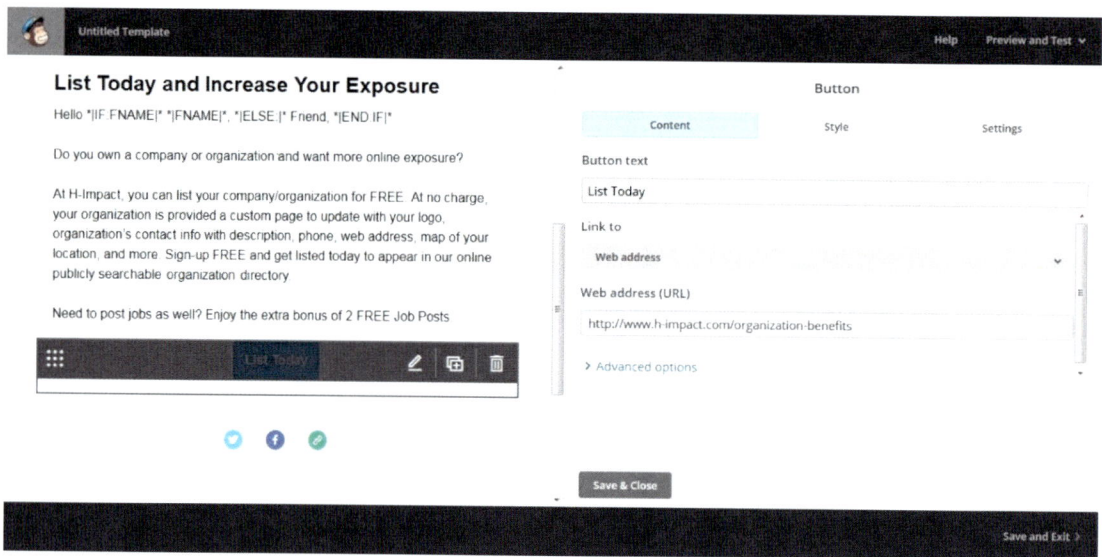

With the **Style** tab selected, under the **Button Style** section:

- Keep the **Border** and **Border radius** defaults.

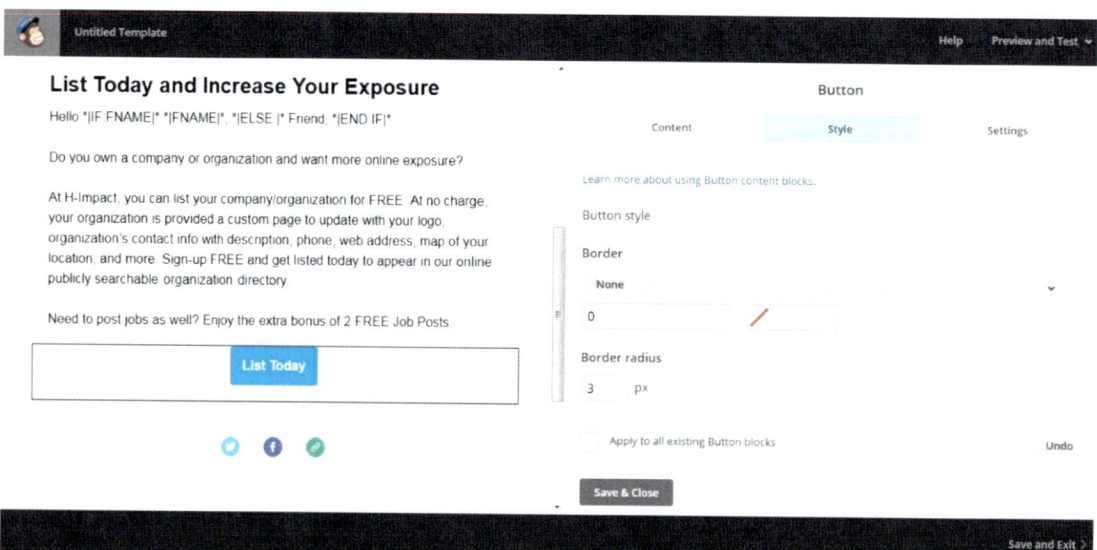

- Update the **Button's Background** to **#ec7425**.

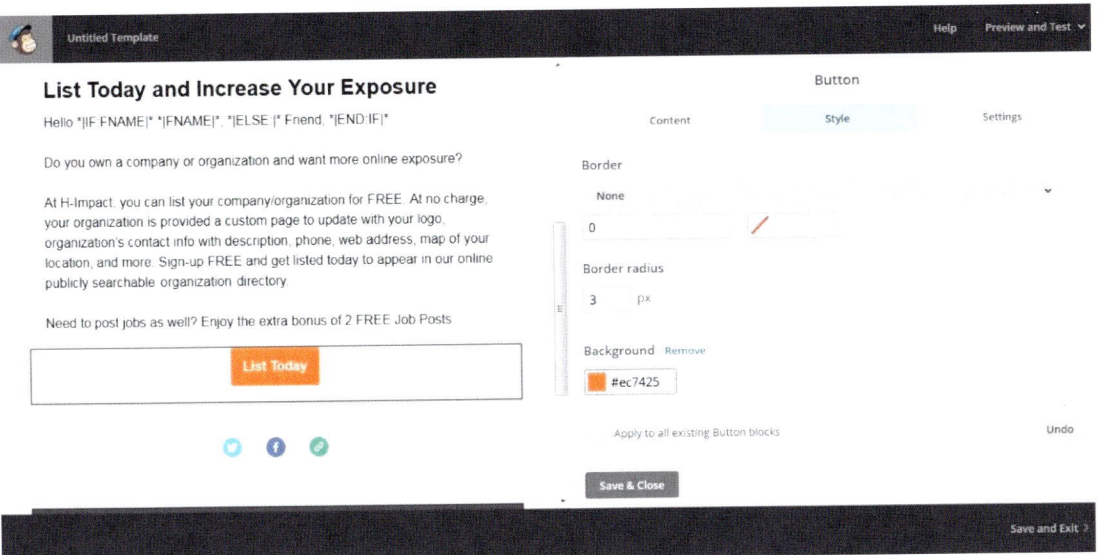

- Use the vertical scroll bar on the far **right** side of the page to scroll to the **Text Style** area.

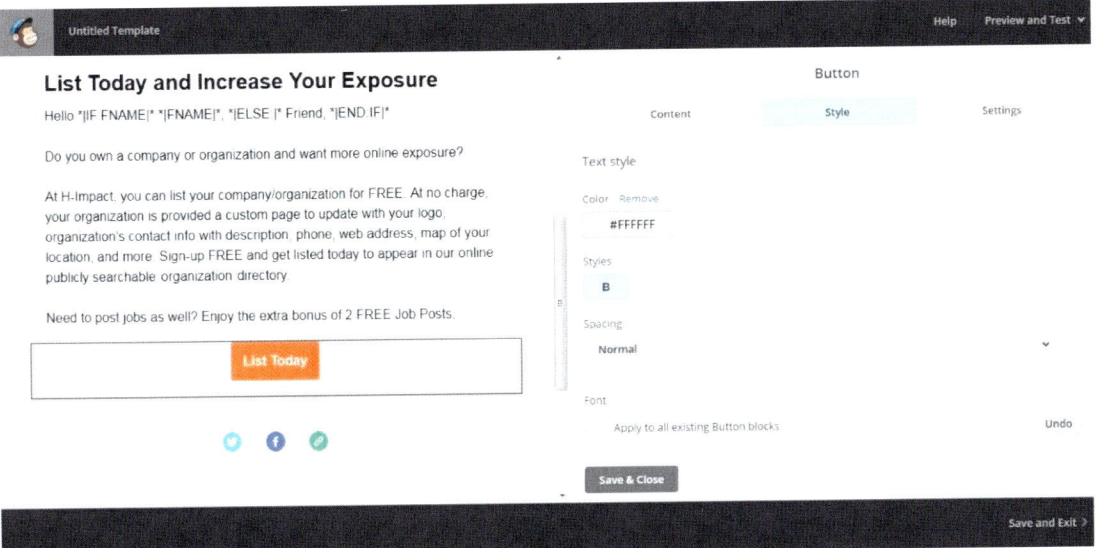

- Accept the defaults for: **Color** #FFFFFF; **Styles** B; **Spacing** Normal; **Font** Arial.
- Change **Size** from 15px to 22px and accept the default for: **Padding** 15.

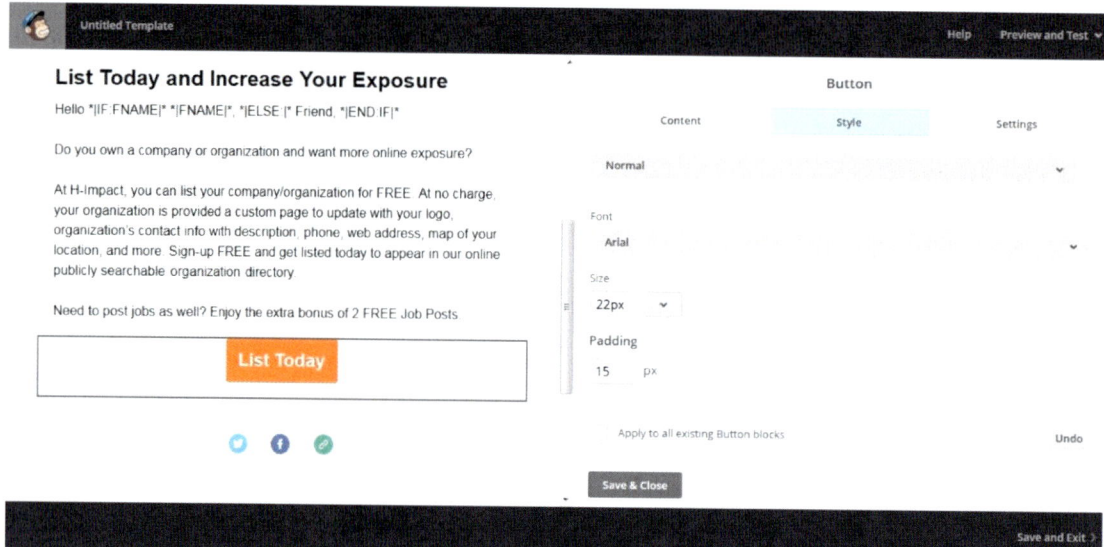

- Click **Save & Close**.

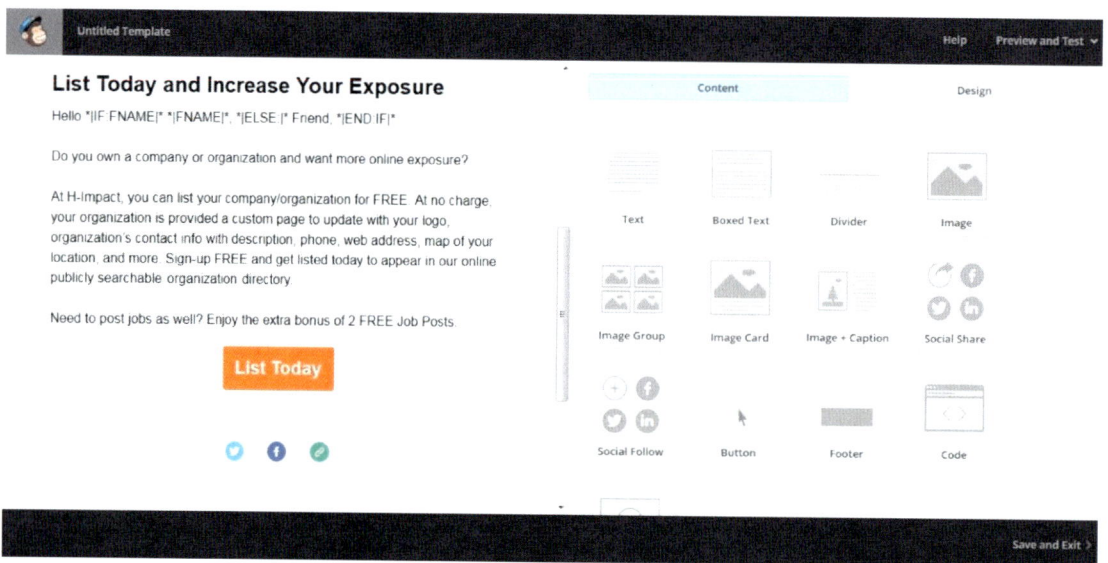

Adding Another Text Content Block for Closing Text

Let's add a closing to this email. To do this we need to add an additional **Text Content Block** to the **Template**. We need to place it below the **Button Content Block**. To add the **Text Content Block** we can drag it from the right pane and place it below the **Button Content Block** in the left pane.

- Click and hold the **Text Content Block** and **Drag it** to the left pane to place it right below the **Button Content Block**. Make sure you place the **Text Content Block** in the body with the white background on the inside of the gray line indicating the bottom of the body area. The **Drop block here** message should appear to help you place the **Text Content Block**.

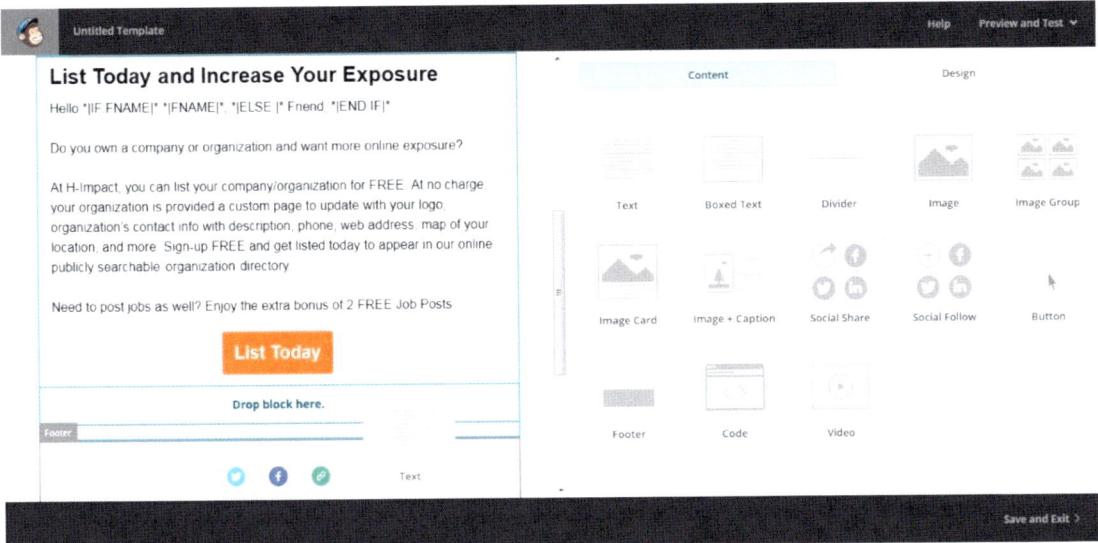

- The **Text Content Block** displays and the editable **WYSIWYG** displays in the right pane.

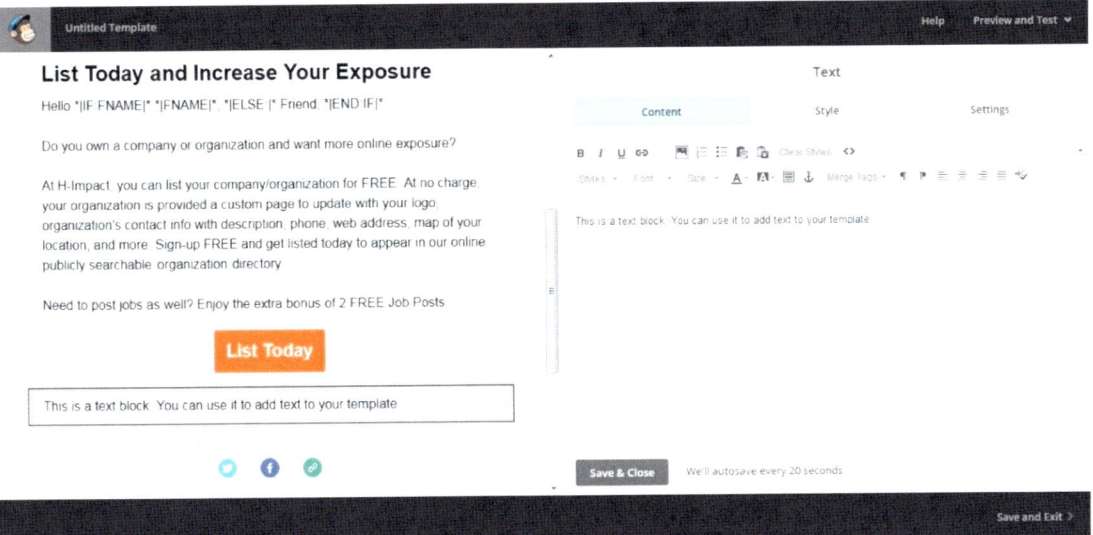

- Update the Text to include a closing and standard signature such as:

We look forward to having you as the next organization listed in our directory.

Sincerely,

Travis Holt

Co-Founder & CEO, H-Impact LLC

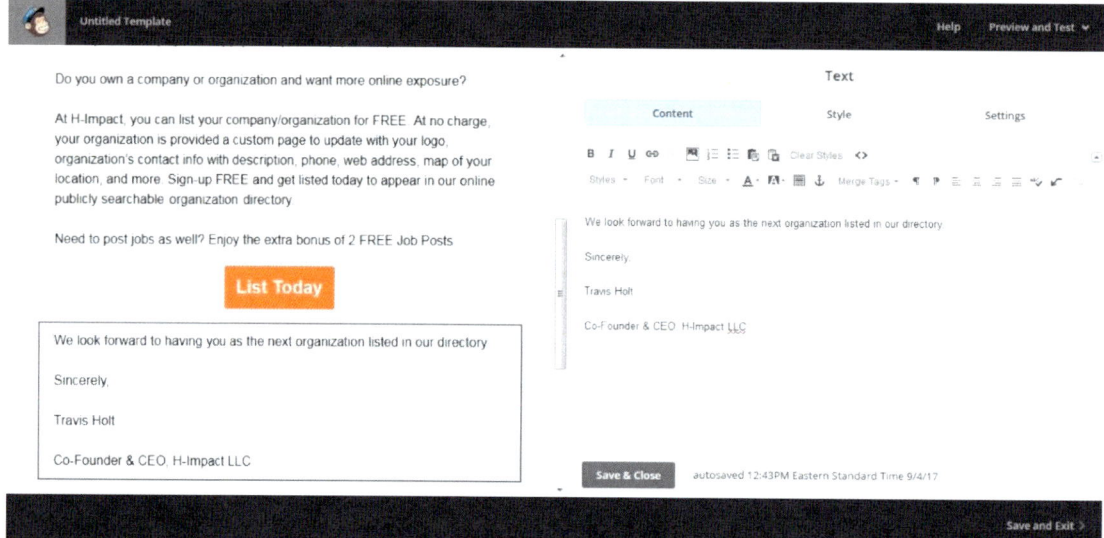

- To add additional styling for emphasis purposes, highlight and click the **Bold Formatting button** identified in the right pane's toolbar with the letter **B.**

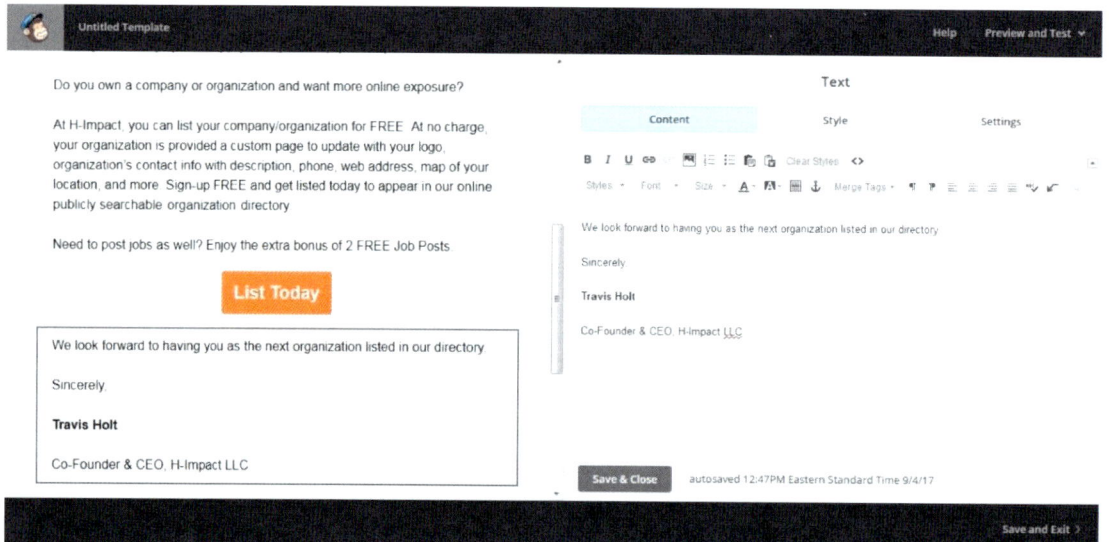

- Click **Save & Close**.

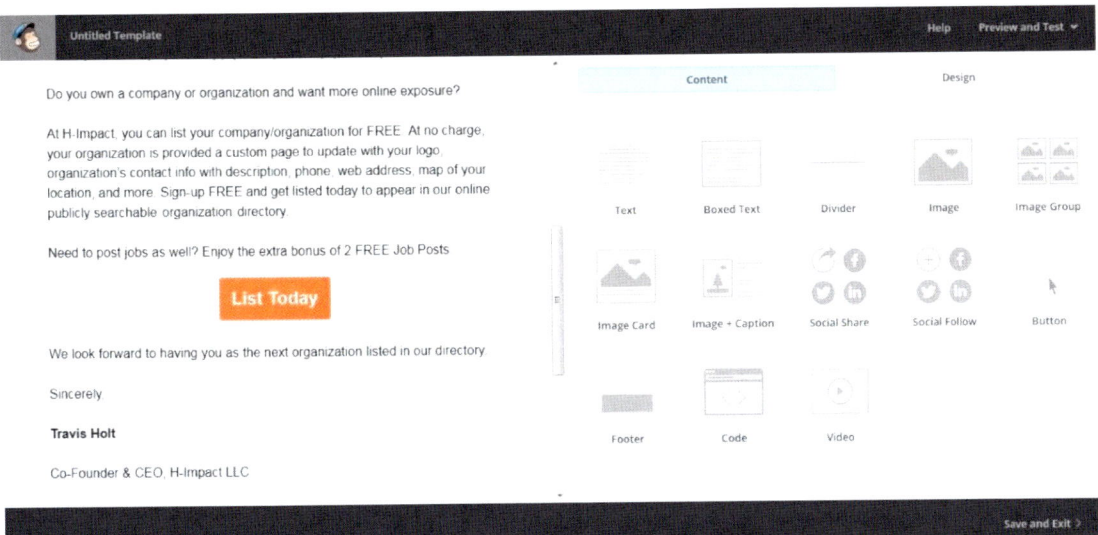

Update Footer's Default Social Share Content Block

We are ready to update the footer. By default the **Template** comes with a **Social Follow Content Block** in the footer which is configurable. We need to update the **Social Media Links' Target URL's** to point to our company's respective **Social Media** websites to allow the recipients of this email to easily navigate to our company's **Social Media** websites. We also have the option of updating an additional icon that points to our company's website.

For each **Social Media Link**, there is a drop down that is used to pick the **Social Media Site**, a **URL** for the **Web address** and **Link** text used optionally if the user chooses to display the **Link Text**. Finally, the links can be reordered using the repositioning handle identified by the three vertical dots at the beginning of each **Social Media** row, as desired to the satisfaction of the user/company sending the email.

Reorder Social Media Icons

Let's reorder the default **Social Media icons**. We need to move the **Facebook icon** in front of the **Twitter icon**.

- Click and hold the **Facebook** handle identified by the three vertical dots and **Drag it** to the 1st slot. You'll notice a black bold border at the top of the **Twitter** row which indicates the **Social Media** row being moved (Facebook) is ready to be dropped to complete the reordering. **Facebook** should now be in the 1st slot and **Twitter** should be in the 2nd slot.

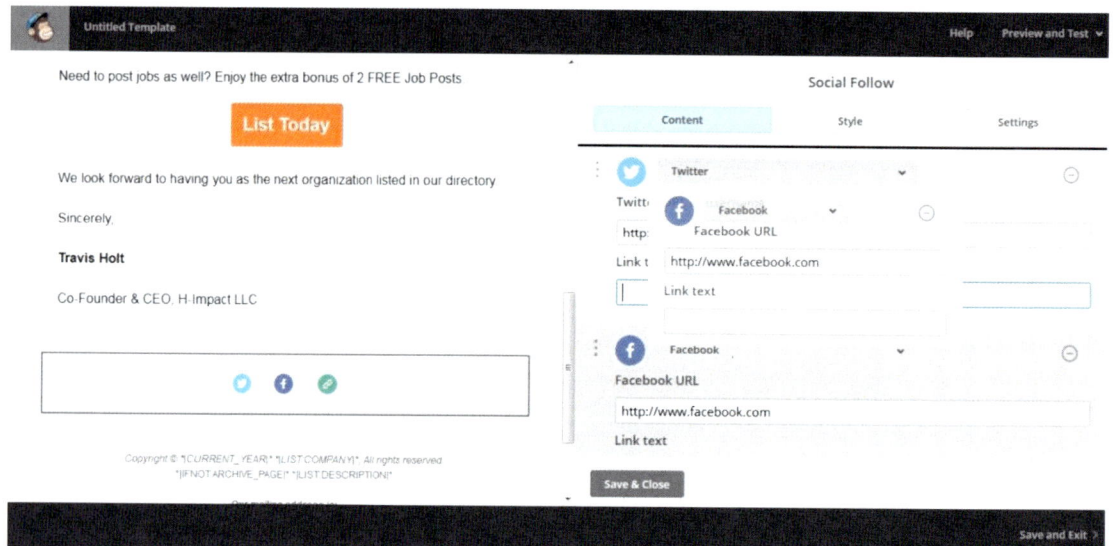

Configure Social Media Details

Now let's update the **Social Media** details for each icon. We will accept all defaults for the **Link** text on each **Social Media** icon. Again, these values will vary based on the company entering the data.

Our company's values for H-Impact are as follows:

- For **Facebook**, enter the **Facebook URL**: https://www.facebook.com/pages/H-Impact/763388233770079.
  Finally enter the **Link** text: Facebook
- For **Twitter**, enter the **Twitter URL or username**: https://twitter.com/HImpactPros.
  Enter the **Link** text: Twitter
- For **Website**, enter the **Website URL**: http://www.h-impact.com/home.
  Enter the **Website** text: Website
  *Note: Alternatively, you may want to define your link with a query string and source code as mentioned previously in the **Defining Links with Source Codes** section.*

Add New Social Media Service References

Now let's **add more services** and reorder them accordingly.

- Scroll to the bottom of the existing icons and click the **Add Another Service** button.

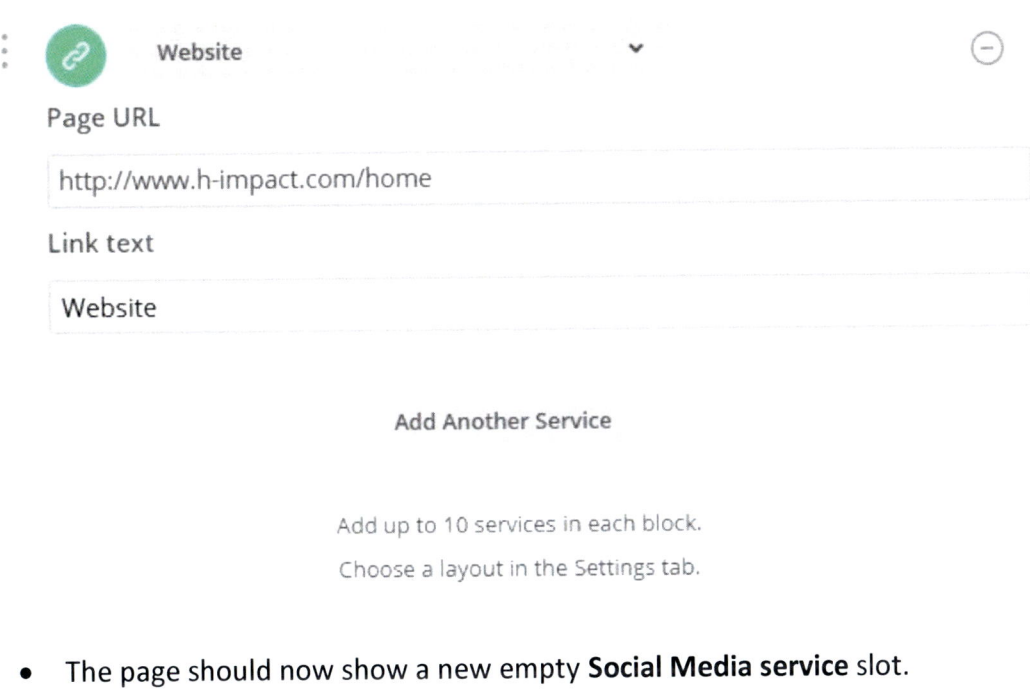

- The page should now show a new empty **Social Media service** slot.

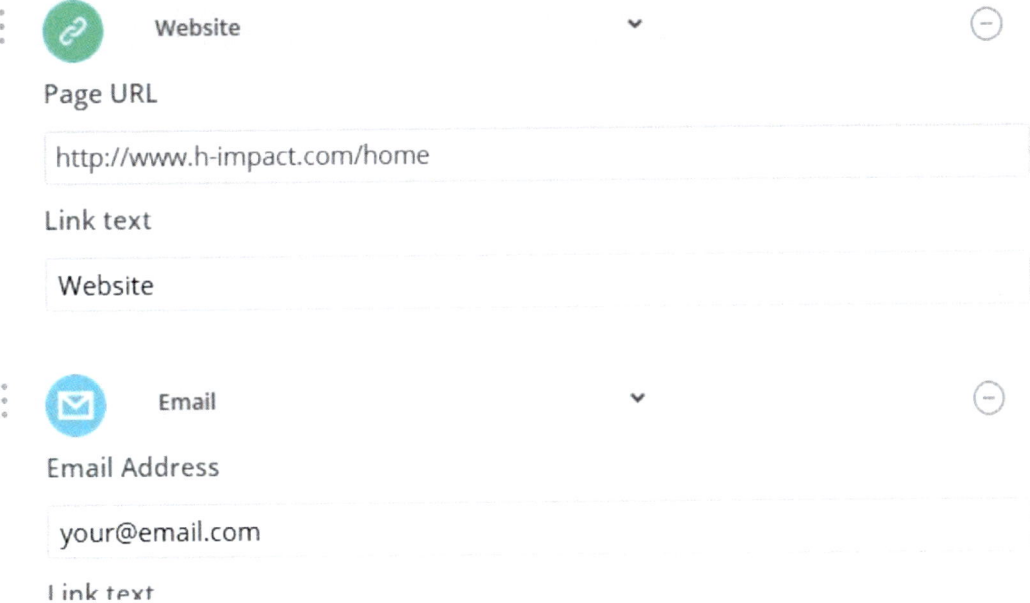

Reorder Social Media Service

Scroll to position the new **Social Media slot** with **Email** as the default. Ensure you are able to clearly see all fields that need to be updated. Let's enter **LinkedIn** information instead of **Email** in this new slot.

- To do so first choose **LinkedIn** from the drop down.

- For **LinkedIn**, enter the **LinkedIn profile URL**: https://www.linkedin.com/company/h-impact.
  Enter the Link text: LinkedIn

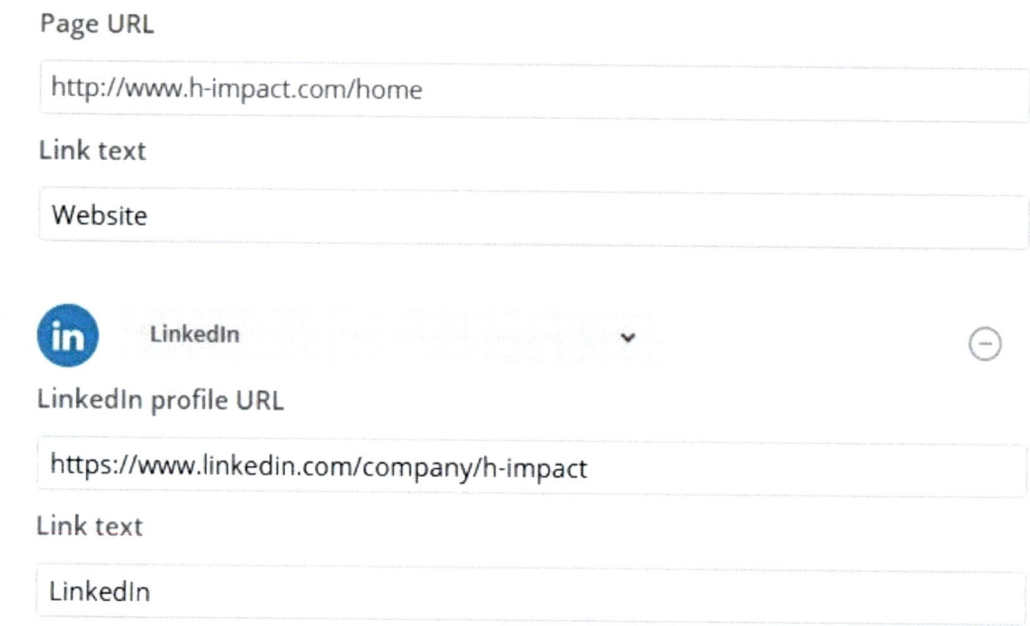

- Reposition to reorder **LinkedIn** below **Twitter** and above the **Website** slot. **Click** and **hold** the **LinkedIn** handle identified by the three vertical dots and **drag it** to the slot right above the **Website** service. Look for the bold black top border which indicates the **Social Media icon** is ready to be dropped.

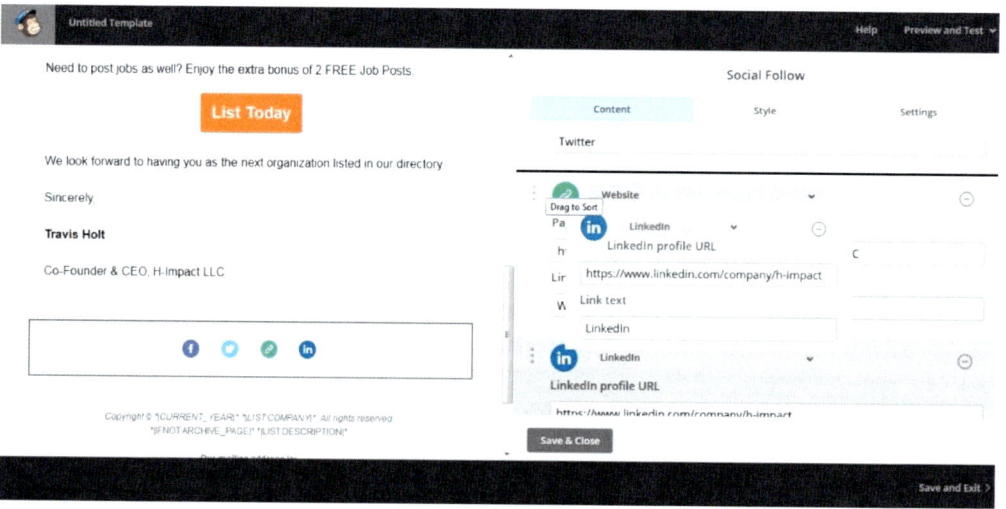

- **LinkedIn** should now appear below **Twitter** and above the **Website** slot.

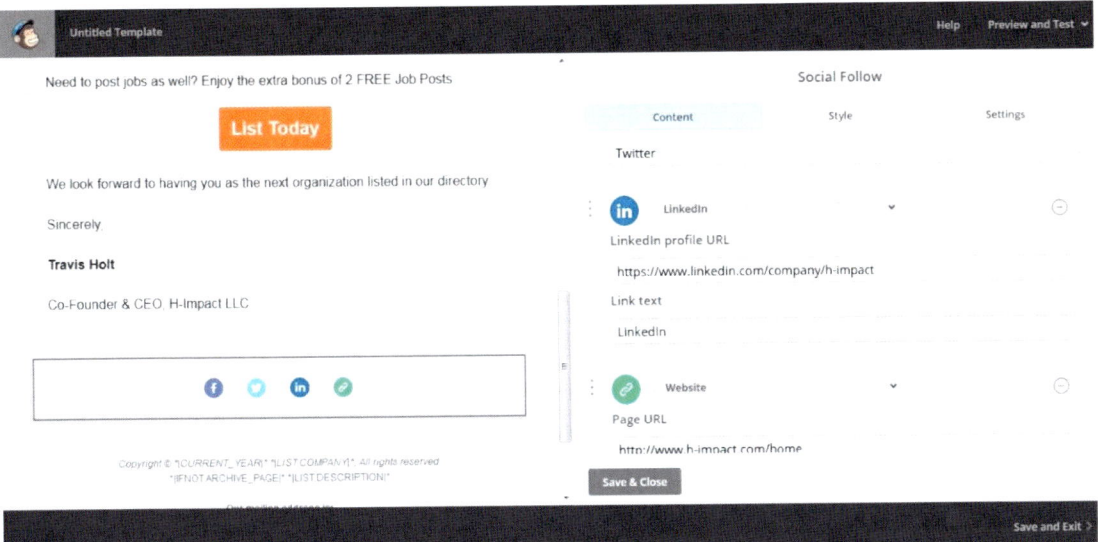

Add, Reorder, and Configure More Social Media Services

- Scroll to the bottom of the **Social Media icons** and locate the **Add Another Service button** to add **YouTube**. Repeat the steps used to add **LinkedIn** by positioning **YouTube** right above the **Website** service.
- For **YouTube**, enter the **YouTube channel URL**: https://www.youtube.com/channel/UCwR9pelif7dLOzVS4cBGRKA.
  Enter the **Link text**: YouTube
- Scroll to the bottom of the **Social Media icons** and locate the **Add Another Service button** to add **Google Plus**. Repeat the steps used to add **LinkedIn** by positioning **Google Plus** right above the **Website** service.
- For **Google Plus**, enter the **Google Plus profile URL**: https://plus.google.com/101189913328700271420/about?hl=en.
  Enter the **Link text**: Google Plus
- Click **Save & Close**.

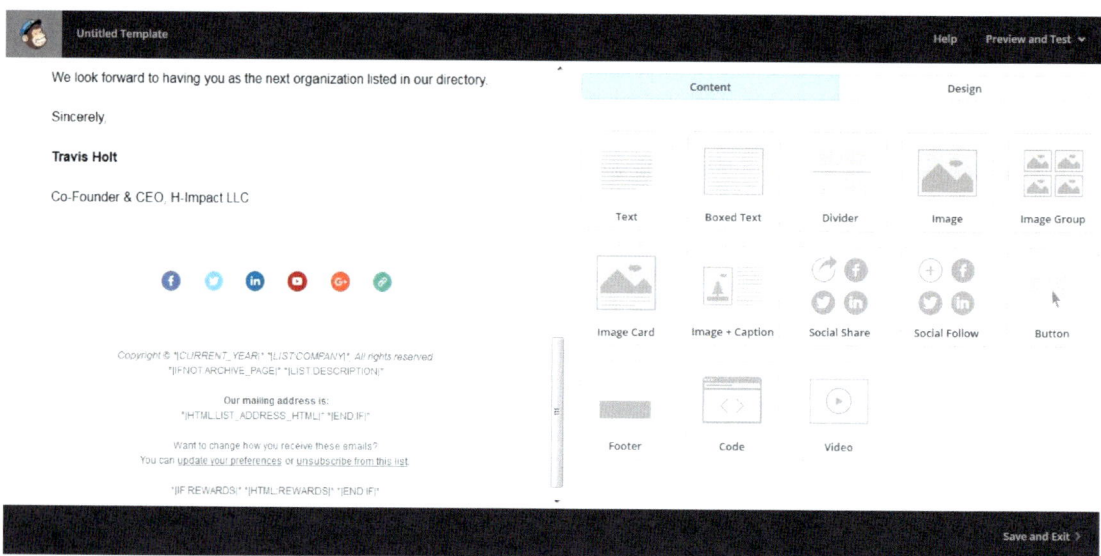

Once completely updated with the respective **Social Media Links** and from the left pane *after clicking to select the newly updated and reordered* **Social Media Follow Content Block**, the **right pane** should resemble the following:

Chapter 3: Templates 69

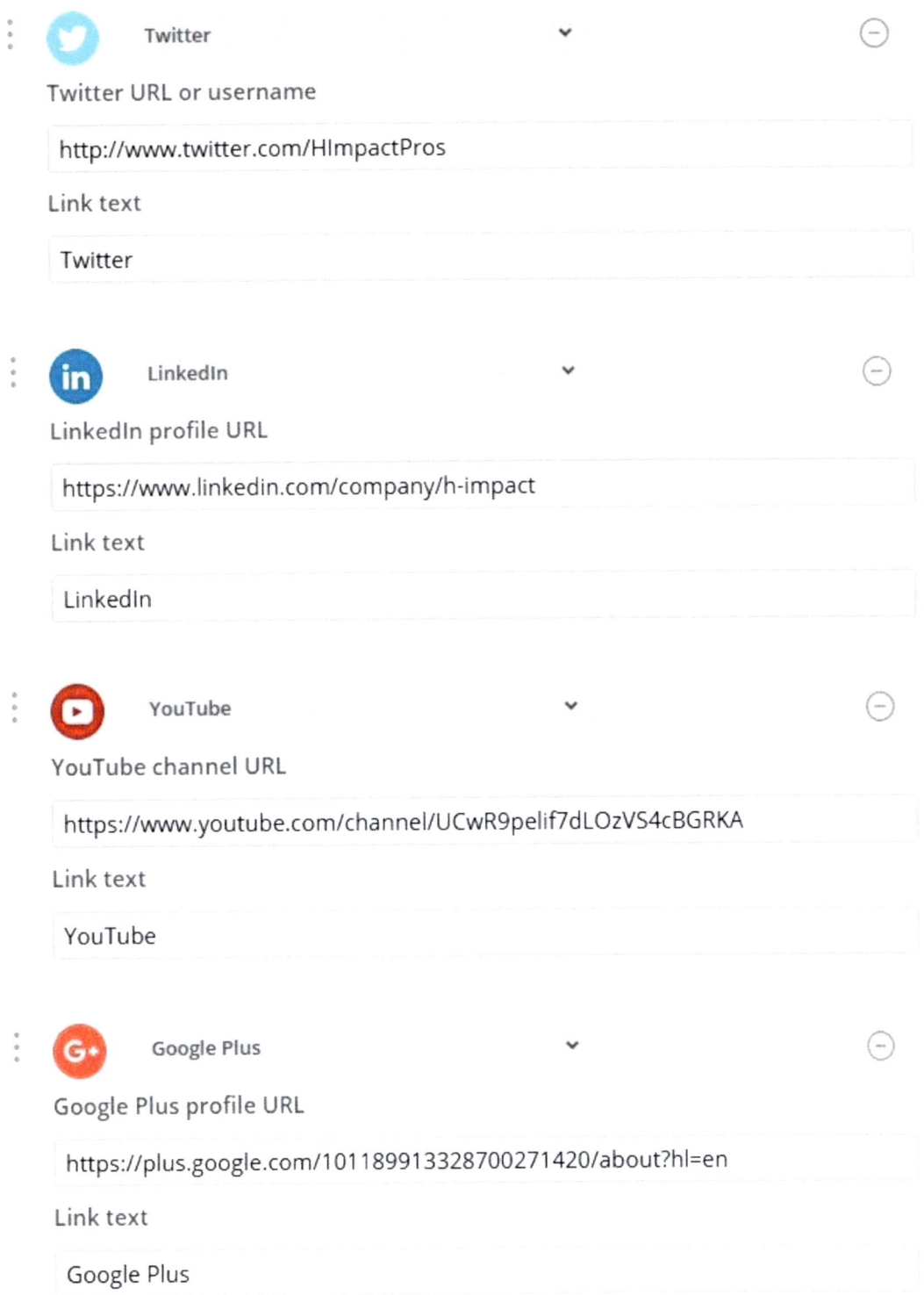

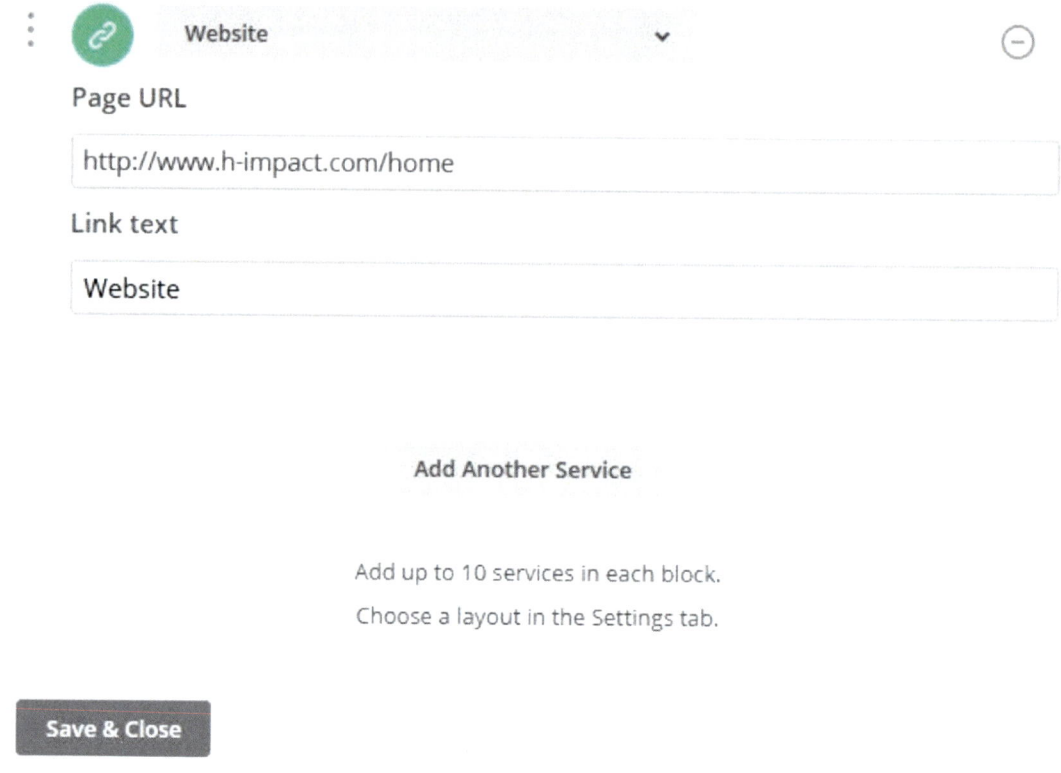

Footer Content Block

The footer also includes a **Footer Content Block** by default. To access the content within this block click hover and click the last content block at the bottom of the template. Just like other Content Blocks the content in this block can be edited, but caution must be applied. Contact Information in this block is required in all campaigns to comply with the CAN-SPAM Act and international spam law. **MailChimp** automatically includes your contact info in the **Footer Content Block**. Similar to the salutation we used earlier, **Merge Field Indicators** are used to dynamically reference contact info provided during registration such as, **company name** and **address**.

In addition, other info included consists of the year for copyright purposes, and **Rewards** fields that indicate the email was generated using **MailChimp**. Also, as a result of the **CAN-SPAM Act**, individuals receiving campaign emails must be provided the ability to cancel or opt-out receiving emails. Individuals may opt-out by using the **unsubscribe from this list link** which allows them to remove their name from the **MailChimp** subscriber list. Once the recipient of the email clicks the link in the footer of the email, they are provided an online form by **MailChimp** to easily complete the unsubscribe process. Once unsubscribed, the recipient, and not the company, may only re-subscribe to receiving the emails again. The **Rewards Merge Field** references convert to a **MailChimp** logo for branding which is required when using the **New Business Forever Free** version of **MailChimp** but not the paid versions.

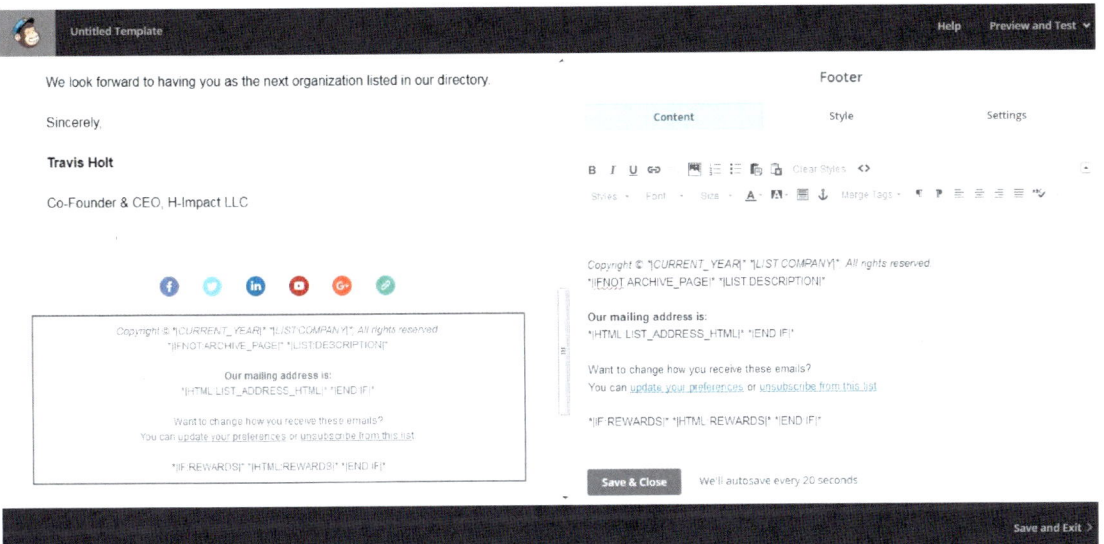

Step 4: Save Your Template

Once your **Template** has been edited, including replacing default text and other content, after clicking **Save and Close** to finish editing **Content Blocks,** we need to save the **Template** itself with a more relevant name to replace its current **Untitled Template** default name. Click **Save and Exit** to **Save the Template**. Enter the name of the new **Template** understanding it may be sent multiple times to various recipients. Unlike a **Campaign** name, the **Template** name should be less specific.

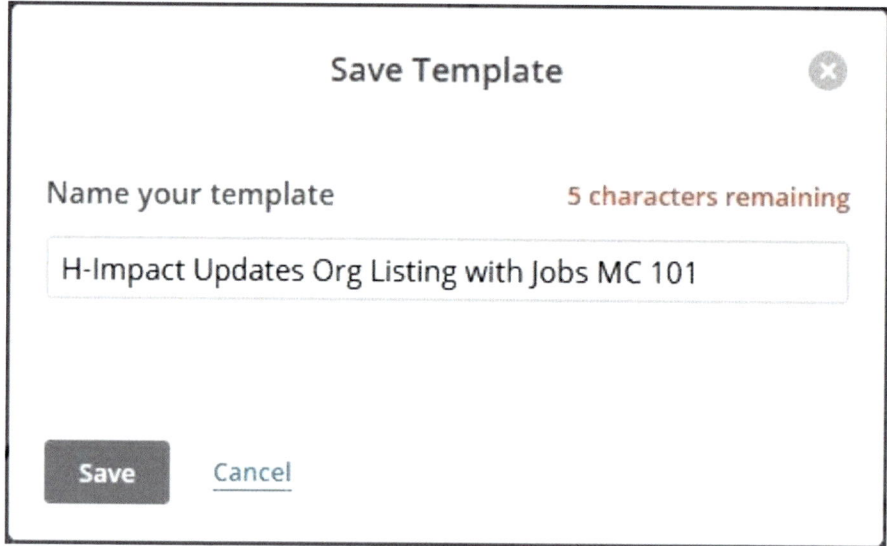

Editing a Template

To **Edit a Template** from the Templates page, identify the **Template** to edit and click the name or use the **Edit** button of the respective row.

Code Your Own Template

By editing a **Code Your Own** template a page will display with the well-formed email layout on the left, but an HTML panel on the right that allows you to edit the HTML directly. Note any edits performed in the **Edit Window** will auto-save within seconds after each update. This is something to keep in mind considering it is possible to lose the original HTML based on how quickly the auto save occurs. It is highly recommended that **Beginners** use the **Drag and Drop** type **Templates** and avoid using the **Code Your Own** Templates. **Code Your Own Templates** require an advanced level of understanding of web design and HTML.

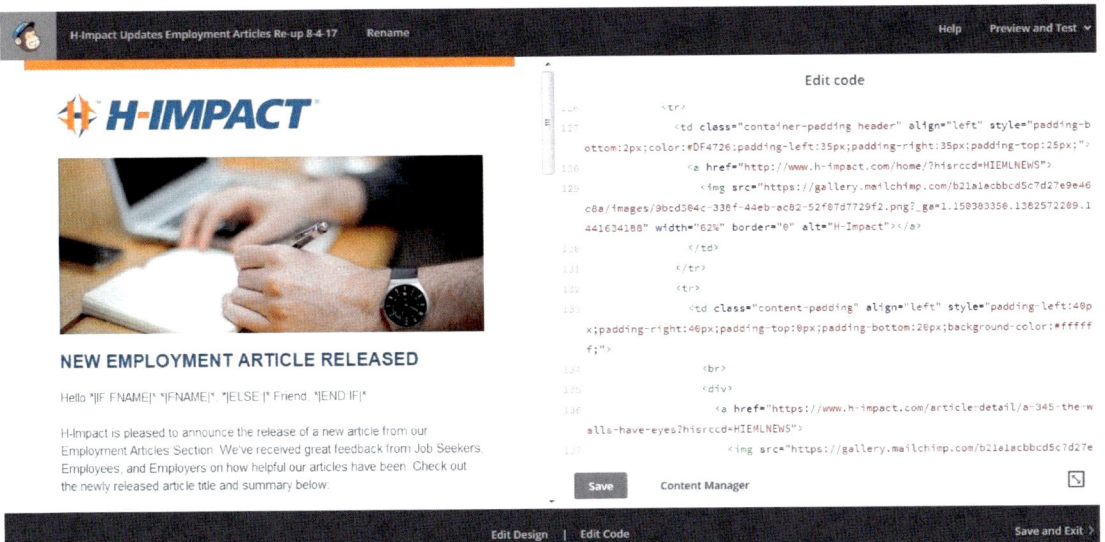

Drag and Drop Template

For users just getting started and may not understand HTML, **Drag and Drop Templates** are recommended. By editing a **Drag and Drop Template** a page will display with the well-formatted email layout on the left but optional **Content Blocks** on the right that can be dragged to the left.

The available default **Drag and Drop Content Blocks** that can be dragged from the right panel to the left panel include:

- Text
- Boxed Text
- Divider
- Image
- Image Group
- Image Card
- Image Caption
- Social Share
- Social Follow
- Button
- Footer
- Code
- Video

By clicking the **Content Block** once positioned in the left side of the screen, you are provided the edit panel on the right side that allows the **Content Block** to be updated. To update the **Content Blocks** on the left, use your mouse to hover over the **Content Block**, until you see a transparent black border around the **Content Block** with icons in the upper right corner resembling a:

- Checkered Square to Reposition
- Pencil to Edit
- Trash to Remove
- A Window with a + Symbol to Duplicate

For example, to edit a **Text Content Block**, hover over the **Content Block** in the left side of the window until the transparent black border displays around the **Content Block**. Once the border displays, hover over the Pencil icon and click it to display the edit pane on the right side of the page. At this point you are able to edit the content of the **Text Content Block** similarly to using a popular word processing program with font style formatting options including **color**, **size**, **bold**, **italics**, and/or **bullets**. After editing the content such as within the **Text Content Block**, be sure to click the **Save and Close** button to update the **Content Block**.

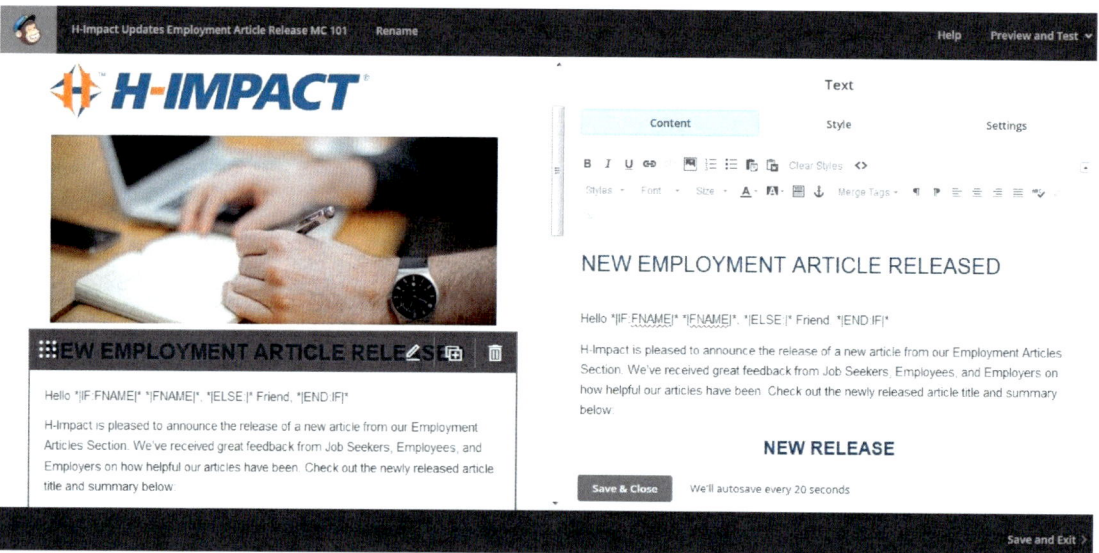

Sometimes you may also need to update an image. Images from the **Content Manager** are easily integrated into Email Templates. To update an Image when using the **Image Content Block**, hover over the **Image Content Block** until you see the transparent black border around the **Content Block**. Click the Pencil icon on the left to bring up the

Image Content Block Control panel on the right. You'll notice the thumbnail of the image with the name and current dimensions. Below the dimensions, you'll notice the links:

- **Replace** - Replace will bring up the **Content Manager** which will allow you to click to select another image or upload a new image. Once the new image has been selected, use the **Insert** button to replace the image.
- **Edit** - Clicking Edit will allow **Photo-editing** with features such as **Cropping**, **Colorization**, **Overlays** and **Frames**.
- **Link** - By clicking Link, a panel will display with a drop down allowing you to link to **Web Address**, **Email Address**, **Anchor Link** and **File**
- **Alt** - You may use the **Alt** link to provide **Substitute text** for when the recipients' email client has images blocked or for when an display error may be resulting.

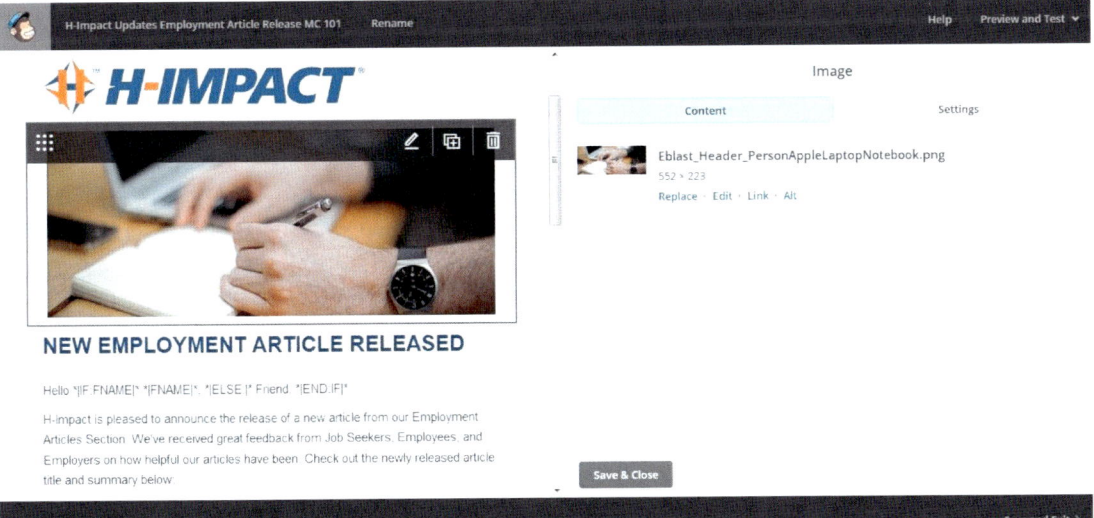

Save Your Template

Again, after editing the **Content Blocks** such as the **Text Content Block**, **Image Content Block** and/or other **Content Blocks,** be sure to click the **Save and Close** button to update the content. To update the **Template**, make sure you click the **Save and Exit** in the bottom right hand corner of the screen.

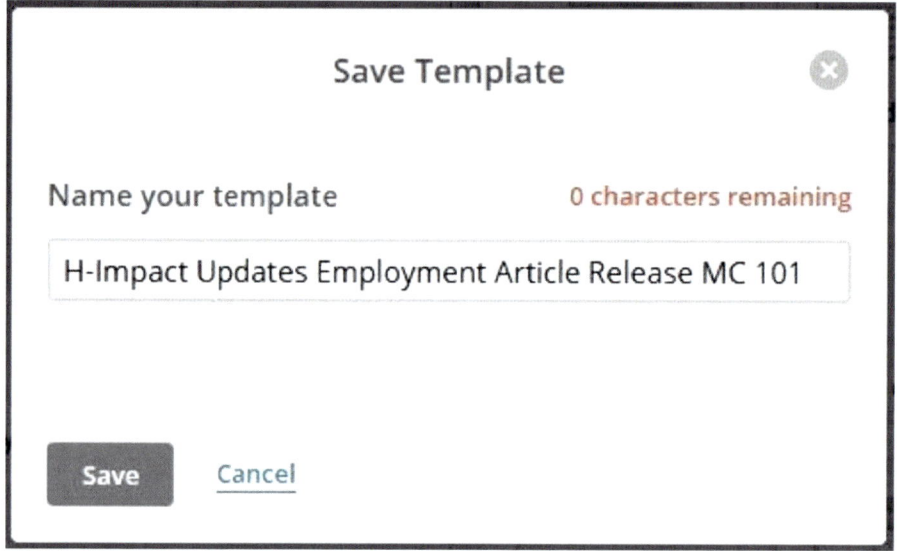

List Management

Creating Lists Overview

To **Create a List**, click the **Lists Menu** from the **Main Menu** at the top of the page. A page displays with either all your **Recipient/Subscriber Lists** you've created or no **List** if you haven't created any yet. If you do have **Lists**, the index should include the **Name** of each **Subscriber Lists**, **Created Date**, and **Rating**. They will also include stats on **Subscriber Count**, **Open Rate**, and **Click Rate**. Along with these **Stats**, there is a gray **Add Subscriber Button** and a **Stats Drop Down**.

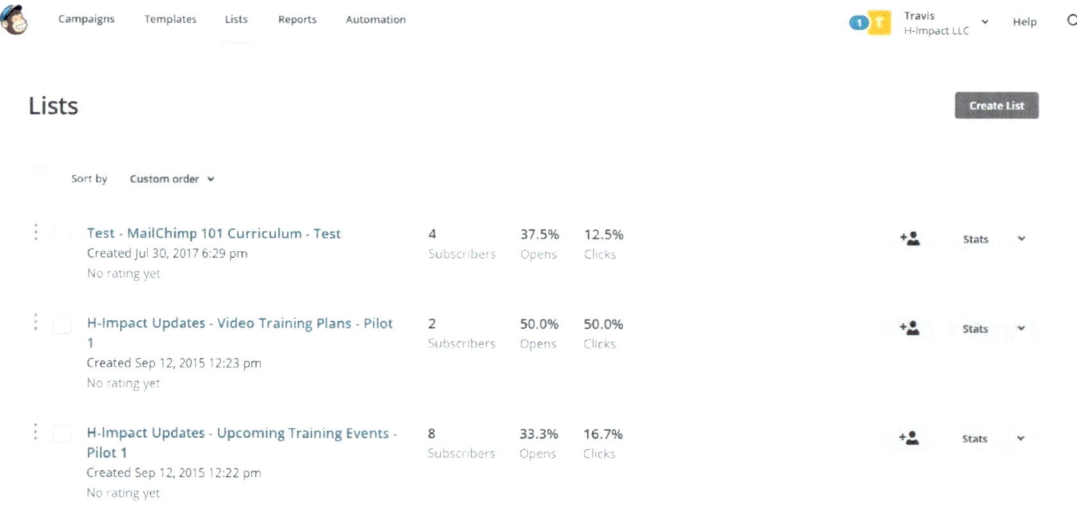

Under the **Stats Drop Down** are the options:

- Manage contacts
- Signup forms
- Settings
- Imports
- Exports
- Replicate list
- Combine lists

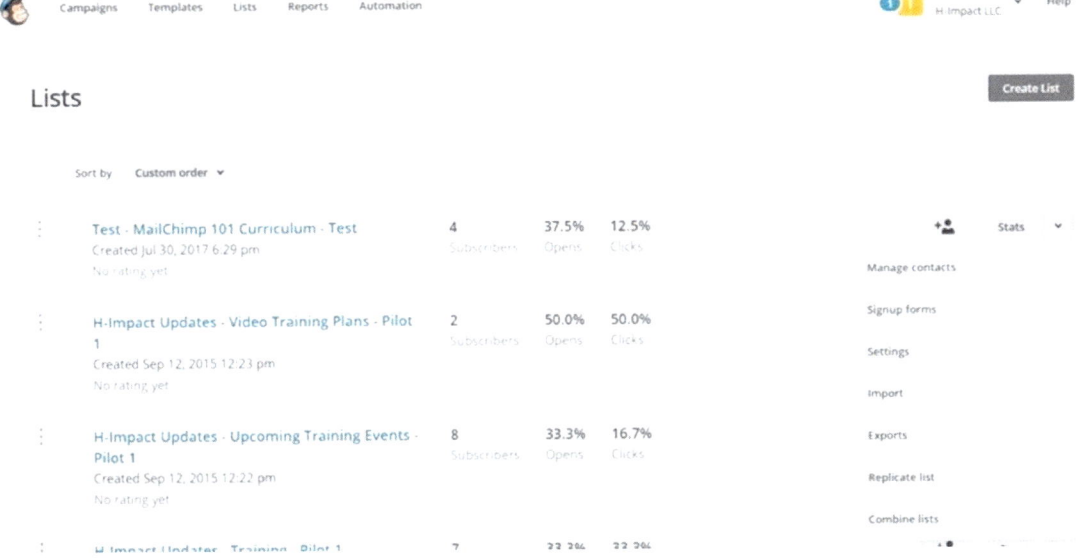

To select a **Subscriber List** click the highlighted **Name**.

The **Subscriber List** should appear showing the minimal default fields for **Email Address**, **First Name**, and **Last Name.**

As a rule of thumb, a Subscriber cannot exist without an Email Address. All other fields are optional.

On the **Subscriber List** page you'll also notice as the title, the **Subscriber List Name** with the **Subscriber Count** as a link. Below the title there is a **Switch List Drop Down link** that allows you to toggle between the available **Subscriber lists**. Following the **Switch List Drop Down** link, there is a secondary menu that allows you to **Manage** and **Configure** the list display with options,

- Stats

- Manage contacts
- Add contacts
- Signup forms
- Settings
- Search

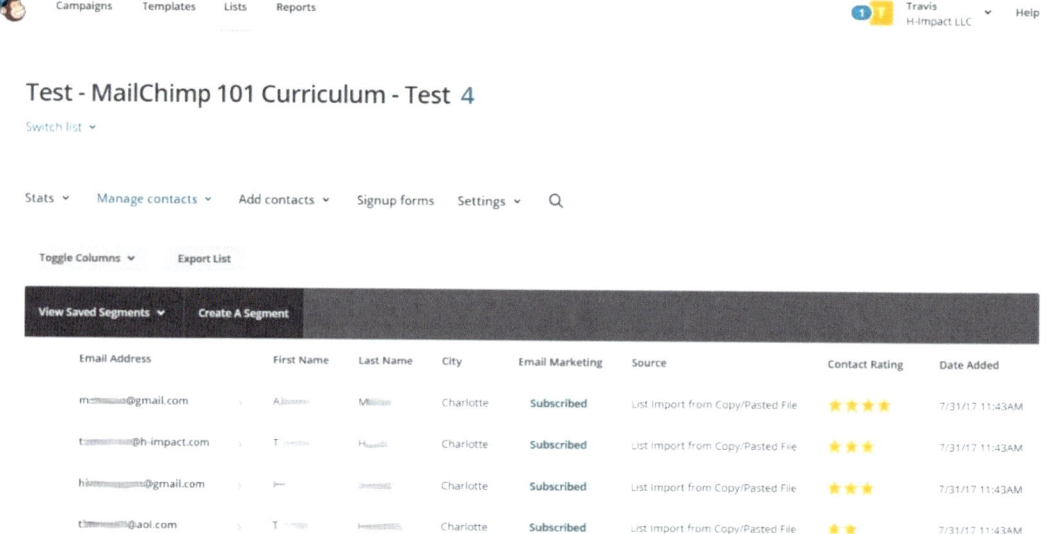

Creating Lists Process Configuration

Click the **Lists Menu** at the top of the page to start the process to create a recipient List. From the **Subscriber Lists Index** page, click the gray **Create Lists** button in the upper right corner of the screen.

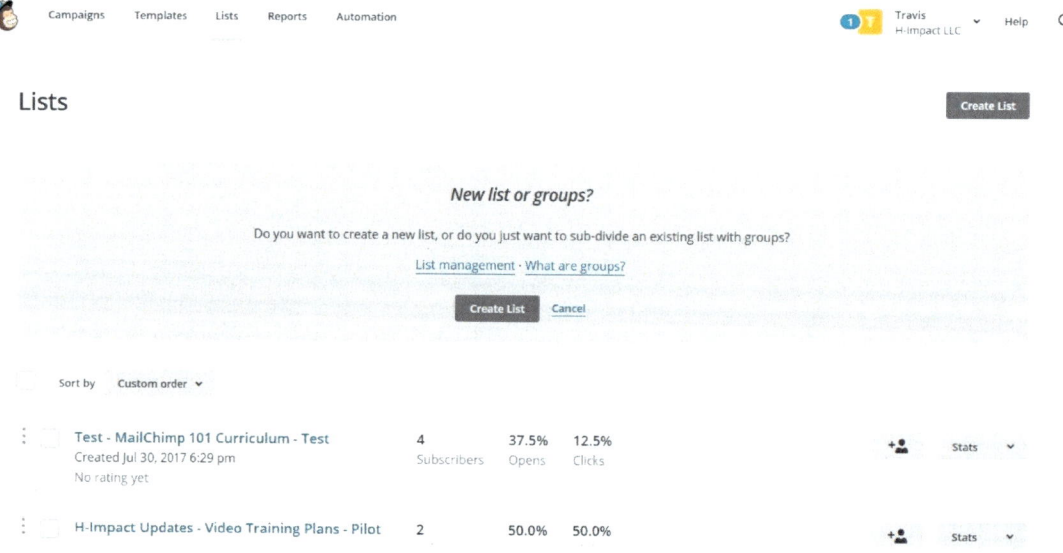

In the gray **New Lists or Groups** box click **Create List**. A page will display titled **Create List** with fields and settings required to setup the **Subscriber List**. Under **List details** you must supply the:

- List Name
- Default From email address
- Default From name
- Short reminder about how the Subscriber joined the list

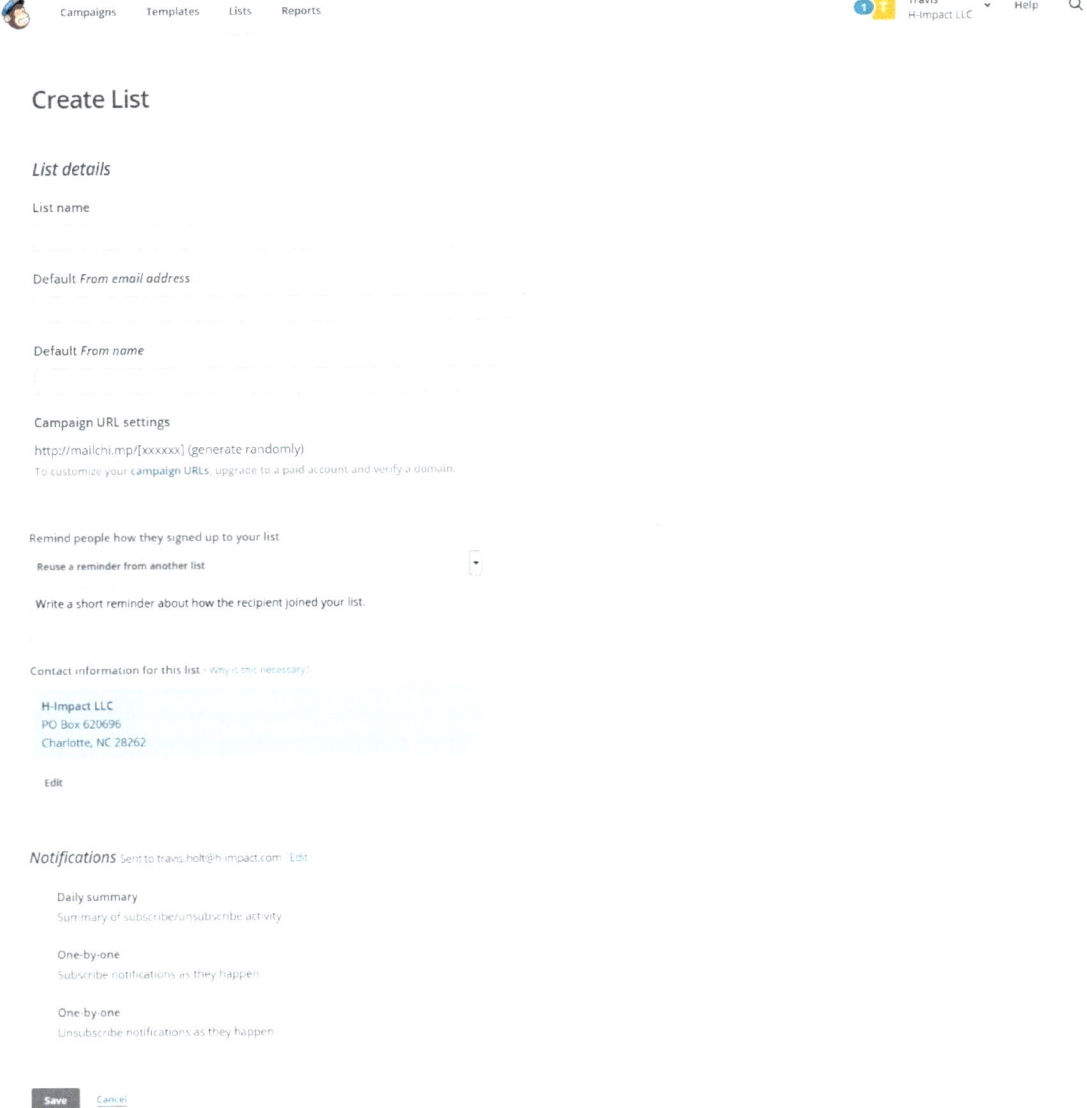

Optionally you may edit the **Office Address** and the **Default Reply-to-email address** setting which should match the email you used to set up the **MailChimp** account.

You can also choose to receive **Summaries** to the default email address for:

- Daily for Subscribe/Unsubscribe activity
- One-by-One Subscribes
- One-by-One Unsubscribes

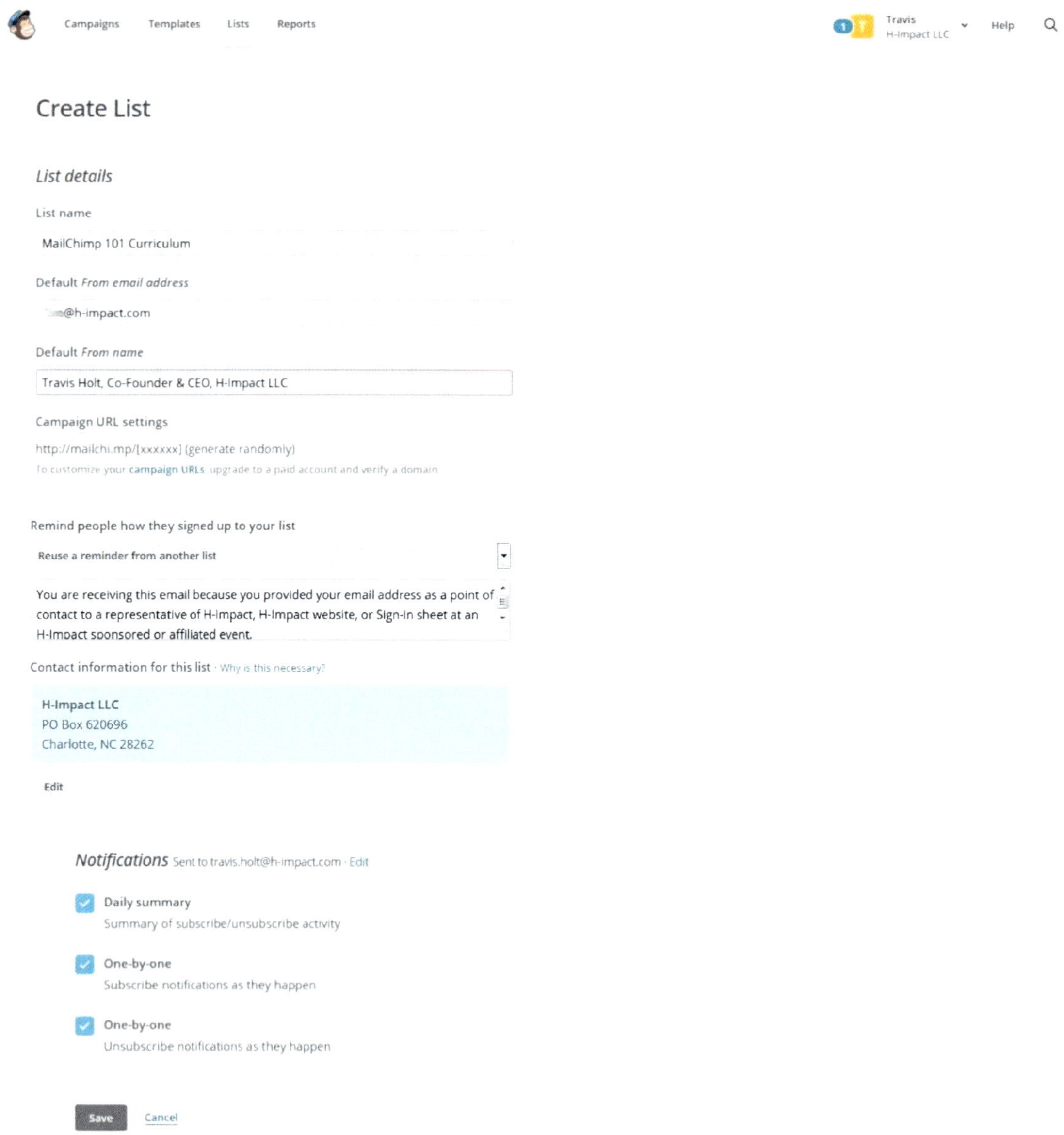

To create the **Subscriber List** click **Save**.

On the Subscriber List page you'll also notice as the title, the **Subscriber List Name**. Below the title there is a **Switch List Drop Down link** that allows you to toggle between the available **Subscriber Lists**. Following the **Switch List Drop Down** link, there is a secondary menu that allows you to Manage and Configure the list display with options,

- Stats
- Manage contacts
- Add contacts
- Signup forms
- Settings
- Search

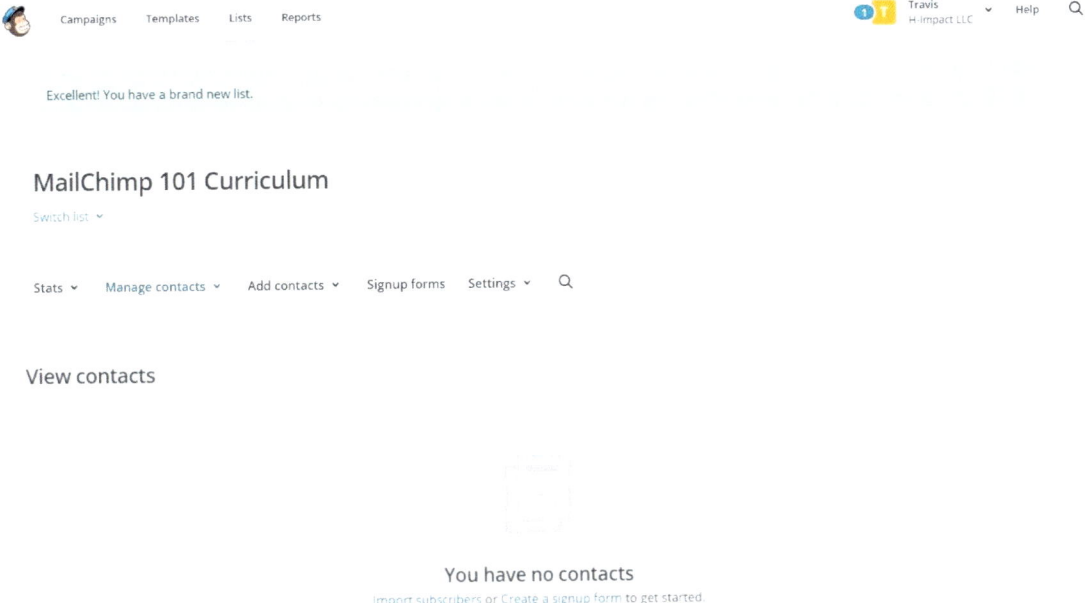

Collect Email Addresses

Before emailing recipients from **MailChimp**, it is recommended that users of **MailChimp** gather a list of recipients which they wish to send emails in order to get started. This is completely up to the **MailChimp** user as to how they carry out this process to compile the list. Some companies or users of **MailChimp** can gather the list of recipients and compile the recipients from:

- Their collections of business cards

- Paper Sign-up List at Company events
- Online Sign-up Forms
- Internal Database Email Subscription List Systems
- Email Contacts in Email Systems like Gmail
- Or Leads from Other Paid for or Non-paid lead systems

Once collected these emails addresses with relevant **Subscriber List** fields may be placed in a single file to be imported into **MailChimp** in batch once the **Subscriber Lists** has been properly configured and the **List Fields** have been defined. For instance **MailChimp** will accept a precompiled list of **Email addresses** that have been added to a **Microsoft Excel Spreadsheet** or a **comma delimited** (*.csv) file. Loading the files in bulk from a precompiled list can help to expedite creating official **Subscriber Lists** inside of **MailChimp**. As an alternative to collecting Email Addresses beforehand, they may be added in real time on an as needed basis using **MailChimp's** administrative forms or online subscriber forms which can be integrated into external websites like a company's official website. These **Add Subscriber** options are described later in this book in detail in the section titled **Add Subscribers.**

Define List Fields and MERGE Tags

From the **Settings** drop down menu option click on the **List fields and *|MERGE|* tags**.

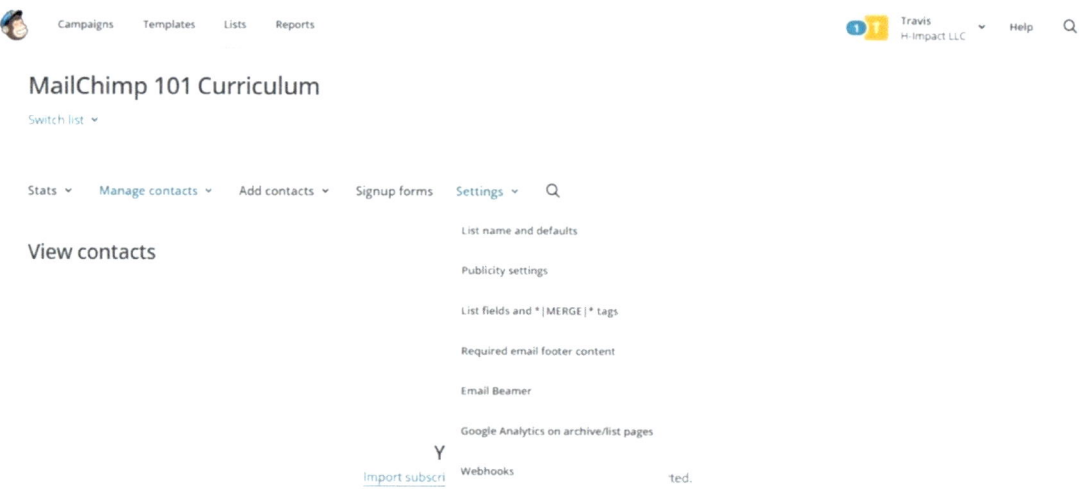

The page will display with a sub heading of **List fields and *|MERGE|* tags**. You will notice a list of fields already present.

They include: **Email Address, First Name** and **Last Name.**

As a rule of thumb, a Subscriber cannot exist without an Email Address.

This page is designed for you to create a layout of the Subscriber List. It allows you to type the text for the Label of the field you would like to display in a Subscriber form or the Subscriber List layout. Along with the field label text, the type of field is defined. These include:

- Text
- Number
- Radio Button
- Date
- Birthday
- Address
- Zip Code (US Only)
- Phone
- Website
- Image

By default the **Email Address** field is an **Email** type, the **First Name** field is **Text**, and the **Last Name** field is **Text**.

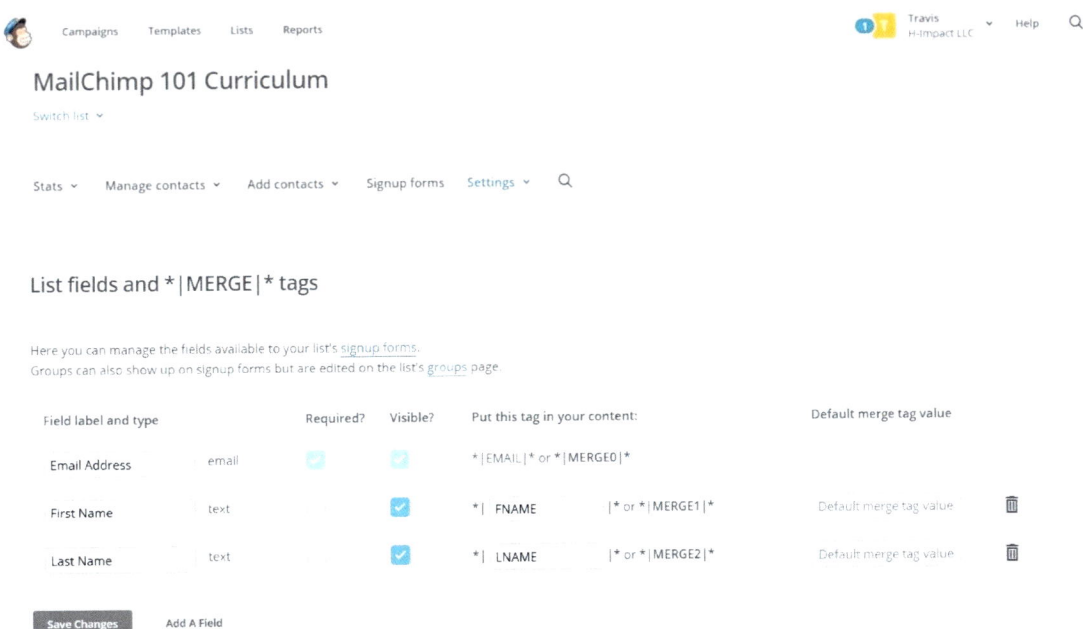

MERGE Field Tags

There are also **MERGE field indicators** that by default resemble ***|MERGE#|***. For each field the **#** is replaced with the sequential order of the field. You can also rename the field to a **Tag** that is more reflective of the actual **Field Name**.

MERGE field indicators are used to dynamically reference data from the **Subscriber list** in **Email Templates** and other places in the **MailChimp** system that can dynamically populate data from the Subscriber list. A prime example is the salutation of an email or letter. For instance Hello ***|FNAME|*** used in a **Template** can dynamically populate the **First Name** for each recipient of the **eBlast**.

Add New Fields

Many times it's advantageous for users to add fields that do not exist by default. For example to add a **City** field just click on the **Add A Field** button at the bottom of the page. This prompts you to click on the type of field you want under **Select a field type to add**.

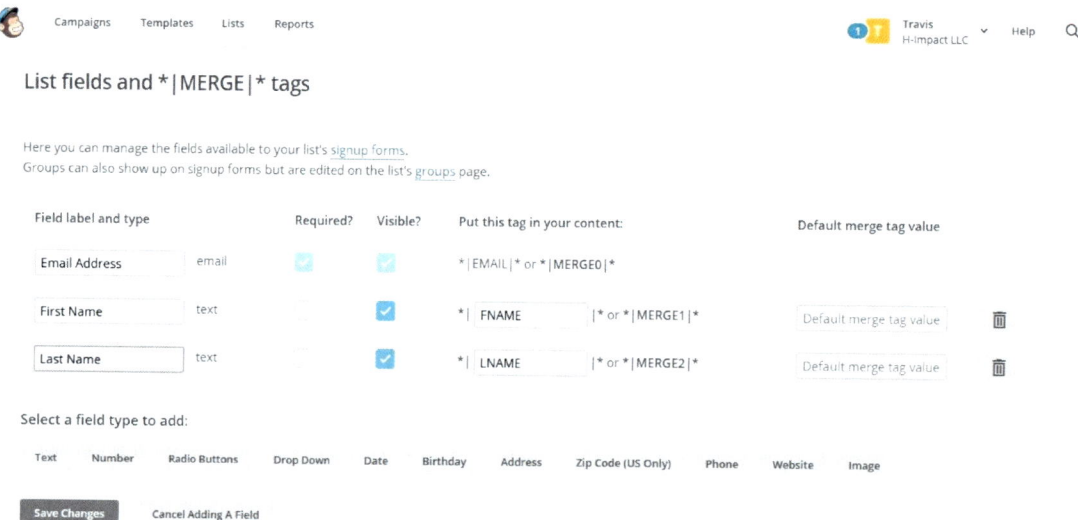

- For our purposes, click **Text**.

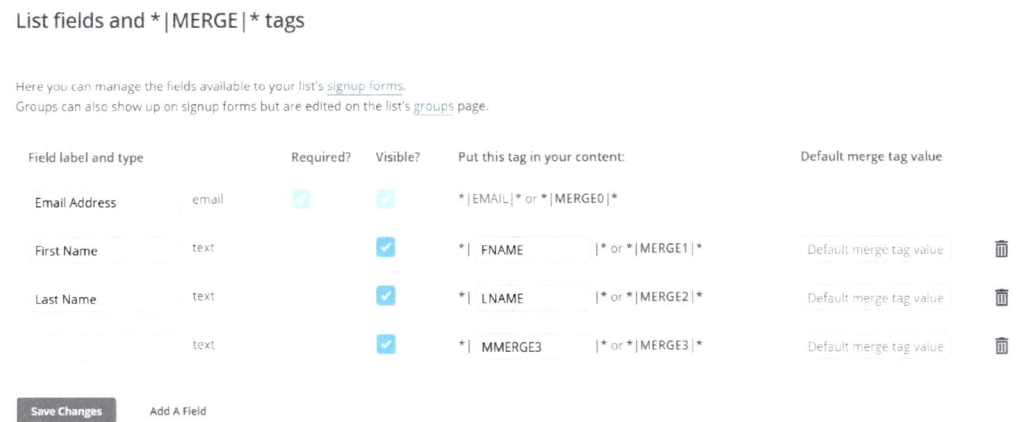

- Next add the name of the field in the **Field Label and Type**. Type **City** in the textbox.
- Also in the 2nd text box replace the text **MMERGE3** with **CITY**.

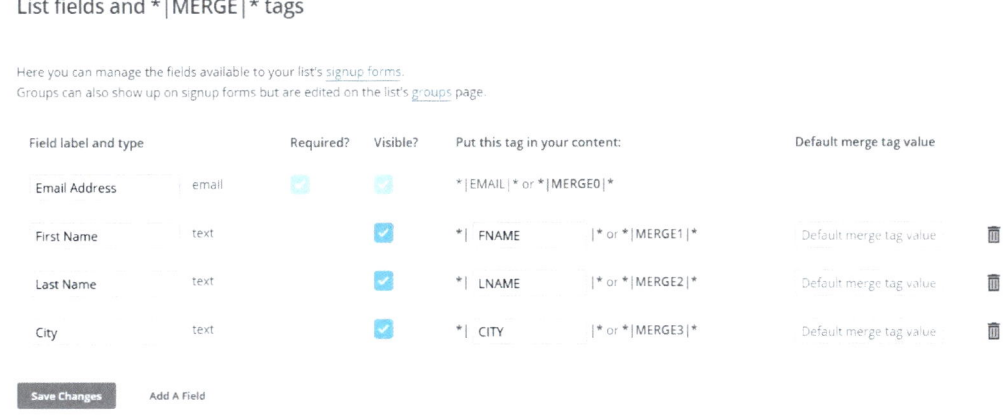

Required and Visible Field Properties

Next you will notice the **Required** and **Visible** checkboxes. The **Required** checkbox will define if a field can be empty or not. The visible checkbox will hide or show the field on the **User Subscriber Forms**.

Save List Changes

Click on the gray **Save Changes** button to save the list changes including the new field.

MailChimp 101 Curriculum

Remove Fields

If you change your mind about a field you can remove it by clicking on the garbage can icon at the end of the row next to the respective field.

Add Subscribers

We are now at a point where we can **Add Subscribers** to our list. There are 4 methods used to **Add Subscribers** to list in **MailChimp**.

We may add subscribers using:

- The Add Subscriber Form for Administrators
- Add Subscriber Form for MailChimp Users
- MailChimp Application Programming Interface (API) calls in conjunction with an External Website
- Copy/Paste or Import them directly into MailChimp using an external data source such as a comma delimited file (CSV) or a Microsoft Excel file

For the purposes of this book we will focus on using Add Subscriber Form to add subscribers *one at a time* and importing them *in batch* into MailChimp using an external data source such as a comma delimited file (CSV) or a Microsoft Excel file.

Add Subscribers Form

Let's look at adding a subscriber using the built in **Add Subscriber** form. To do this, simply click on the **Add Contacts** drop down and select **Add Subscriber**. The Add Subscriber form displays.

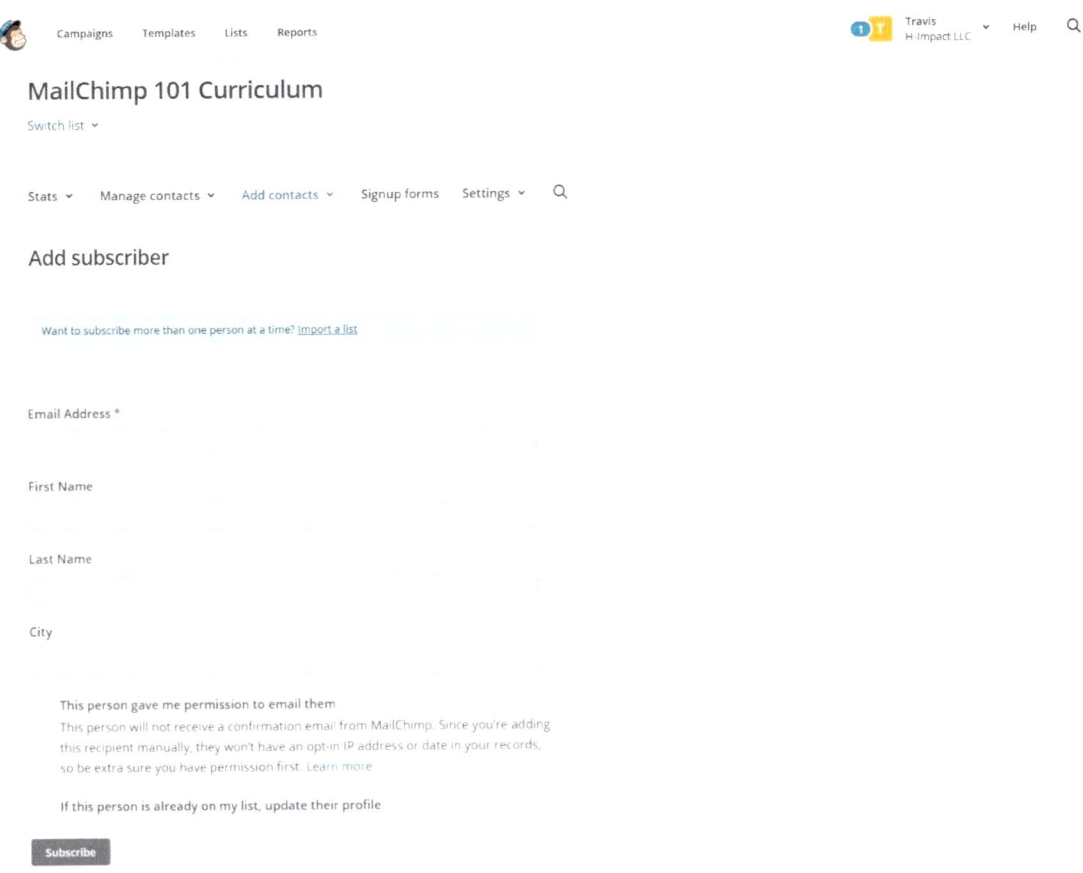

Simply complete the form with the **Subscriber List** data for the following fields:

- Email Address
- First Name
- Last Name
- City

For Example:

- Enter [**Your Email Address**] like *youremail@yourcompany.com* for **Email Address**
- Enter [**Your First Name**] for **First Name**
- Enter [**Your Last Name**] for **Last Name**
- Enter [**Your City**] for **City**
- Also check the box for: **This person gave me permission to email them.**
- For the next check, also check the box: **If this person is already on my list, update their profile.**

- Click **Subscribe** to add the subscriber.

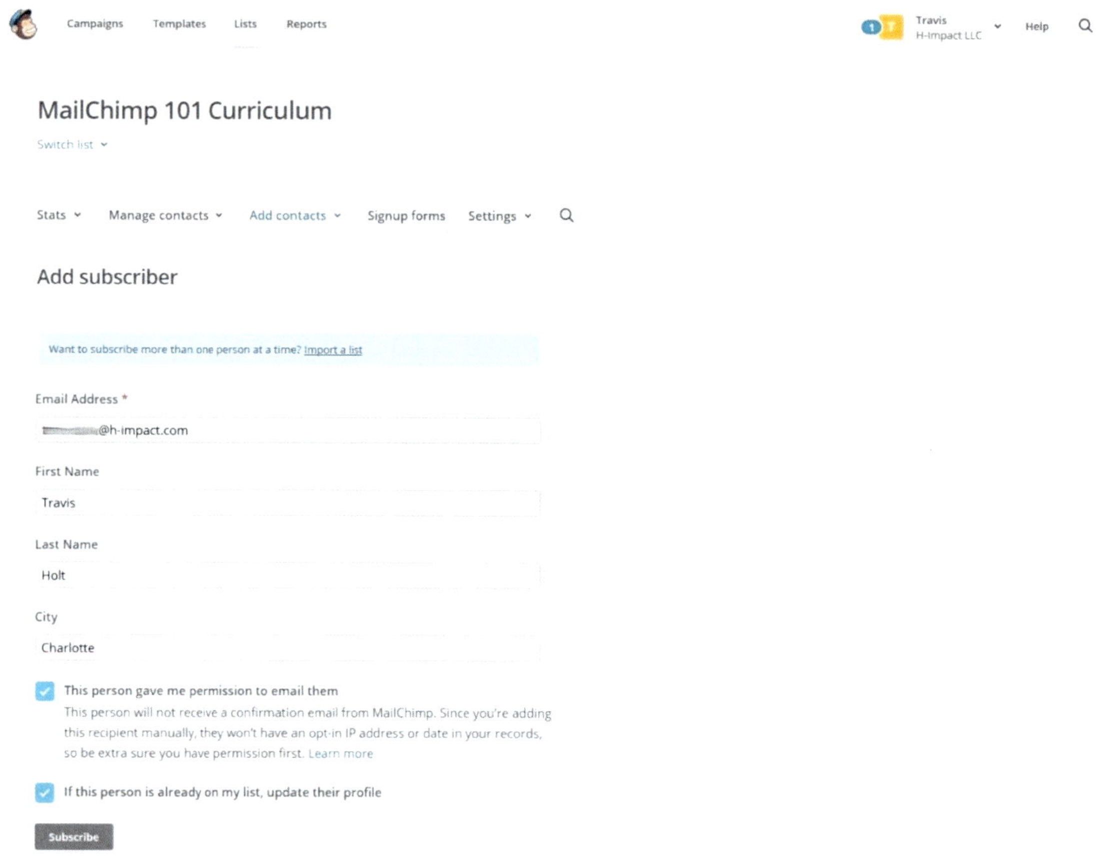

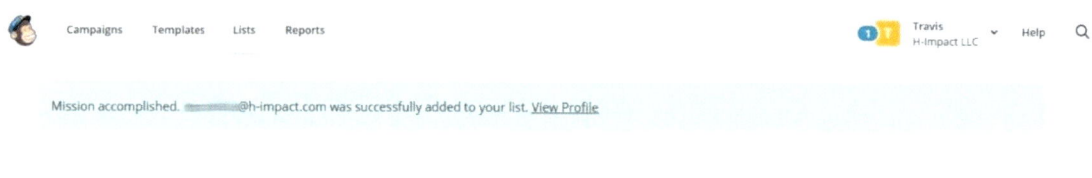

A confirmation message should display as follows:

Repeat this process using additional subscribers until you have finished adding all your subscribers.

Import Subscribers

Adding Subscribers can be accomplished one at a time using the **Add Subscriber** form like described above. This is effective for quick additions that are few in number. But when there is a need to import multiple subscribers at once, the form may not be practical. When there is a need to import **Subscribers** in a batch or in higher volume all at once, **MailChimp** allows the user to import subscribers in a file format using CSV or an excel file. To make this as seamless as possible, the file used to import the subscribers should have fields that match the fields outlined in the corresponding **MailChimp** Subscriber list. Those fields that do not match will display as unmatched and can either be manually mapped at the time of import or skipped and not imported at all.

Let's take a look at how to import data from an Excel file data source. To do this, simply click on the **Add Contacts** drop down and select **Import contacts**. When presented the question:

Where do you want to import contacts from?

- **CSV or tab-delimited text file**
  Import contacts from .csv or .txt files
- **Copy/paste from file**
  Copy and paste contacts from .cls or .xlsx files
- **Integrated service**
  Import contacts from services like Google Contacts, Salesforce, Zendesk, and more

We will use the **Copy/paste** option to import our data.

- Select **Copy/paste from file**
- Click the button at the bottom of the page with the text **Next>**

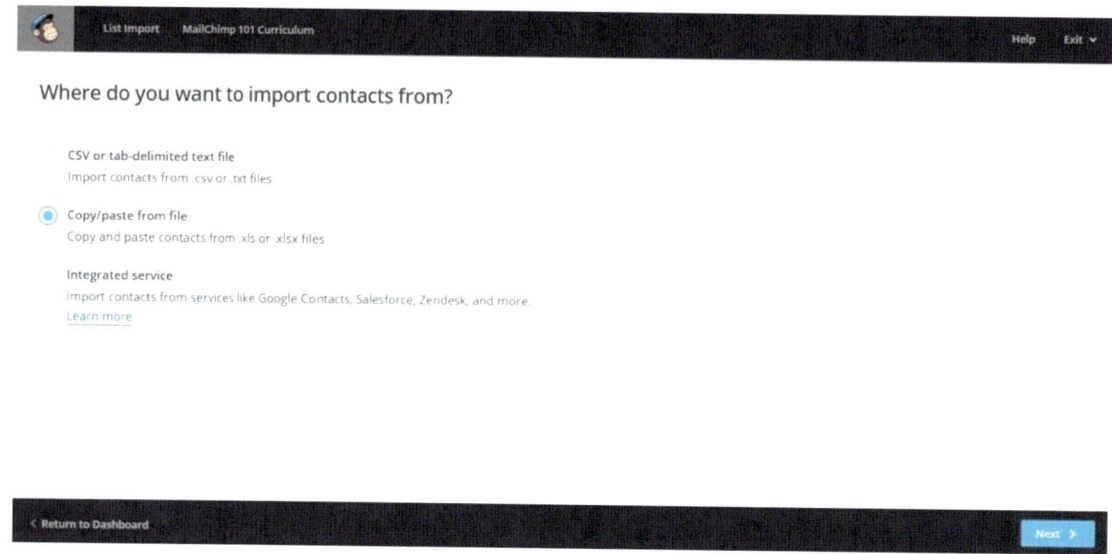

The Next page displays with the title **Copy/pasted file.**

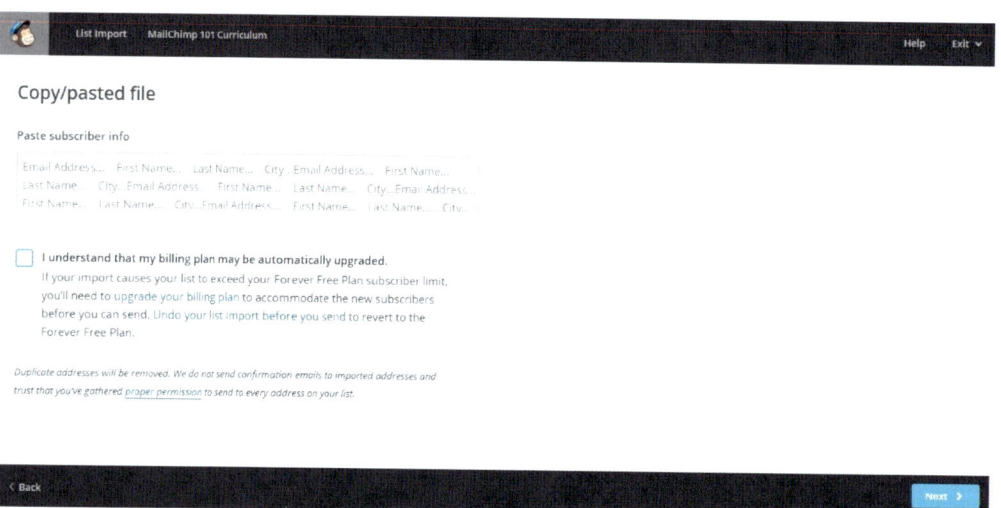

- Open the Excel file with your contacts.

	A	B	C	D
1	Email Address	First Name	Last Name	City
2	_____@h-impact.com	Travis	Holt	Charlotte
3	_____@h-impact.com	Charles	Morgan	Charlotte
4	_____@gmail.com	Mark	Patterson	Charlotte
5	_____@aol.com	Terry	Holmes	Charlotte

- In Excel, highlight and **Copy** the *data including Field names* (Note: In our case, our field names should match our MailChimp field names. As a preliminary step, we created the Excel file knowing the exact field names we would need to import into MailChimp.).
- In **MailChimp**, in the box at the top of the page, place the cursor at the beginning of the watermarked text and **Paste it**.
- Check the box that states: **I understand that my billing plan may be automatically updated.**
- Click the button at the bottom of the page with the text **Next >**

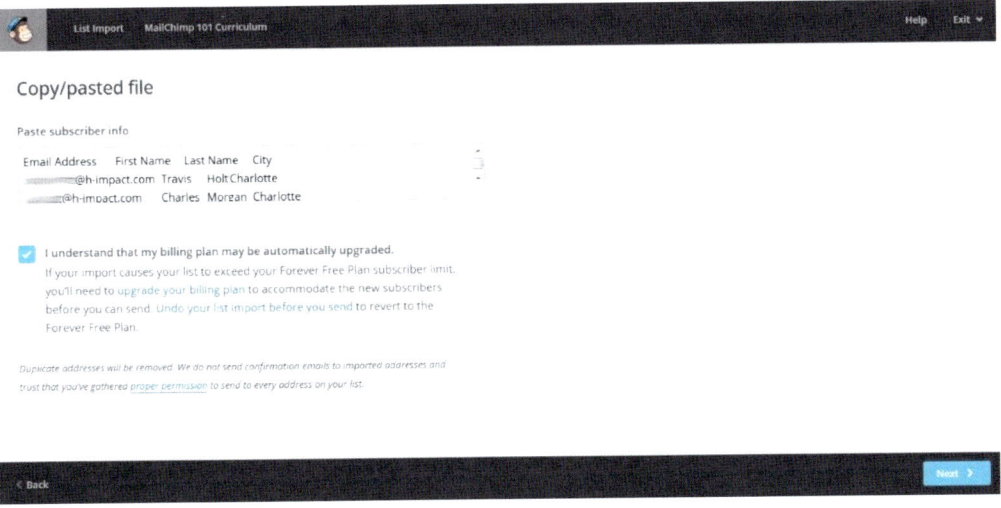

The Next page displays with the heading **Import contacts.**

- Notice the bar at the top of the page which should state **All columns are matched.**
- **Click Next below to Finish.**

Because we took some preliminary measures to make sure our Field names in our **MailChimp** Subscriber list matched the Fieldnames in the Excel file we are importing from, all field names synched without issue. If some of our fields didn't match they would appear below in red and we would then need to use the drop down in each unmatched field to match the fields properly. With the exception of **Email Address** or any other required field, if we determine that we do not wish to import a field we can simply click **Skip** for the matched and unmatched fields.

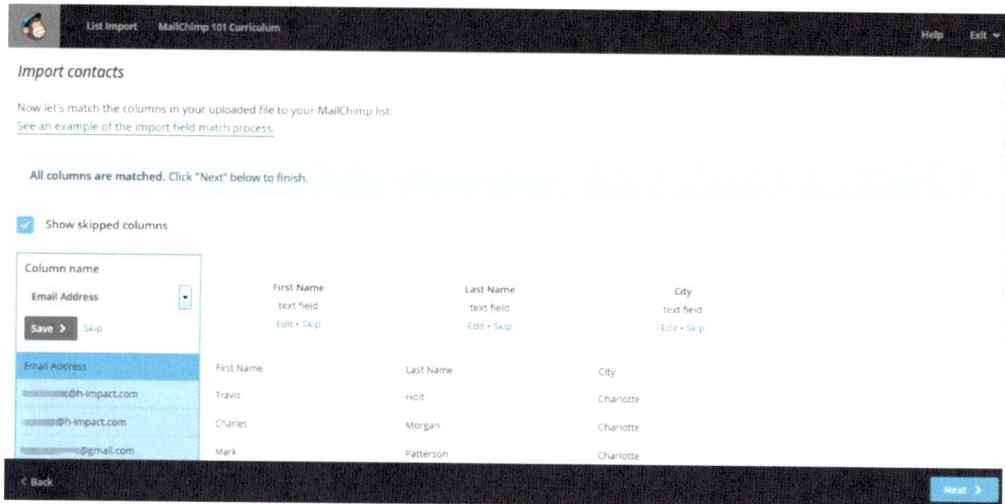

Per the successful confirmation message indicating all our columns matched,

- **Click the Next button below to Finish.**
- The Next page displays with the heading: **You're all set to import!**

The page should also display the following:

Please review the selections below importing your data Import.

- **Import method** Copy/Paste
- **Importing 4 of 4 Columns (Edit using the gray Edit button to modify fields being Imported)**

Categorize the imported contacts as:

- Subscribed
- Unsubscribed
- Cleaned

Mark the imported contacts as **Subscribed** and proceed to import:

- **Choose Subscribed** to ensure all contacts can be contacted as needed with the next **Campaign.**

- Click the **Import button** to complete the **Import.**

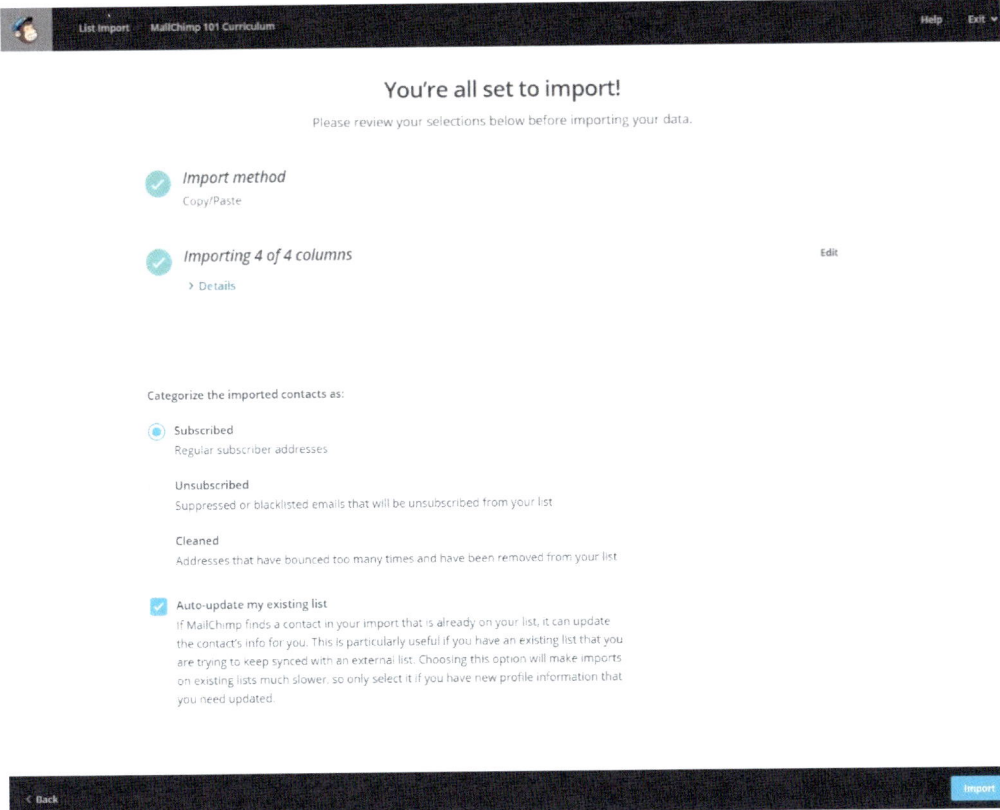

A confirmation message appears at the top of the next page stating **# contacts were imported successfully.**

The data should now show as imported in the grid at the bottom of the **Subscriber List** detail page.
Note the data loaded in the bottom of the screen with the data indicating the date imported and type of **Import Source** as **Copy/Pasted File**.

How to Unleash Email Marketing with MailChimp

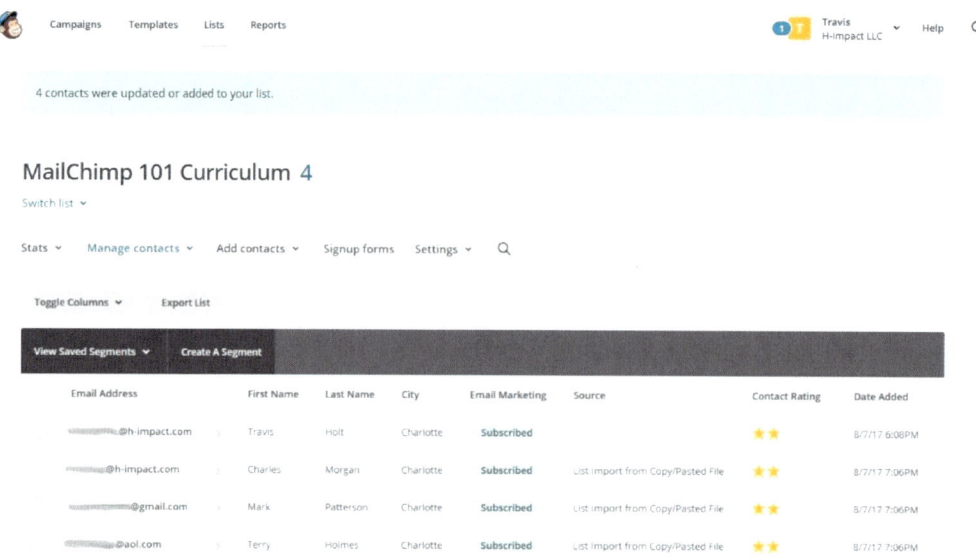

Chapter 4: **Creating Campaigns**

In this chapter we will create 2 **Campaigns** and send out 2 resulting emails respectively. These **Campaigns** will use **Drag and Drop Templates** that were designed and stored in the **Templates** section. One **Template** was created earlier under the section titled **Create Drag and Drop Template - Step-by-Step.** This template will be used later to generate the email titled **Example A** in the **Resulting Emails** section. We created the second template prior to the publication of this book using a similar **Drag and Drop** design method. This template will be used later to generate the email titled **Example B** in the **Resulting Emails** section.

To create a new **Campaign**, click **Campaigns** from the **Main Menu** at top of the page. Then click the **Create Campaign** button at the top right of the page.

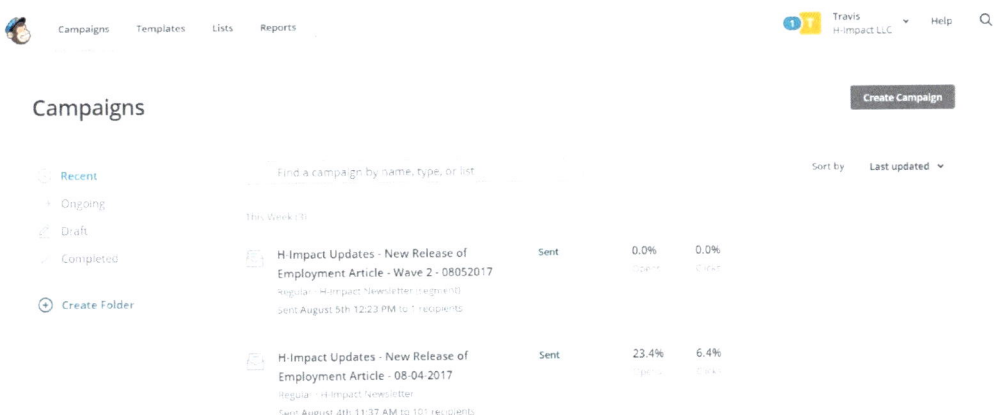

A modal dialogue window will display with a Search bar with the question, "**What do you want to create**?" From here you have the option of:

- Clicking a **button** with the text **Let us guide you** to help you decide.
- Clicking a **Create an Email** link
- Clicking **Create an Ad** link

For the purposes of this book, click the **Create an Email** link.

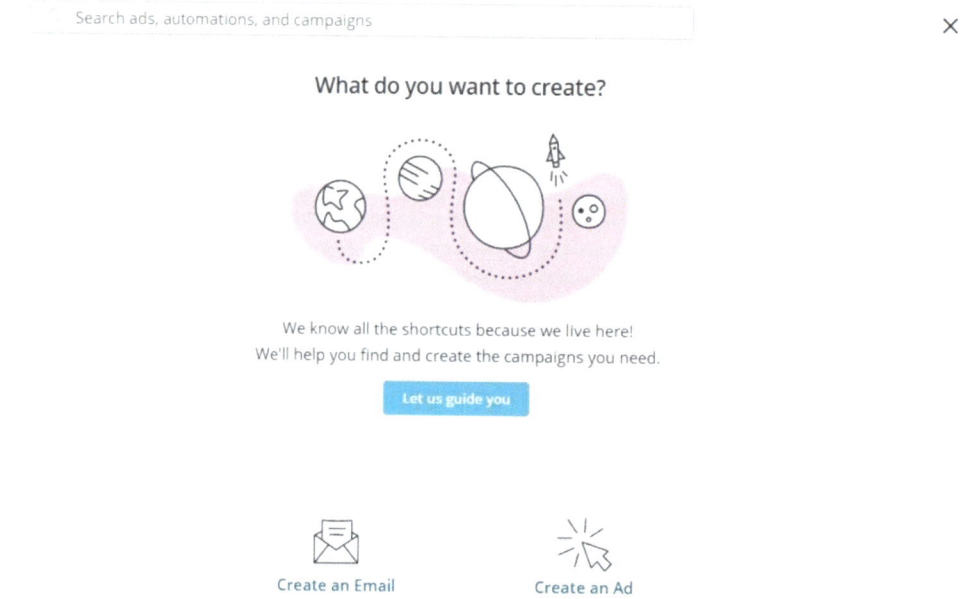

In the next window that appears, titled **Create an Email: Regular**, ensure **Regular** is selected and **Enter** the campaign name in the textbox at the bottom of the page. Name the **Campaign** something which you and your interoffice staff can recognize pretty easily. Make the name specific to the purpose of the communication.

Old Versus New Campaign Builder Process

MailChimp is constantly improving its system to make it more efficient and effective for its end users. At the time this book was published, **MailChimp** was in the process of releasing a newer and faster way to send out **Campaigns.** Depending on your previous **Campaign** mode, you will be presented with the options to complete your **Campaign** using the **Old Campaign Builder Process** or the **New Campaign Builder Process**. If you are brand new to **MailChimp,** and **MailChimp** has yet to phase out the **Old Campaign Builder Process** you will more than likely be presented an option to switch to the **New Campaign Builder Process** after entering your **Campaign Name**. This book demonstrates how to send a Campaign using the **Old Campaign Builder**

Process or the **New Campaign Builder Process**. Enter your Campaign name as requested to see if you will be using the **Old Campaign Builder Process** or be allowed the option to switch to the **New Campaign Builder Process**.

If you already know which Campaign Builder you would like to use or will be using:

For the **Old Campaign Builder Process** and for *Resulting Email Example A*, enter "**New Promo – Org Listing with 2 Free Job Posts - 11072017**".

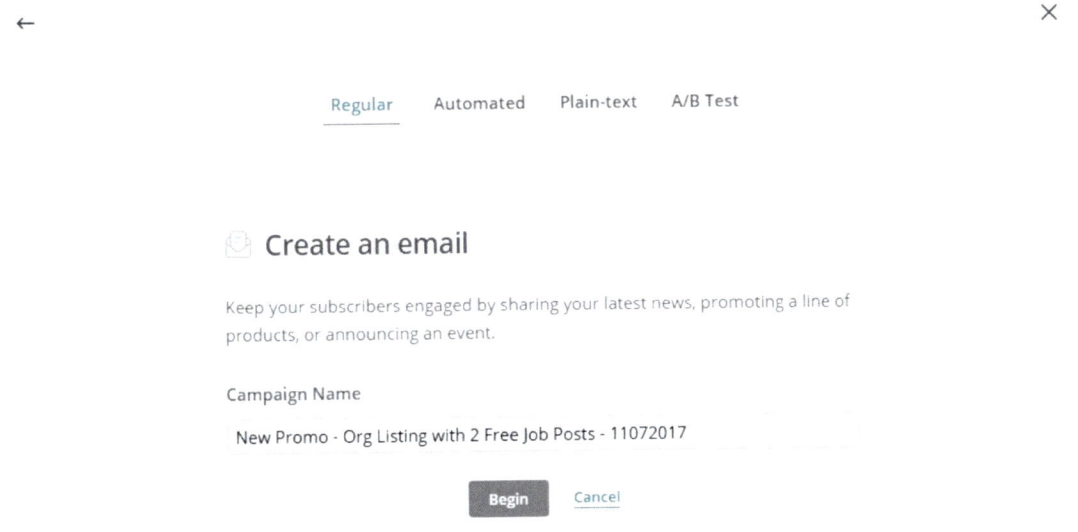

Click the gray **Begin** button.

For the **Old Campaign Builder Process** and for *Resulting Email Example B*, enter **"New Article Release – The Walls Have Eyes - 08082017"**

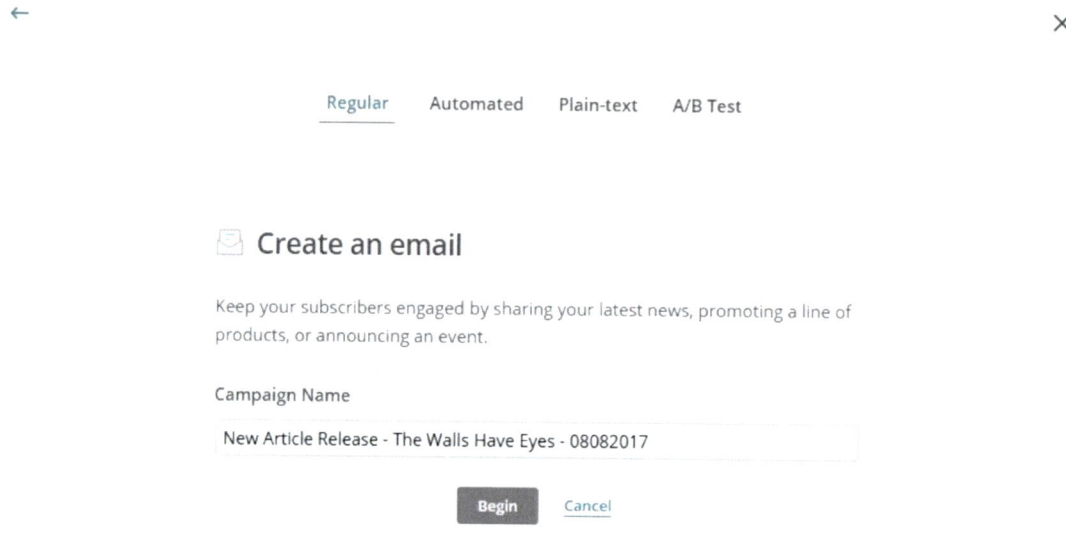

Click the gray **Begin** button.

For the **New Campaign Builder Process** and for *Resulting Email Example A*, enter "New Promo – Org Listing with 2 Free Job Posts – New Campaign Builder – 11092017".

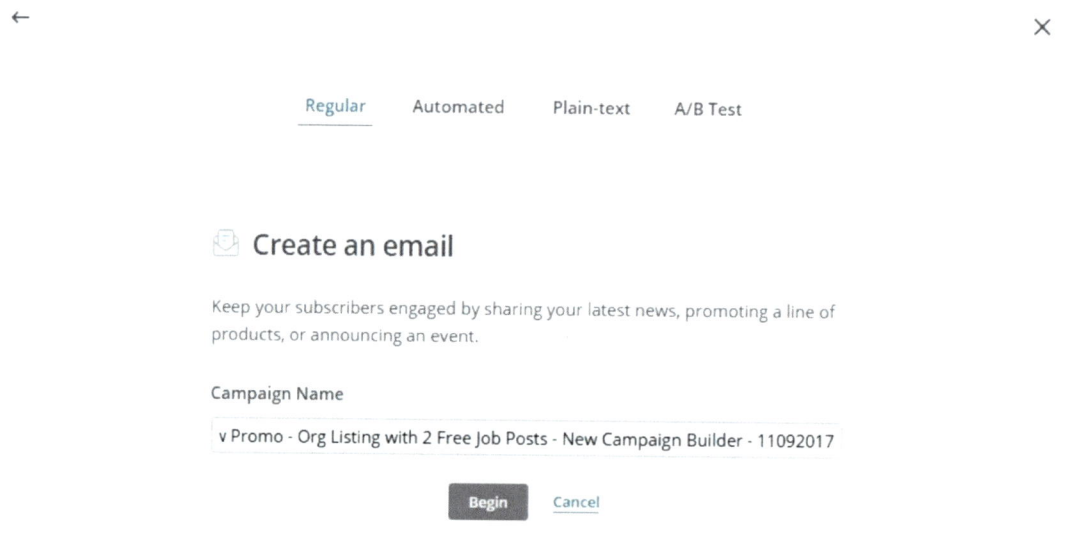

Click the gray **Begin** button.

Again, this name is for interoffice/internal business use only and will not be seen by the recipients/subscribers of the email.

The next page appears titled "**Who are you sending to?**" Choose the **Subscriber list** using the **Choose a list** drop down. Note the number of subscribers below each list.

For *Resulting Email Example A*,

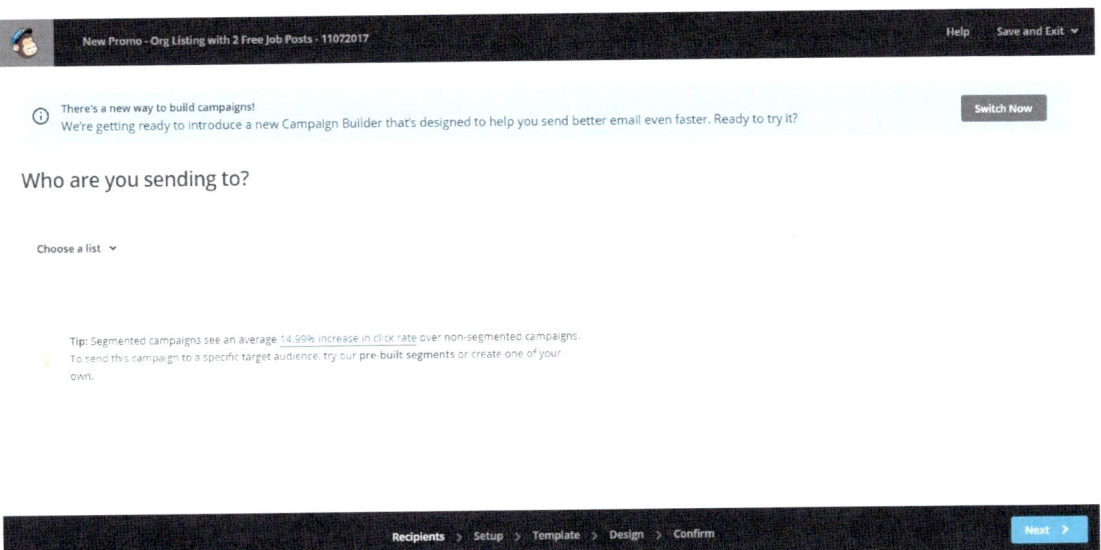

For *Resulting Email Example B*,

To users wanting to **Switch** and use the **New Campaign Builder Process** you may be presented a message that includes a button to **Switch** to the **New Campaign Builder**.

If you are presented this option and would like to proceed using the **New Campaign Builder**, click the **Switch Now** button. If you are not presented the option to Switch, there is a very good chance that you are already using the **New Campaign Builder**. Users that choose to switch to the **New Campaign Builder** are able to switch back to the **Old Campaign Builder** as long as **MailChimp** provides the option and hasn't phased the **Old Campaign Builder** out yet. The resulting campaign will generate the email in the **Resulting Emails** section for **Example A** later on in this chapter.

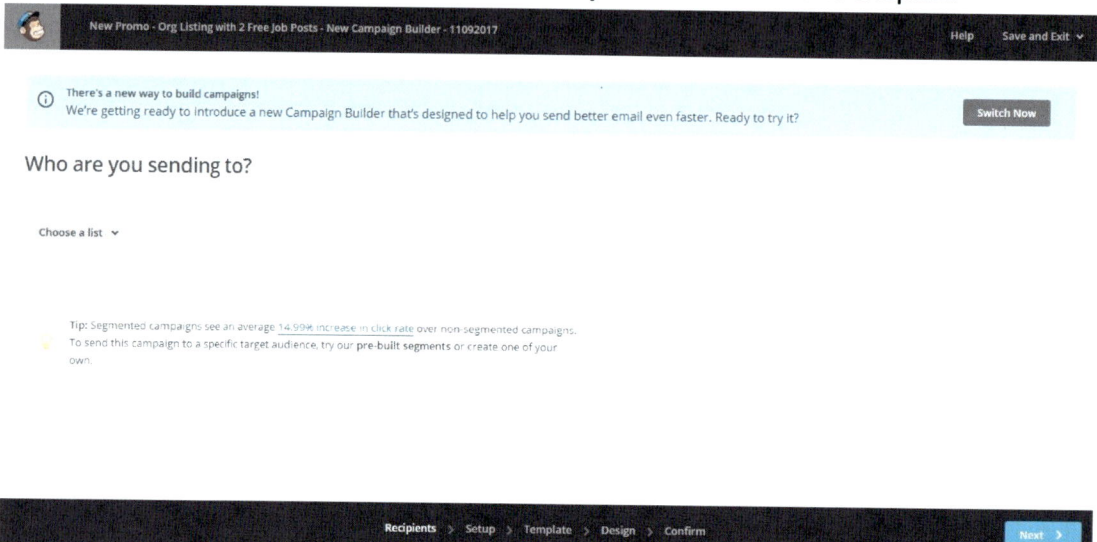

Click **Switch Now** to switch to the new **Campaign Builder** when presented the option.

Old Campaign Builder Process

Notice the header now displays from left to right the **MailChimp** logo, the name of the **New Campaign** (**New Promo – Org Listing with 2 Free Job Posts – 11072017 or New Article Release - The Walls Have Eyes – 08082017**), a **Help** link along with a **Save and Exit** link. The footer displays all steps including the current Recipients step required to create the **Campaign**. They are:

1. Recipients
2. Setup
3. Template
4. Design
5. Confirm

There is also a **Next** button in the footer. Click this button to proceed to the **Setup** Step.

Recipients

The page then displays 3 options:

- Entire list
- Saved segment or prebuilt segment
- Group or New segment

For the purposes of this book we will select **Entire list** and click the **Next >** button.

For **Resulting Email Example A,**

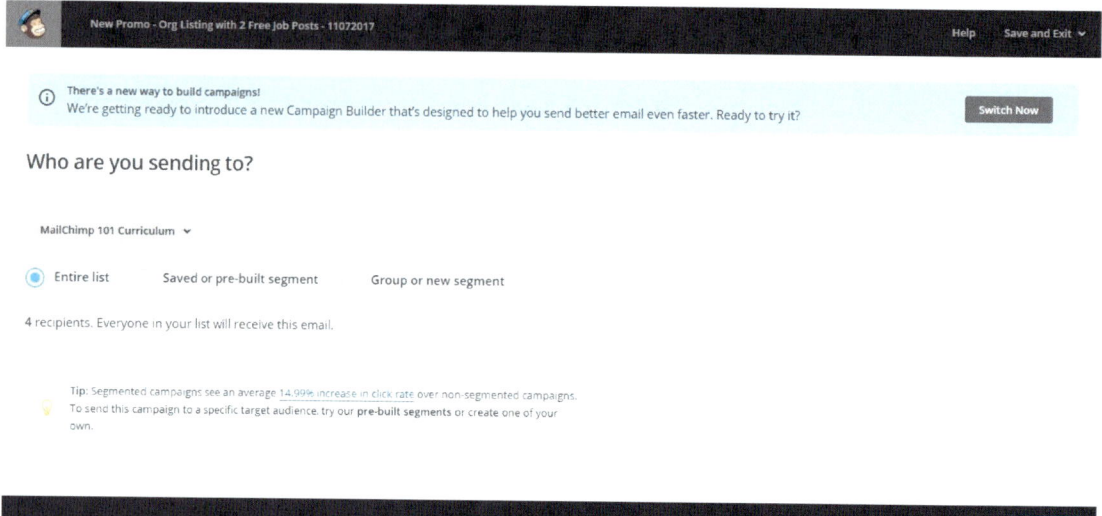

For **Resulting Email Example B,**

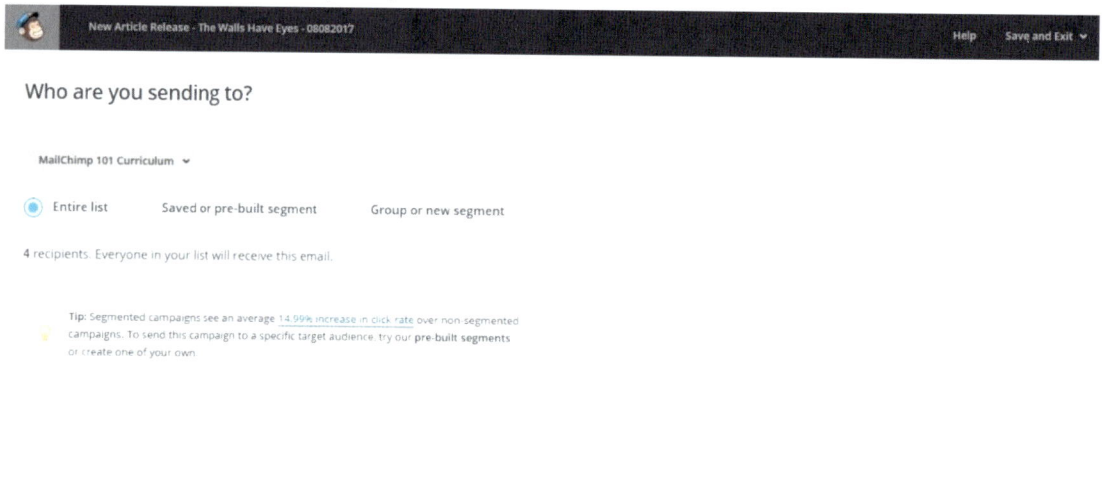

Setup

The **Setup** page appears requiring more info about the **Campaign**. From the **Setup** step to the **Confirm** step, you will notice the **Back** button that is also available in the footer to allow you to go back to the previous step if desired.

For *Resulting Email Example A,*

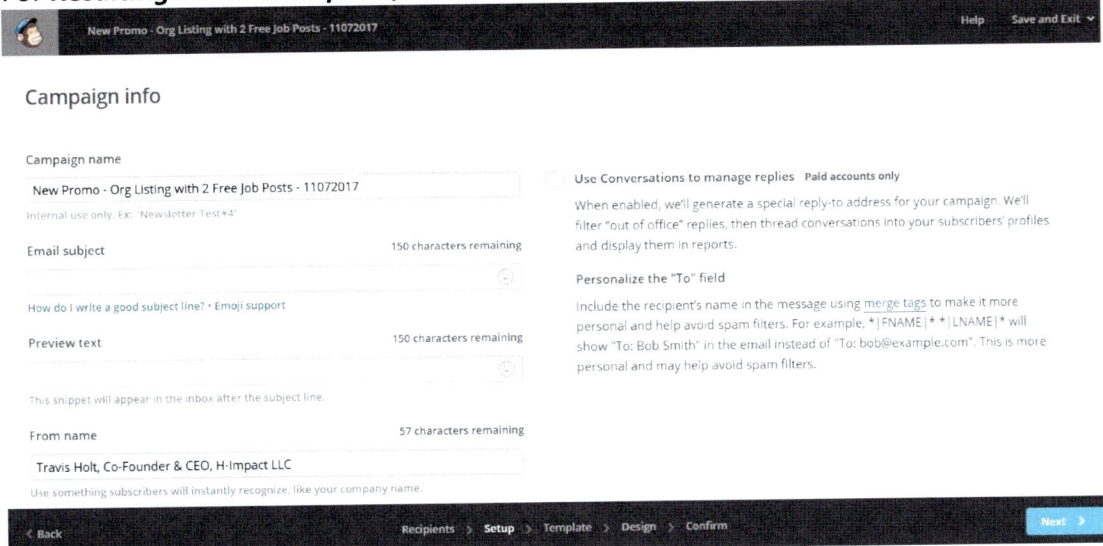

For *Resulting Email Example B,*

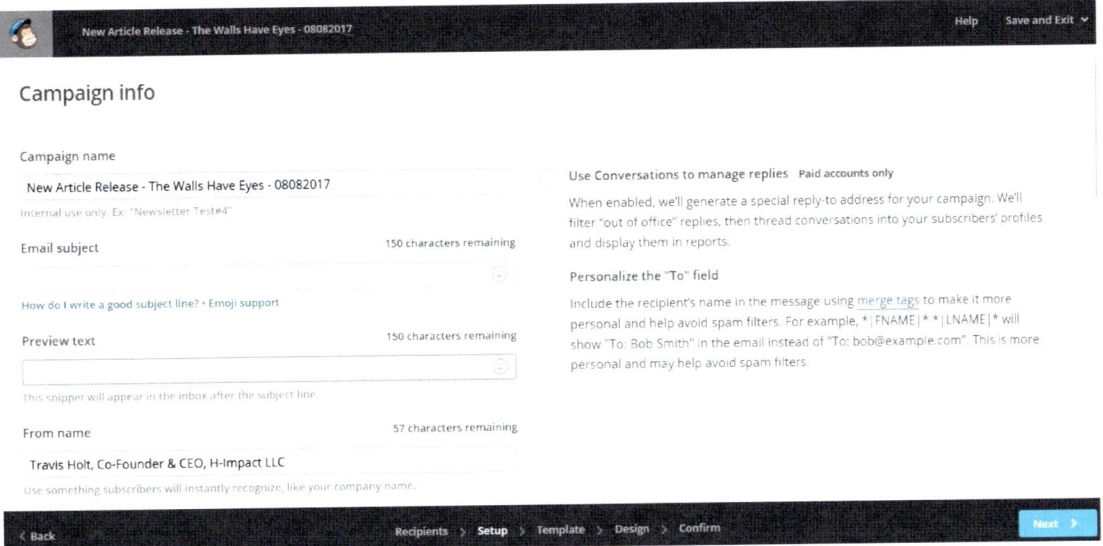

Enter the:

- Email Subject (Enter a subject that peeks the recipient's interests about how reading the email can benefit them. Ensure there are no misspellings or grammar errors.)

- Preview Text (Enter a preview text that acts as a brief summary that peeks the recipient's interests about how reading the email can benefit them. Ensure there are no misspellings or grammar errors.)
- From Name (For companies, try a pattern like First Name Last Name, with Job Position, Company Name or Web Address. Ex: John Doe, CEO, ABZ Company(or ABZ.com))
- From Email Address (This can be the email address of the recipient or a group email accessible by multiple users. Keep in mind when users reply to the eBlasts, someone will need to continue to check the email addresses inbox to ensure all replies are acknowledged, replied to or processed.)

Personalize the To Field: Recommendation: **Check this Field** to minimize the emails you send from being trapped in the spam filters of your recipients, it is recommended that you use MERGE fields for the First Name *|FNAME|* and Last Name *|LNAME|* for the To Field. Entering *|FNAME|* only in the available textbox will result in the First Name and entering *|FNAME|* *|LNAME|* in the textbox will result in the Full name.

In the section titled Tracking accept the values for:

- Track Opens with **Checked** value
- Track Clicks with **Checked** value (required for Free accounts)
- Track Plain-text Clicks with **Checked** value (required for Free accounts)

Accept all other **unchecked** defaults for **Google Analytics**, **Ecommerce link tracking**, **Click-tale link tracking**, and **Salesforce link tracking**.

Accept the defaults on the page for Social media and video convert to **not** include them (ie unchecked values).

Social Media Connection

Along with **Social Cards, MailChimp** users can send posts out to **Social Media** platforms when **Email Campaigns** are sent.

Campaign URL

Prior to connecting our campaign to the **Social Media** platforms, let's edit the **Campaign URL** to make it more user friendly. The **Campaign URL** is a reference to a web page created and hosted by **MailChimp**. It will be used when **MailChimp** posts users' **Campaign** content to **Social Media** platforms or when a user would like to share the email's content on line with any one regardless if they received the email or not. This **URL** will be redirected to, from the **Social Media** platforms and will display a page that contains the same content and similar layout included in the **Campaign** email that is sent to the recipients. **MailChimp** allows you to change the page name part of the **Campaign URL**. From the **Setup** step, to edit the **Campaign URL,** click the **edit** link.

For **Resulting Email Example A**, let's edit the **Campaign URL**.

Campaign URL
http://mailchi.mp/[xxxxxx]/list-your-company-with-h-impactcom-at-no-cost-and-get-2-job-posts-for-free-1478521 edit

The **Edit Campaign URL** dialogue box appears.

Edit Campaign URL

Your default campaign URL includes a domain name and email subject line.

The domain name part of your campaign URL is generated randomly. You can edit the email subject part of the URL path here.

68 characters remaining

http://mailchi.mp / [Generate Randomly] / o-cost-and-get-2-job-posts-for-free-1478521

Save   Cancel

Let's remove the auto number placed at the end of the **Campaign URL**. Click **Save**.

Edit Campaign URL

Your default campaign URL includes a domain name and email subject line.

The domain name part of your campaign URL is generated randomly. You can edit the email subject part of the URL path here.

76 characters remaining

http://mailchi.mp / [Generate Randomly] / tcom-at-no-cost-and-get-2-job-posts-for-free

Save   Cancel

Upon clicking **Save**, the **Campaign URL** should now display without the auto number previously at the end the **URL**.

Campaign URL
http://mailchi.mp/[xxxxxx]/list-your-company-with-h-impactcom-at-no-cost-and-get-2-job-posts-for-free edit

For **Resulting Email Example B**, let's edit the **Campaign URL**.

Campaign URL
http://mailchi.mp/[xxxxxx]/the-walls-have-eyes-1578622 edit

The **Edit Campaign URL** dialogue box appears.

Let's remove the auto number placed at the end of the **Campaign URL**. Click **Save**.

Upon clicking **Save**, the **Campaign URL** should now display without the auto number previously at the end of the **URL**.

Now let's connect to the **Social Media** platforms which will link to the **Campaign URL**. **MailChimp** offers **Social Media Auto post** and **Auto-tweet** options for **Facebook** and **Twitter** that simultaneously post to these **Social Media** platforms upon sending **Email Campaigns**. In order to take advantage of the **Social Media Auto Post** option, you must configure **MailChimp** to use your **Facebook** or **Twitter** accounts by supplying the username and password credentials for the respective **Social Media** platform.

To connect to **Twitter**, click the **Connect Twitter** button.

Social media

☐ Auto-tweet after sending   ☐ Auto-post to Facebook after sending

Connect To Twitter   Connect To Facebook

Click **Authorize app** upon entering **Twitter** credentials.

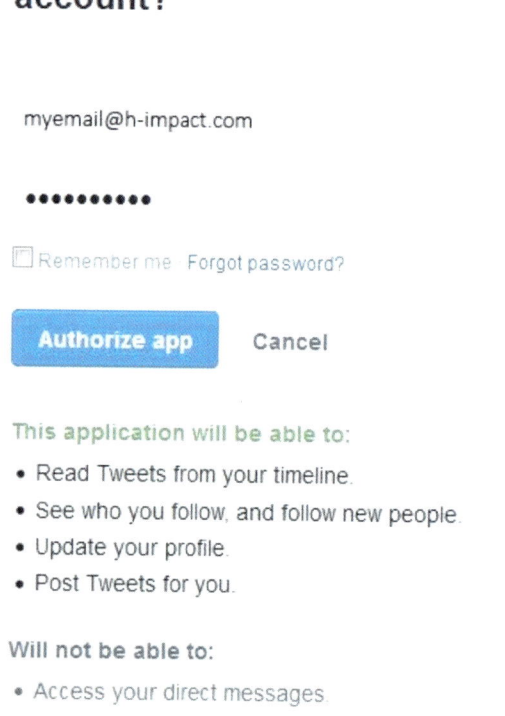

Note Possible Navigation Error and Workaround: After connecting to a **Social Media** platform, Sometimes **MailChimp's** Old Campaign Builder steps may redirect the user to a step beyond the **Setup** step used to connect to **Social Media** sites. If after entering the **Twitter** credentials, you are moved to a step beyond the **Setup** step, click the **Setup** step at the bottom of the **Campaign Builder** to navigate back to the **Setup** step.

Upon returning back to the **Setup** step, notice the **Twitter** option now reads **Auto-tweet campaign as [your Twitter username]**.

Now check the **Twitter** checkbox to edit the **post message**.

Review the message in the **Twitter** textbox for accuracy and edit the message as needed. Note that the **MERGE field** tag ***|URL|*** references the Url which is represented by the **Campaign Url** link which links to a **MailChimp** hosted version of the **Campaign Email**.

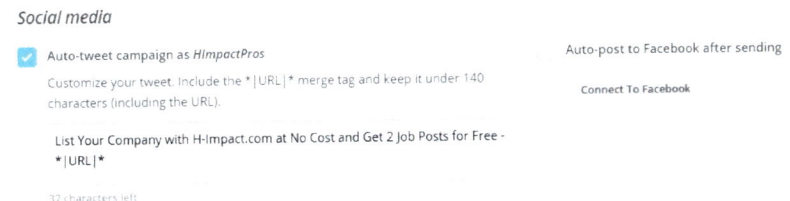

Once you have finished reviewing and editing your **Twitter** message, you may move on to connecting to **Facebook** to setup the **Auto-post**.

To connect to **Facebook** under the **Social media** section, click the **Connect to Facebook** button to display the **Facebook** login page.

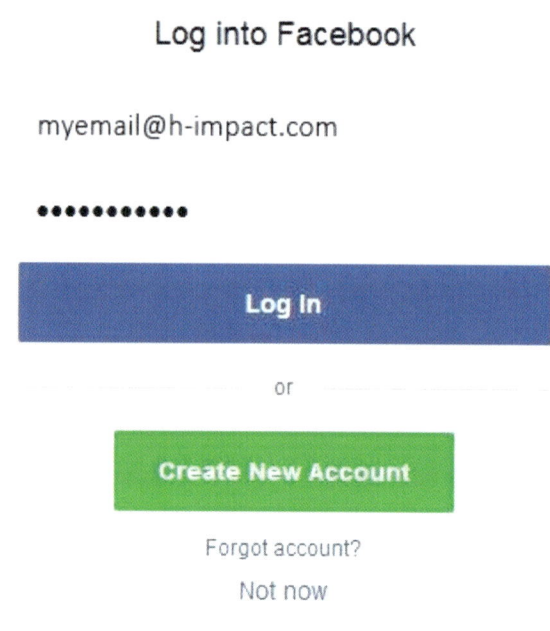

Click **Log In** upon entering your **Facebook** credentials. Make sure **Auto-tweet campaign as [your Twitter username]** is still selected.

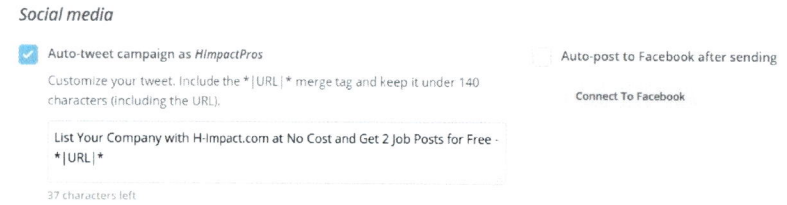

Now check the **Facebook** checkbox to edit the **publishing profile** or **page** and **post message**.

Review the message in the **Facebook** textbox for accuracy and edit the message as needed. Note for **Facebook**, the **MERGE field** tag ***|URL|*** reference will be added to your post text although it doesn't show in the textbox. The **Campaign Url** links to a **MailChimp** hosted version of the **Campaign Email**. Finally, use the checkboxes below the textbox to choose the personal profile or a page to post from. For this example we will select **H-Impact (Fan Page)** in order to post to and post as the **H-Impact** Page.

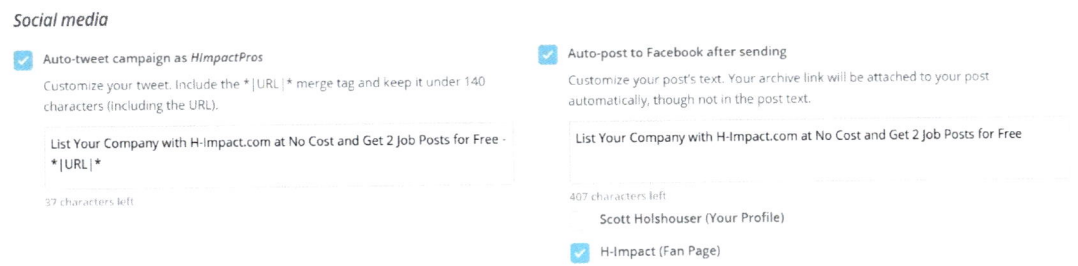

Note: The **video convert option** is useful if we were embedding a video which may cause issues being opened in certain email clients. Considering, we are not referencing a video for this book we do not need to check this option. If we were referencing a video we highly recommend checking this option.

For **Resulting Email Example A**

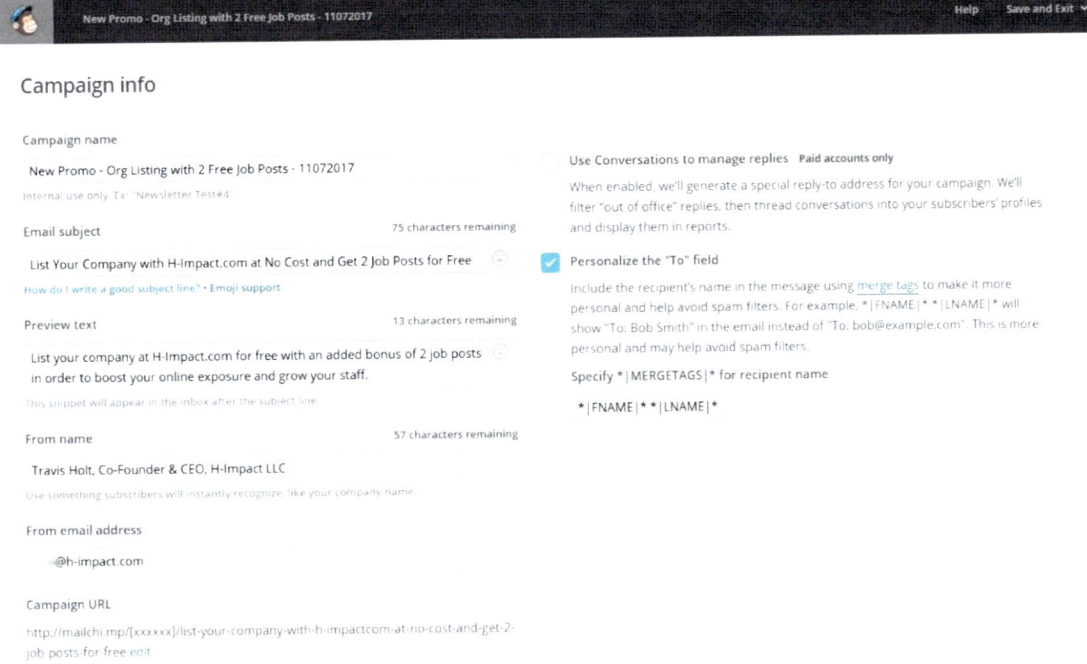

Tracking

☑ **Track opens**
Discover who opens your campaigns by tracking the number of times an invisible web beacon embedded in the campaign is downloaded. Learn more

☑ **Track clicks** Required on free accounts
Discover which campaign links were clicked, how many times they were clicked, and who did the clicking.

☑ **Track plain-text clicks** Required on free accounts
Track clicks in the plain-text version of your email by replacing all links with tracking URLs. Learn more

☐ **Google Analytics link tracking** Google Integration or Shopify must be enabled
Track clicks from your campaigns all the way to purchases on your website.
Requires Google Analytics on your website or Shopify Integration.

☐ **E-commerce link tracking**
Track visitors to your website from your MailChimp campaigns, capture order information, and pass that information back to MailChimp. Then you can view purchase details, conversions, and total sales on the reports page. You can also set up segments based on your subscribers' purchase activity. Learn more

☐ **ClickTale link tracking**
Gain insight to how subscribers interact with your email content.
Requires ClickTale on your website.

☐ **Track stats in Salesforce**
First, enable Salesforce in Account > Integrations.

Social media

☑ **Auto-tweet campaign as** *HImpactPros*
Customize your tweet. Include the *|URL|* merge tag and keep it under 140 characters (including the URL).

> List Your Company with H-Impact.com at No Cost and Get 2 Job Posts for Free - *|URL|*

37 characters left

☑ **Auto-post to Facebook after sending**
Customize your post's text. Your archive link will be attached to your post automatically, though not in the post text.

> List Your Company with H-Impact.com at No Cost and Get 2 Job Posts for Free

407 characters left

☐ Travis Holt (Your Profile)
☑ H-Impact (Fan Page)

More options

Auto-convert video
Turn this on, and we'll scan your content for embedded videos (which don't always render properly in email apps), then auto-convert them to use our email-friendly video merge tags instead.

< Back   Recipients > **Setup** > Template > Design > Confirm   Next >

Chapter 4: Creating Campaigns

For **Resulting Email Example B**

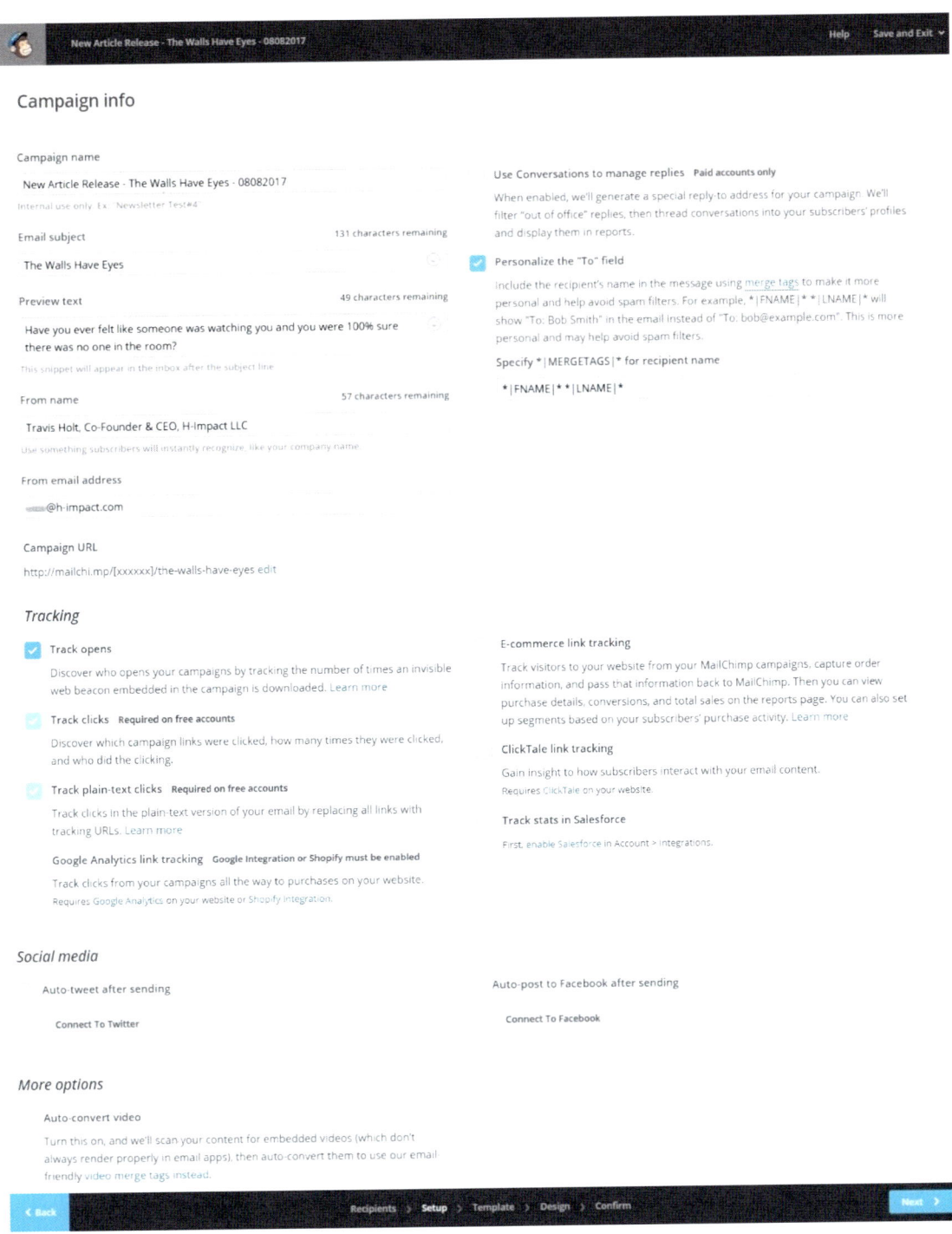

Click **Next** to proceed to the **Templates** step.

Templates

Select a Template appears as the title for the **Templates** step.

From the menu:

- Layouts
- Themes
- Saved Templates
- Campaigns
- Code your own

Earlier from the **Template** instructions around creating a **Template**, we focused on the **Drag and Drop** option to create a **Template**. Alternatively we could have used the more advanced **Code your own** option designed more for advanced users. These templates once saved are accessible under the **Saved Templates** section.

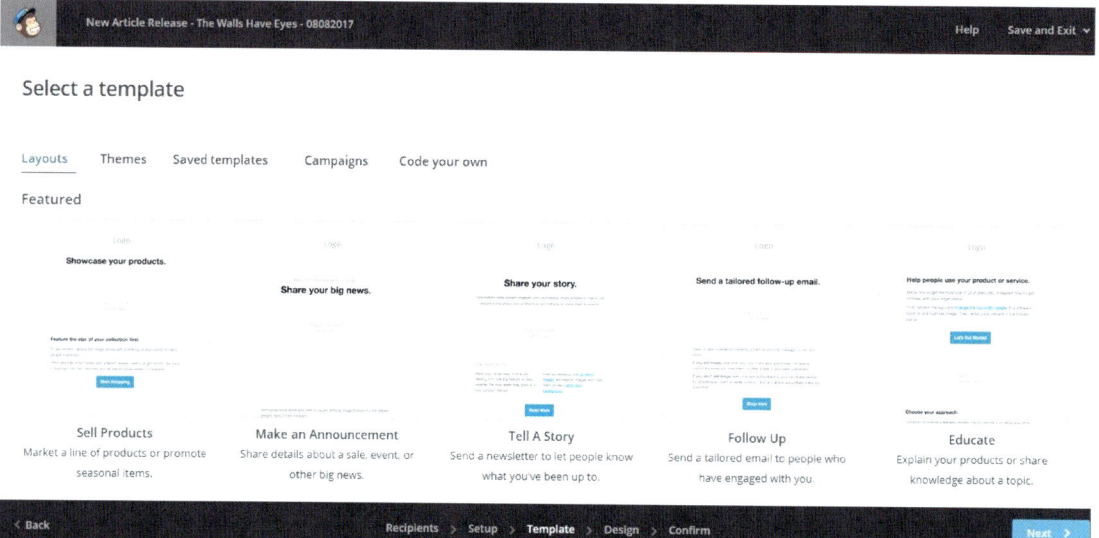

On the **Select a template** page, select **Saved templates**.

Select the **Template** via the thumbnail of the **Email** you wish to use for this **Campaign**.

For **Resulting Email Example A**, select the **Template** named **H-Impact Updates Org Listing with Jobs MC 101**.

For **Resulting Email Example B**, select the **Template** named **H-Impact Updates Employment Article Release MC 101**.

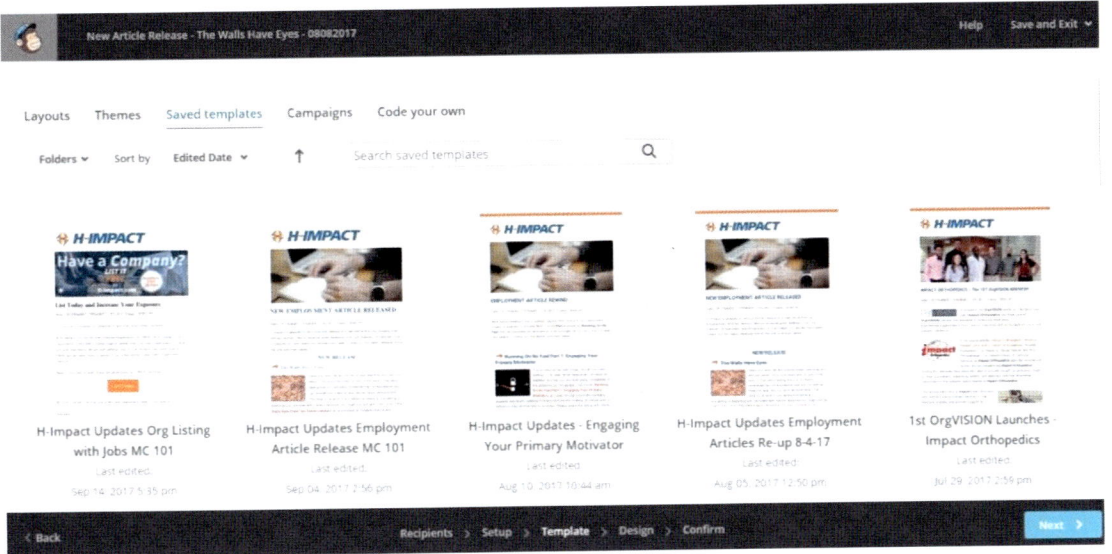

Click **Next** to proceed to the **Design** step. (**Note:** As an alternative to proceed to the **Design** step, **Double click** the thumbnail for the selected **Template**.)

Design

With the **Design** step, a page will display with the well-formatted email layout on the left but optional **Content Blocks** on the right that can be dragged to the left. If the **Template** was created using the more advanced **HTML based Code your own** type, the editable HTML would appear on the right instead of the **Drag and Drop Content Block controls**.

Important: Regardless of the type of **template**, **Drag and drop** or the **Code your own**, please make sure the format is in good shape (including testing in various email clients), there are no typos or grammar errors in the text, and all links point and make it to their expected target URL or the expected downloadable file. As a matter of quality, this review is very important, considering once the email is sent to your recipients there is no way to retrieve it from their inboxes. So make sure the **Email Template** is as error free as possible to ensure your email's primary message is received clearly. It's quite possible that one typo may damage the message you are trying to convey and may create a negative impression of the email you are sending now or any you send in the future.

The formatted template includes:

- **Image Content Block** for the **Logo** that links back to H-Impact.com

- **Image Content Block** for the **Header Image** that links back to a Highlighted Article
- **Text Content Block** that includes **Title** of the Email and Body
- **Button Content Block** that links back to a Highlighted Article

For **Resulting Email Example A,**

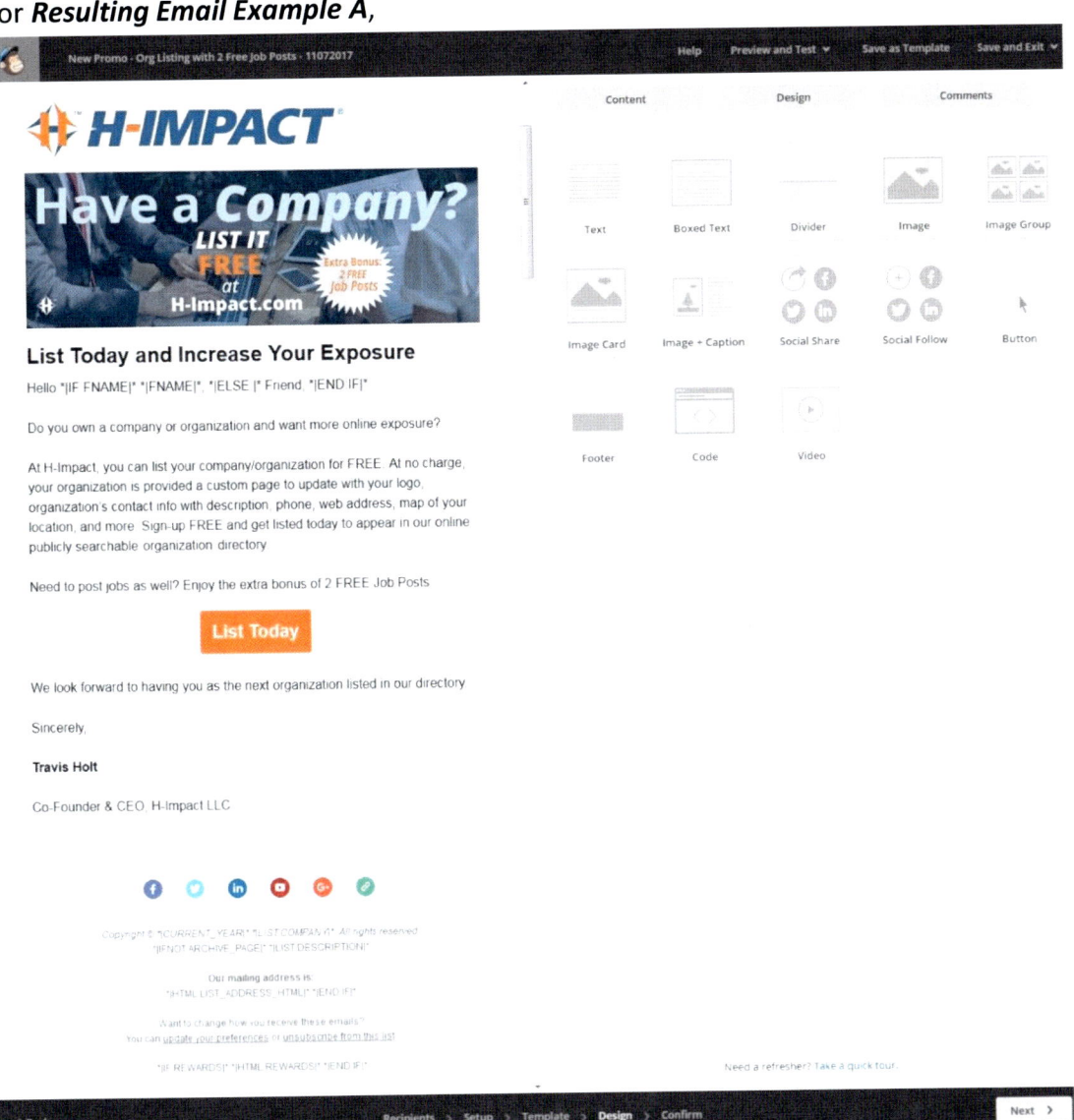

For **Resulting Email Example B,**

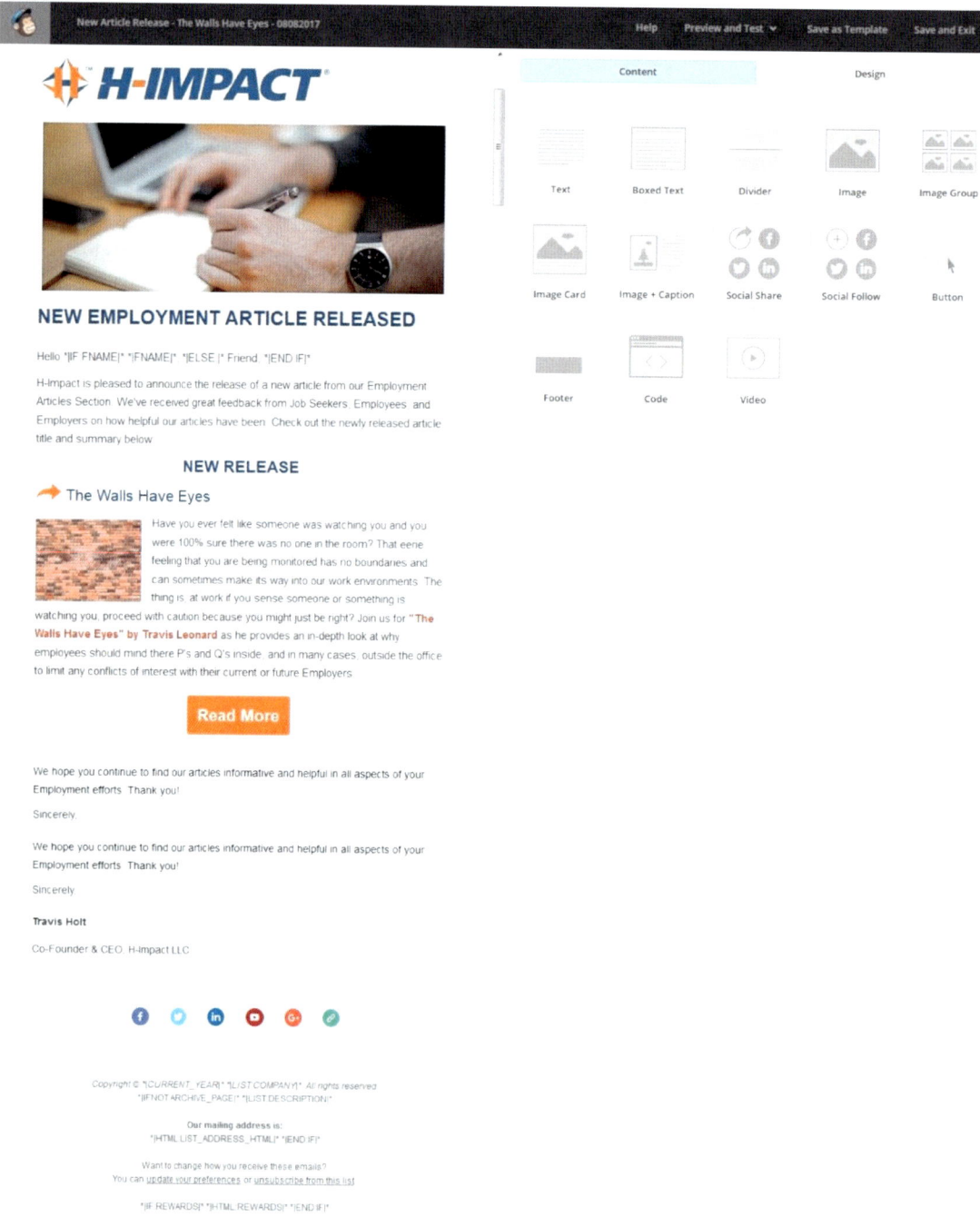

As a precaution, **MailChimp** has placed a **Preview and Test** Dropdown at the top of the Template. This link is a convenient way to test the email without sending it to intended recipients. Use the **Preview and Test** to display a dialogue box to enter the test email or emails. Here is an example of what a test might look like. Notice there is a message text box that is optional and can be sent along with the test email.

Send a Test Email

Send a test to

myemail@h-impact.com, coworker@h-impact.com

Use commas to separate multiple emails.

∨ Include instructions and a personal message
  (optional)

We are testing the email before going live. How does it look?

Send Test   Cancel   Privacy and Terms

Click **Ok** to return back to the **Campaign Builder**.

The recipients of the **Test Email** may provide feedback by responding to the test email. The test recipients' comments will also appear in the comments tab. Depending on your business processes, you may then proceed in carrying out the remaining steps for the **Email Campaign Launch**. **Test Emails** are optional but can be handy in catching errors that might otherwise slip through the cracks. Click **Ok** to complete this **Test Email** process.

Note: As far as the Template examples, notice the footers, which include the closing with configurable **Drag and Drop** built-in **Social Media Follow Content Blocks**. The footers also include a **MailChimp** unsubscribe link required by **MailChimp** and the US **Federal Trade Commission's CAN-SPAM Act** which requires a quick and easy opt-out for recipients of email solicitations from businesses or organizations. For more information on the **CAN-SPAM Act** visit the **Federal Trade Commission's website** at www.ftc.gov. The footer text and associated ***|MERGE|* Fields** are built-in and will populate upon sending this **Template** as a part of our **Email Campaign**.

Click **Next** to proceed to the **Confirm** step.

Confirm

The **Confirm** page displays titled **"You're all set to send!"** MailChimp provides this page as a means to review the **Campaign** prior to completing it. It summarizes the critical elements of the campaign and allows you to edit them if needed before sending the **eBlast** to the recipients.

Each element appears in a list format with their **current value** with a gray **Edit** button that allows you to edit the value if you wish. There is a **Green Check mark** at the beginning of each row that shows each element has been completed. A **yellow caution Exclamation mark** will show if the element may need your attention.

The elements with their current values include:

- List
- Subject line
- Preview text
- Replies (with **current From name and From email address**)
- Tracking
- Sharing and Social Media
- HTML Email
- Plain-text email
- Social Cards
- Monkey rewards (identifies a **MailChimp** link with logo as an affiliate. Required for the **New Business Forever Free** version of **MailChimp**.)

Notice the gray **Schedule** button next to the **Send** button in the bottom right corner of the **Confirm** step. The **Schedule** button can be used to schedule **Campaigns** which you may prepare in advance but send at another date in time. For the purposes of this book, we will send our **eBlast** manually and in real-time. As a result, the scheduling feature will not be covered. For more information on scheduling **Campaigns** please visit www.mailchimp.com.

For **Resulting Email Example A,**

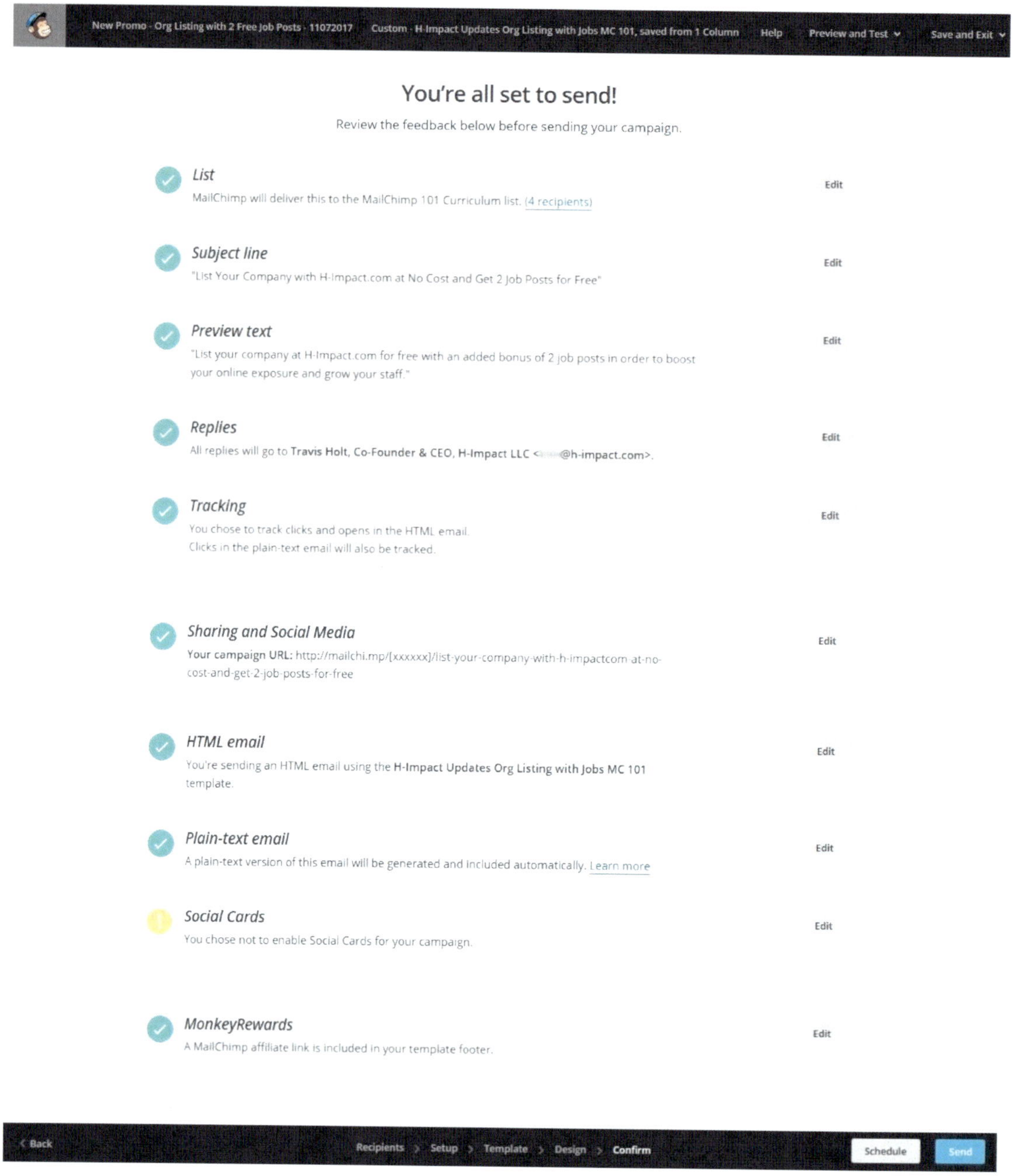

For **Resulting Email Example B,** we **will not auto post** to **Facebook** or **Twitter** and **will not** enable **Social Cards**.

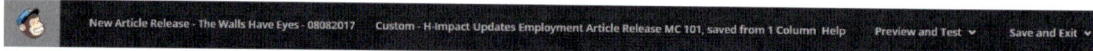

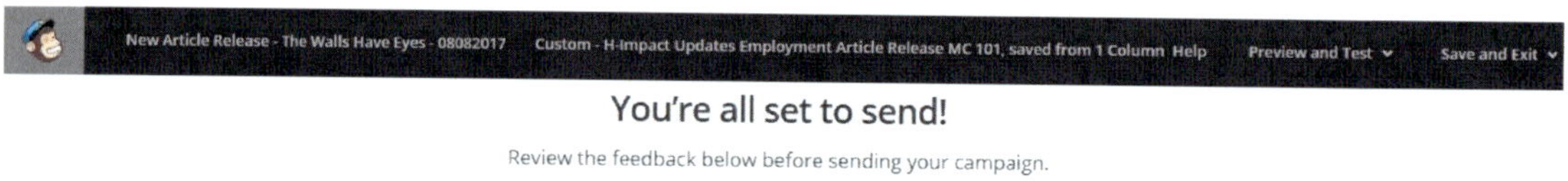

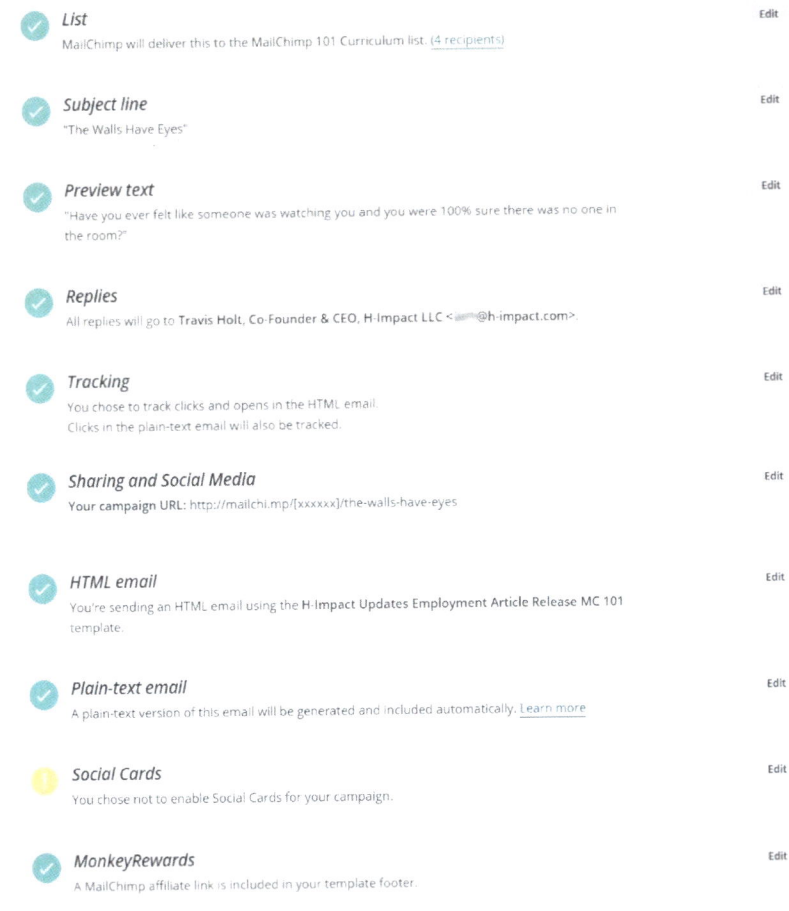

For **Resulting Email Example B,** we **will not** enable **Social Cards** and the **Social Media Auto-post** and **Auto tweet** features. After you've reviewed all the elements of your **Campaign** from the list, you are ready to complete the **Campaign** and send the **eBlast**. To proceed, click the **Send** button. Then skip ahead to the **Send Campaign** section to send your **Campaign**.

On the other hand, for **Resulting Email Example A,** we **will** enable **Social Cards** and the **Social Media Auto-post** and **Auto tweet** features. As a result, Continue on to the **Social Cards** section.

Social Cards

Now, let's enable **Social Cards**. **MailChimp** created **Social Cards** to allow users the ability to easily integrate **Email Campaigns** into popular social media platforms. **Social Cards** are optional. **Social Cards** are digital representations of the content we include in our **Campaign Emails**. At the time this book was written **Social Cards** were available on **Facebook**, **Twitter** and **Pinterest**. Once configured properly, and the **Campaign** is sent with social media auto post enabled, **Social Cards** will appear in news feeds and on **Social Media** pages and can be easily shared amongst social media networks. Each **Social Card** may include a **Title**, **Description** and **Image**. A **Social Card** by default links back to a **MailChimp** hosted version of the **Campaign Email** being sent. Valid accounts on the respective social media platforms are required in order to take advantage of **Social Cards**.

To enable **Social Cards**, click the link titled **Enable Social Cards to share your campaign.**

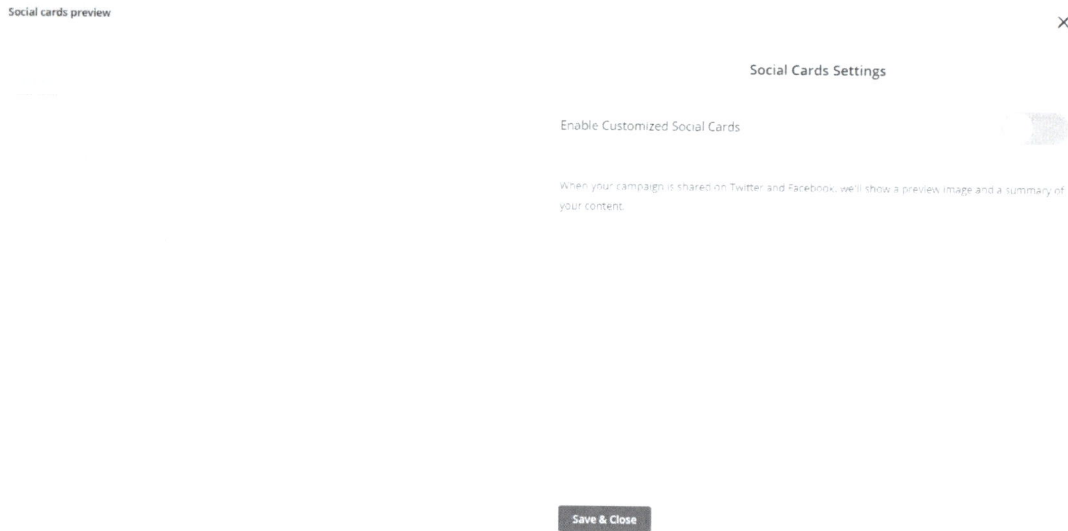

On the **Social cards preview** page **Enable Customized Social Cards** by clicking the toggle slide button under **Social Cards Settings.**

Notice the **Social Card preview** on the left and the configuration panel on the right. Notice the three **Social Media** platform tabs on the left for **Twitter**, **Facebook** and Pinterest. For the purposes of this book, we will configure and implement the **Social Cards** for **Twitter** and **Facebook**.

MailChimp approximates what image to include using the **Email Template** associated with the **Campaign. Title,** and **Description** text boxes are available to supply the **Title** and **Description** of your **Social Card**.

Neither of the image approximations that have been chosen by **MailChimp** displays properly for **Twitter** or **Facebook**.

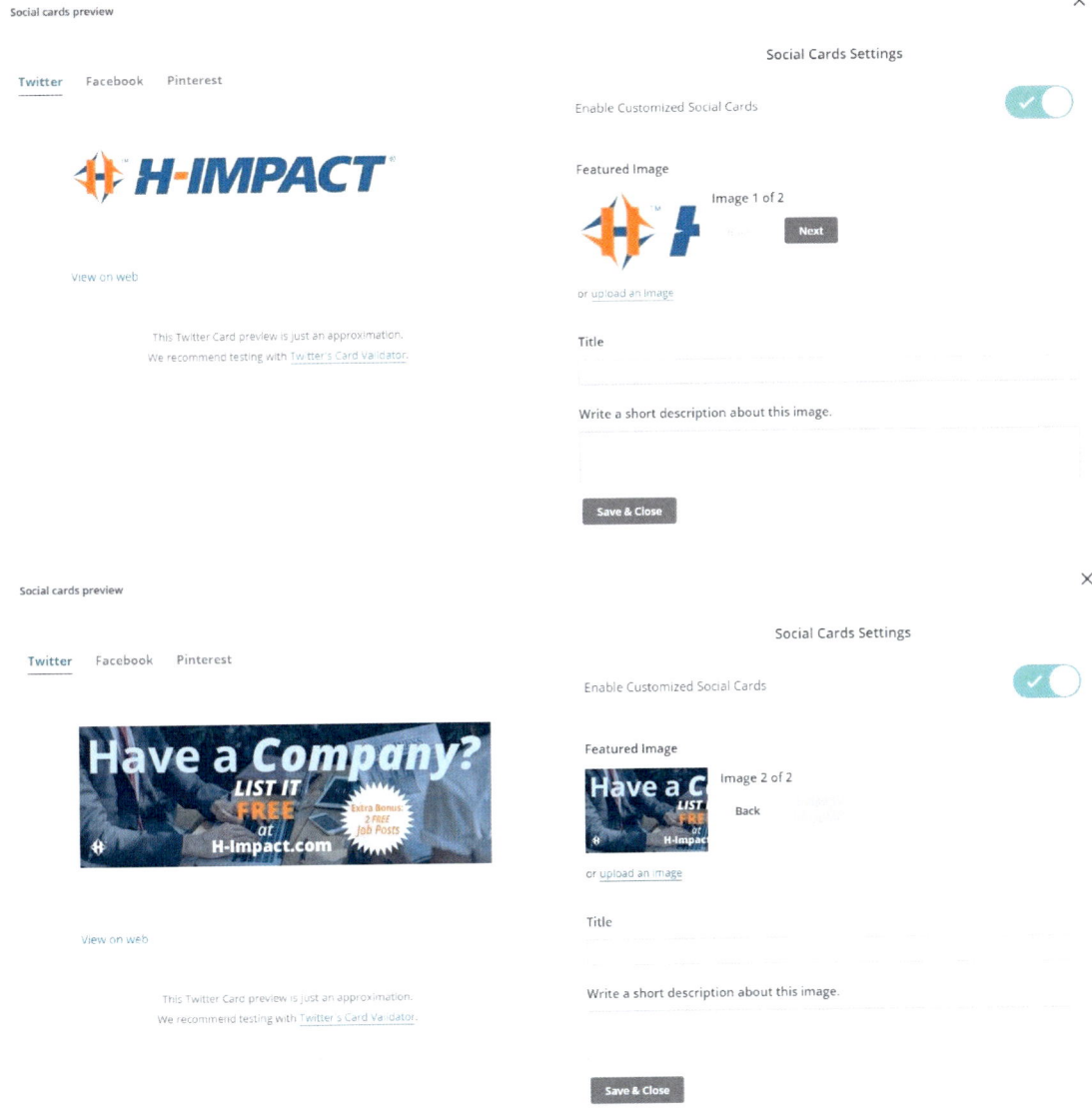

For the best post display of the image, prior to this chapter we prepared and uploaded an image similar to the second image with dimensions of a **477 px width** and a **245 px height**. This image with the desired width and height has been uploaded into the **Content Manager** and is ready to be selected for our **Social Card**.

Note: For each **Social Media platform,** the dimensions that results in the best display for the **Social Card** image may vary.

To select the newly uploaded image with proper dimensions, click the **upload an image** link.

The **Content Manager** displays.

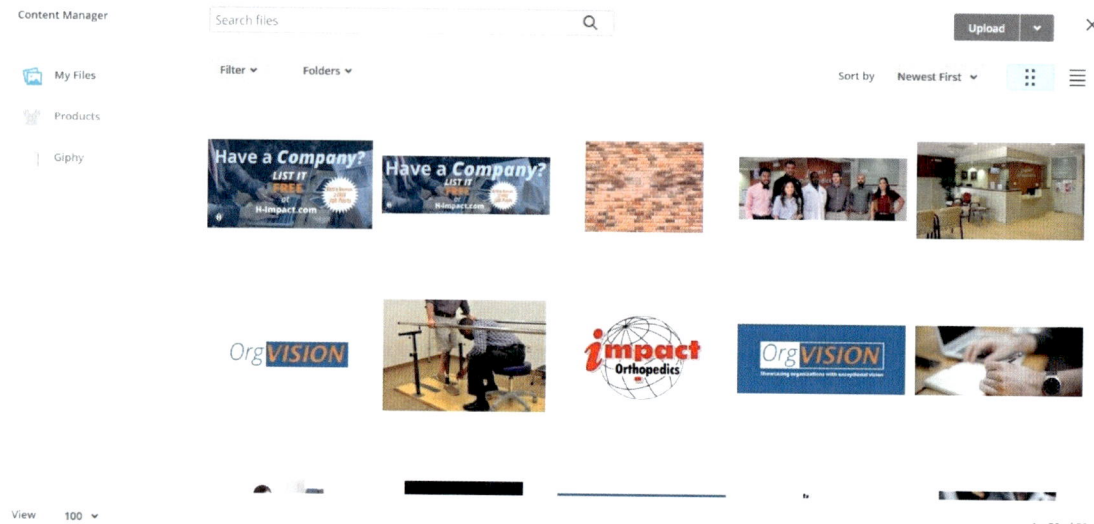

Select the first image with the text **Have a Company?**. This image is very similar to the image we used in our **Email Template**. The first image has the proper dimensions of a **477 px width** and a **245 px height** which will display nicely on **Twitter** and **Facebook** in our **Social Card**. Now click the **Insert** button at the top right corner of the screen.

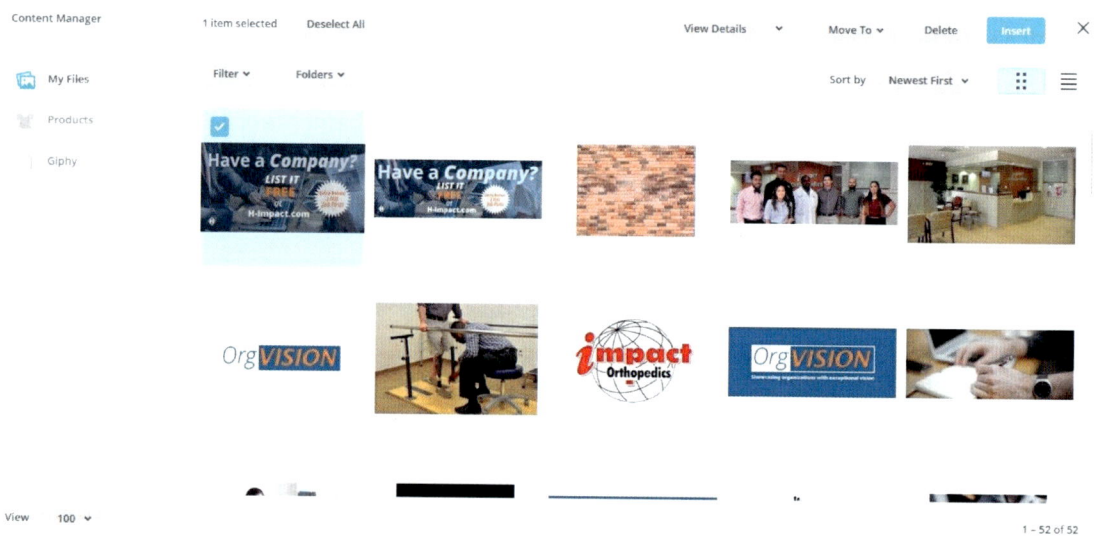

Chapter 4: Creating Campaigns

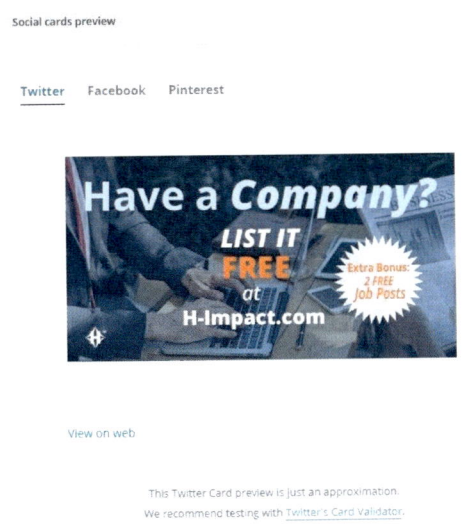
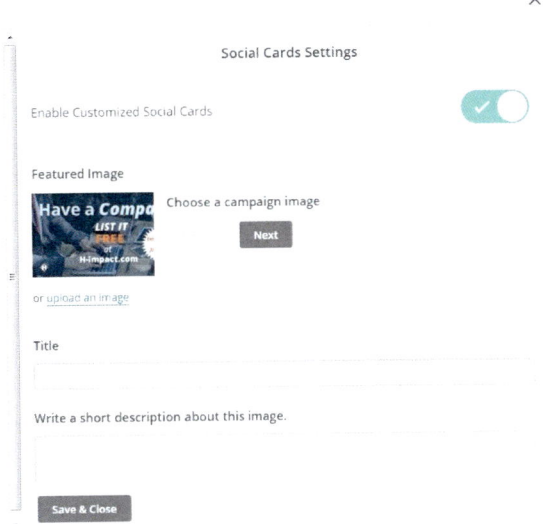

Complete the **Title** and **Description** of the **Social Card**.

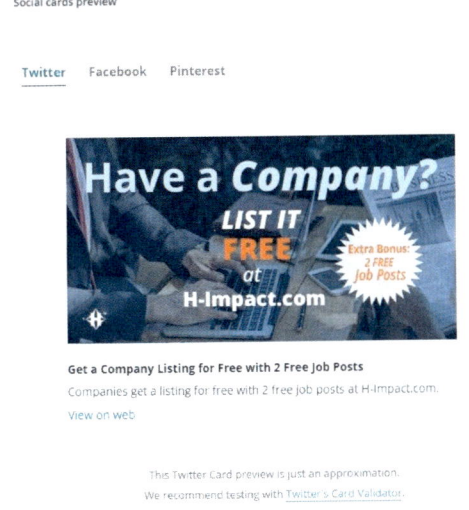
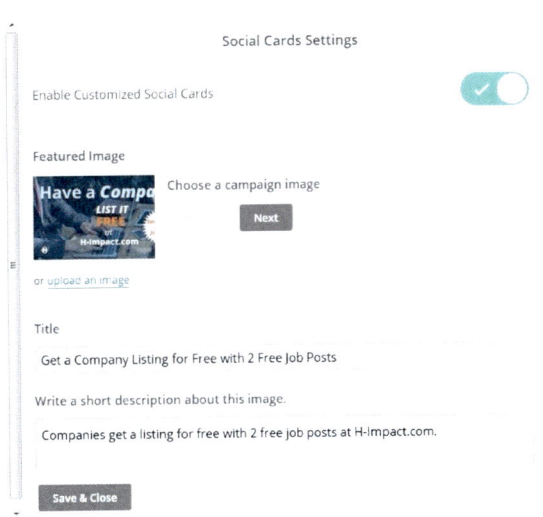

To finish customizing the **Social Cards**, click **Save & Close. Social Cards** is now enabled.

For *Resulting Email Example A,*

How to Unleash Email Marketing with MailChimp

✓ **List** — Edit
MailChimp will deliver this to the MailChimp 101 Curriculum list. (4 recipients)

✓ **Subject line** — Edit
"List Your Company with H-Impact.com at No Cost and Get 2 Job Posts for Free"

✓ **Preview text** — Edit
"List your company at H-Impact.com for free with an added bonus of 2 job posts in order to boost your online exposure and grow your staff."

✓ **Replies** — Edit
All replies will go to Travis Holt, Co-Founder & CEO, H-Impact LLC <___@h-impact.com>.

✓ **Tracking** — Edit
You chose to track clicks and opens in the HTML email.
Clicks in the plain-text email will also be tracked.

✓ **Sharing and Social Media** — Edit
Your campaign URL: http://mailchi.mp/[xxxxxx]/list-your-company-with-h-impactcom-at-no-cost-and-get-2-job-posts-for-free

You chose to share this campaign on social media after sending.
Auto-tweet campaign: List Your Company with H-Impact.com at No... - http://mailchi.mp/[xxxxxx]/list-your-company-with-h-impactcom-at-no-cost-and-get-2-job-posts-for-free
Auto-post to Facebook: List Your Company with H-Impact.com at No Cost and Get 2 Job Posts for Free

✓ **HTML email** — Edit
You're sending an HTML email using the H-Impact Updates Org Listing with Jobs MC 101 template.

✓ **Plain-text email** — Edit
A plain-text version of this email will be generated and included automatically. Learn more

✓ **Social Cards** — Edit
Excellent! Your social card is ready to roll.

Get a Company Listing for Free with 2 Free Job Posts
Companies get a listing for free with 2 free job posts at H-Impact.com.

✓ **MonkeyRewards** — Edit
A MailChimp affiliate link is included in your template footer.

< Back   Recipients > Setup > Template > Design > **Confirm**   Schedule   Send

Again, for **Resulting Email Example B,** we will **not auto post** to **Facebook** or **Twitter** and will not enable **Social Cards**.

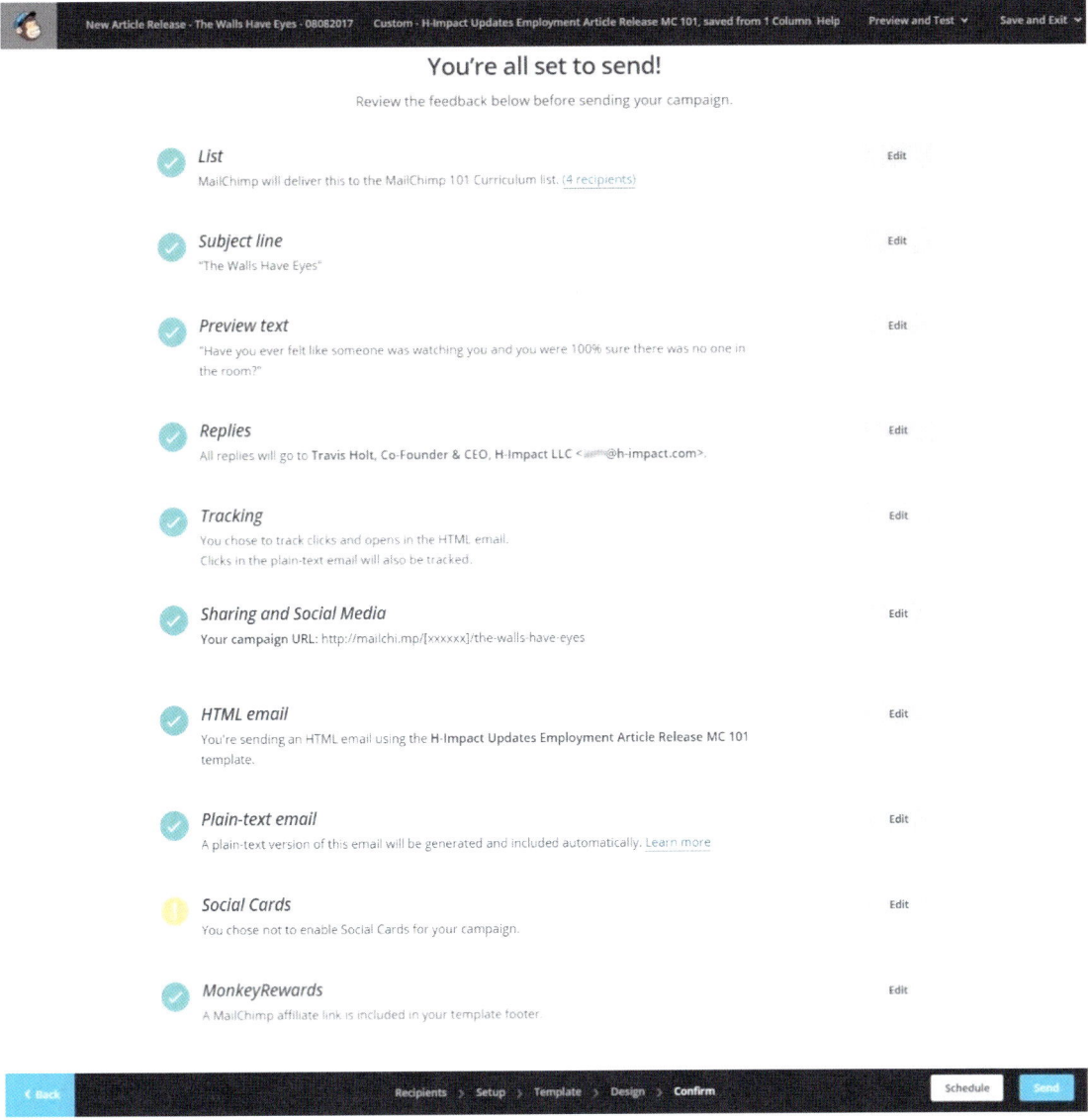

After you've reviewed all the elements of your **Campaign** from the list, you are ready to complete the **Campaign** and send the **eBlast**. To proceed click the **Send** button.

Please skip ahead to the **Send Campaign** section to send your **Campaign** using the **Old Campaign Builder Process**.

New Campaign Builder Process

MailChimp is constantly improving its system to make it more efficient and effective for its end users. At the time this book was published, **MailChimp** was in the process of releasing a newer and faster way to send out **Campaigns**. As an alternative to the **Old Campaign Builder Process** above, the section below demonstrates how this new **Campaign Builder** can be used to send **Campaigns**.

You should have arrived here after switching to the new way of building **Campaigns** or after the old way of building Campaigns has been phased out by **MailChimp** and is no longer available.

Upon navigating to the **Create Campaign** page in the **New Campaign Builder**, you will notice the following page requiring **Campaign** setup information including **To, From, Subject, Content, Social Media Connections, Settings,** and **Tracking**:

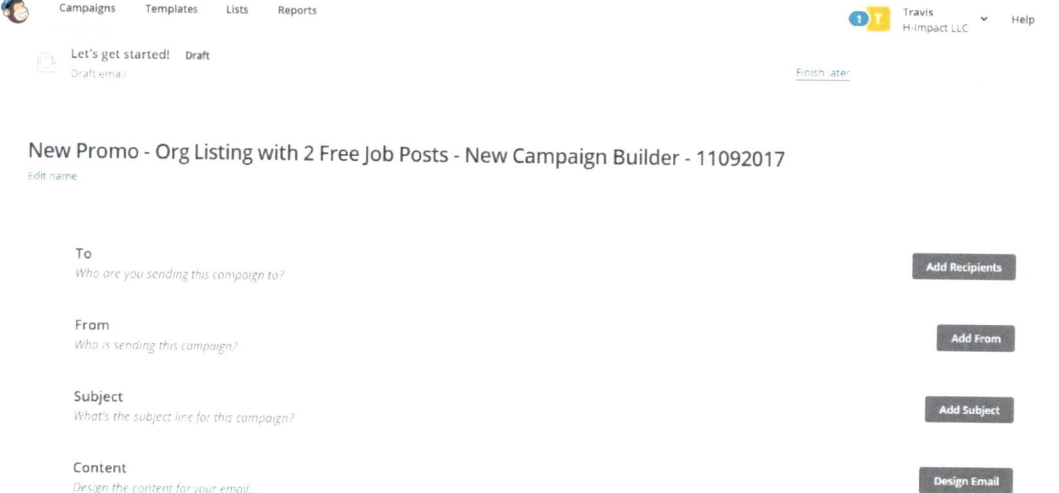

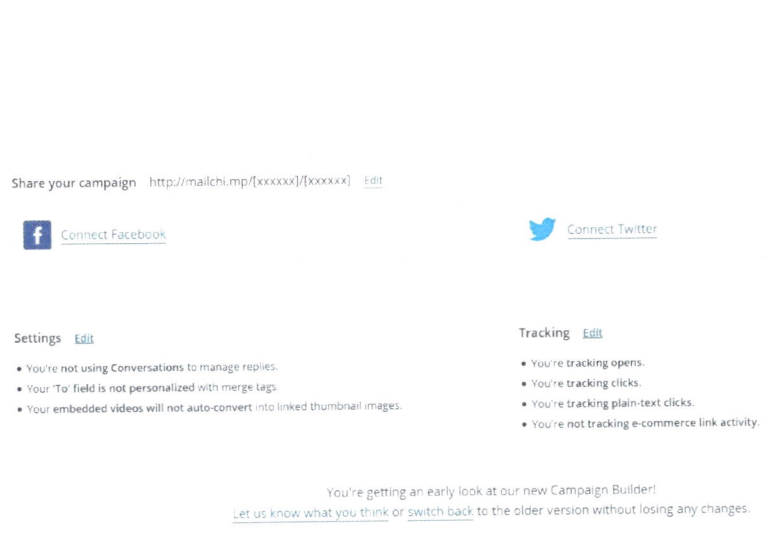

Also notice the switch back link at the bottom of the page indicating that the option is still available to switch back to the **Old Campaign Builder** if the user chooses.

To

Click **Add Recipients**. When the section expands use the **List** dropdown to select **MailChimp 101 Curriculum.** For this example keep the **Segment** dropdown **default** selection **All subscribers on list.**

Save

Click **Save.**

A **check mark** will now appear next to the **To** label indicating that section has been completed. The **Recipients** selection can be modified by clicking **Edit Recipients**.

From

Name

Under the **From** section, which asks, **"Who is sending this campaign?"** click **Add From**. For companies, try a pattern like First Name Last Name, with Job Position, Company Name or Web Address. Ex: John Doe, CEO, ABZ Company(or ABZ.com)

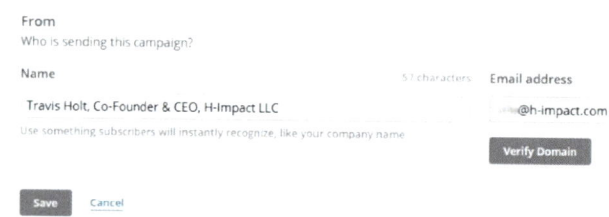

Email Address

Verify your domain by clicking **Verify Domain. MailChimp** will send you a verification email that will include a **Verify Your Domain link** that will send you back to **MailChimp.com** to automatically verify your domain and email address. **MailChimp** will also include a code that can be used to enter into the dialog form to verify domain and email address. For the purposes of this exercise, we will enter the verification code from the verification email into the MailChimp verification dialog form.

Click **Send Verification Email** to verify the domain.

Verify Domain

We need to verify that you have access to an email address at h-impact.com. Enter an address, and we'll send you a verification email. Learn more.

Email address

email@h-impact.com

Enter an address that contains h-impact.com.

> Still getting this message after verifying your domain?

Send Verification Email   Cancel

Enter the **Verification Code** that was sent in the email. Click **Verify**.

Verify Domain

Your verification email is on the way!

We sent an email to `email@h-impact.com` to verify the domain h-impact.com. (11/9/17 9:14PM). To verify h-impact.com, click *Verify Domain Access* in the email. Or enter the verification code in this field.

Enter verification code

e066cf730ffd

Verify   Cancel

Click **Done** to complete the **Domain Verification** process.

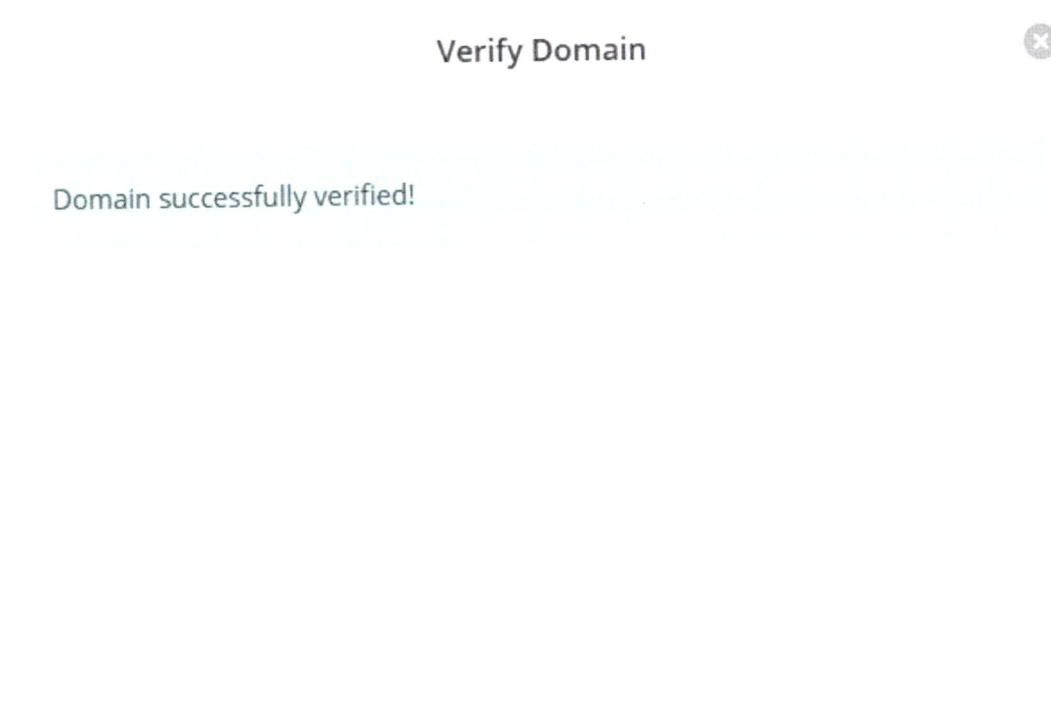

Save

Click **Save** to complete the **From** section of the **New Campaign Builder**.

Once saved the **From** value may be edited by clicking **Edit From**.

Subject

Under the **Subject** section, which asks, "**What's the subject line for this campaign?**" click **Add Subject**.

Subject

Enter a **Subject** that peeks the recipient's interests about how reading the email can benefit them. Ensure there are no misspellings or grammar errors.

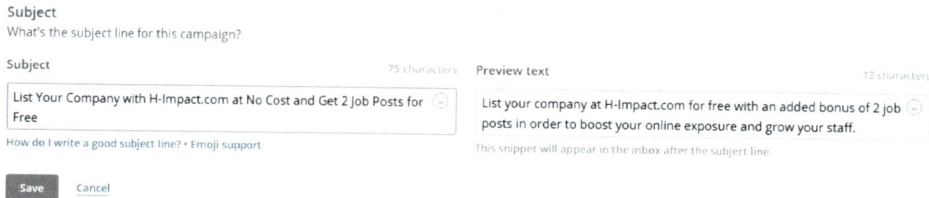

Preview Text

Enter a preview text that acts as a brief summary that peeks the recipient's interests about how reading the email can benefit them. Ensure there are no misspellings or grammar errors.

Save

Click **Save** to complete the **Subject** section of the **New Campaign Builder**. Once saved the **Subject** data may be edited by clicking **Edit Subject**.

Content

Under the Content section where it states "**Design the content for your email**", click **Design Email**.

Select a Template

Select a Template appears as the title.

From the menu:

- Layouts
- Themes
- Saved Templates
- Campaigns
- Code your own

Earlier from the **Template** instructions around creating a **Template**, we focused on the **Drag and Drop** option to create a **Template**. Alternatively we could have used the more advanced **Code your own** option designed more for advanced users. These templates once saved are accessible under the **Saved Templates** section.

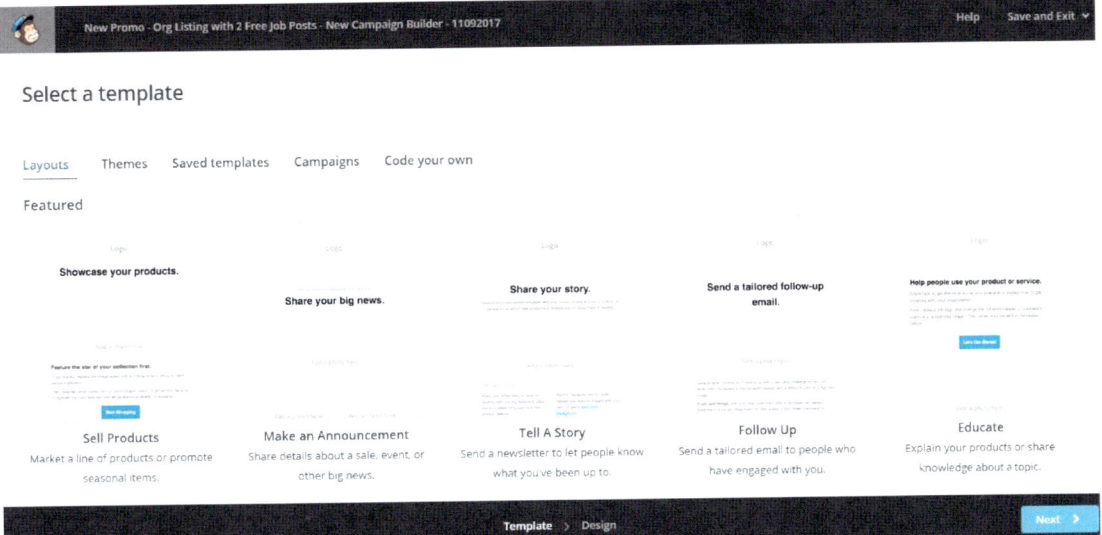

On the **Select a template** page, select **Saved templates**.

Select the **Template** via the thumbnail of the **Email** you wish to use for this **Campaign**.

For **Resulting Email Example A**, select the **Template** named **H-Impact Updates Org Listing with Jobs MC 101**

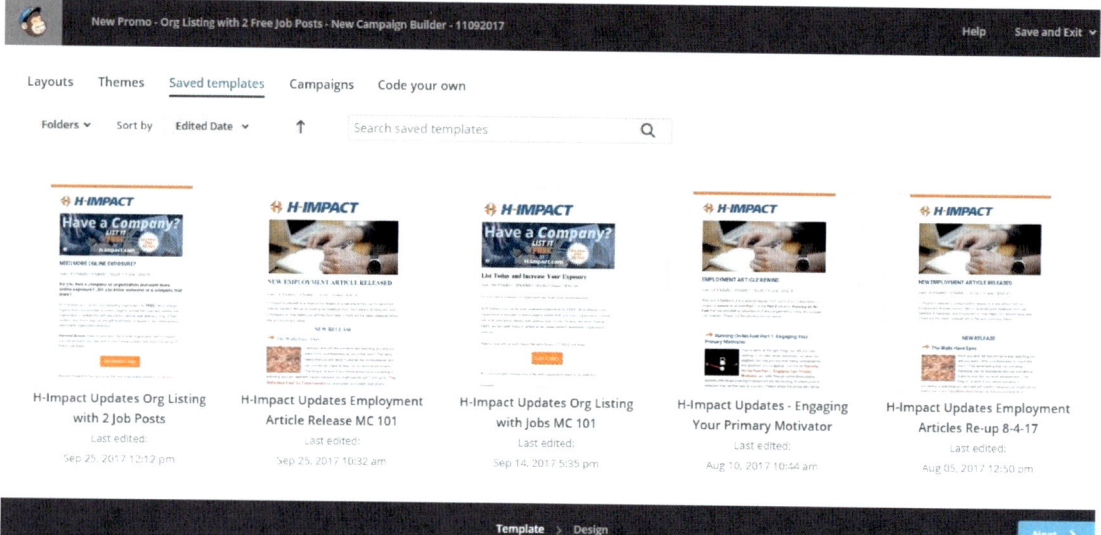

Click **Next** to proceed to the **Design** step. (**Note:** As an alternative to proceed to the **Design** step, **Double click** the thumbnail for the selected **Template**.)

Design

With the **Design** step, a page will display with the well-formatted email layout on the left but optional **Content Blocks** on the right that can be dragged to the left. If the **Template** was created using the more advanced **HTML based Code your own** type, the editable HTML would appear on the right instead of the **Drag and Drop Content Block controls**.

Important: Regardless of the type of **template**, **Drag and drop** or the **Code your own**, please make sure the format is in good shape (including testing in various email clients), there are no typos or grammar errors in the text, and all links point and make it to their expected target URL or the expected downloadable file. As a matter of quality, this review is very important, considering once the email is sent to your recipients there is no way to retrieve it from their inboxes. So make sure the **Email Template** is as error free as possible to ensure your email's primary message is received clearly. It's quite possible that one typo may damage the message you are trying to convey and may create a negative impression of the email you are sending now or any you send in the future.

The formatted template includes:

- **Image Content Block** for the **Logo** that links back to H-Impact.com
- **Image Content Block** for the **Header Image** that links back to a Highlighted Article
- **Text Content Block** that includes **Title** of the Email and Body
- **Button Content Block** that links back to a Highlighted Article

For **Resulting Email Example A**,

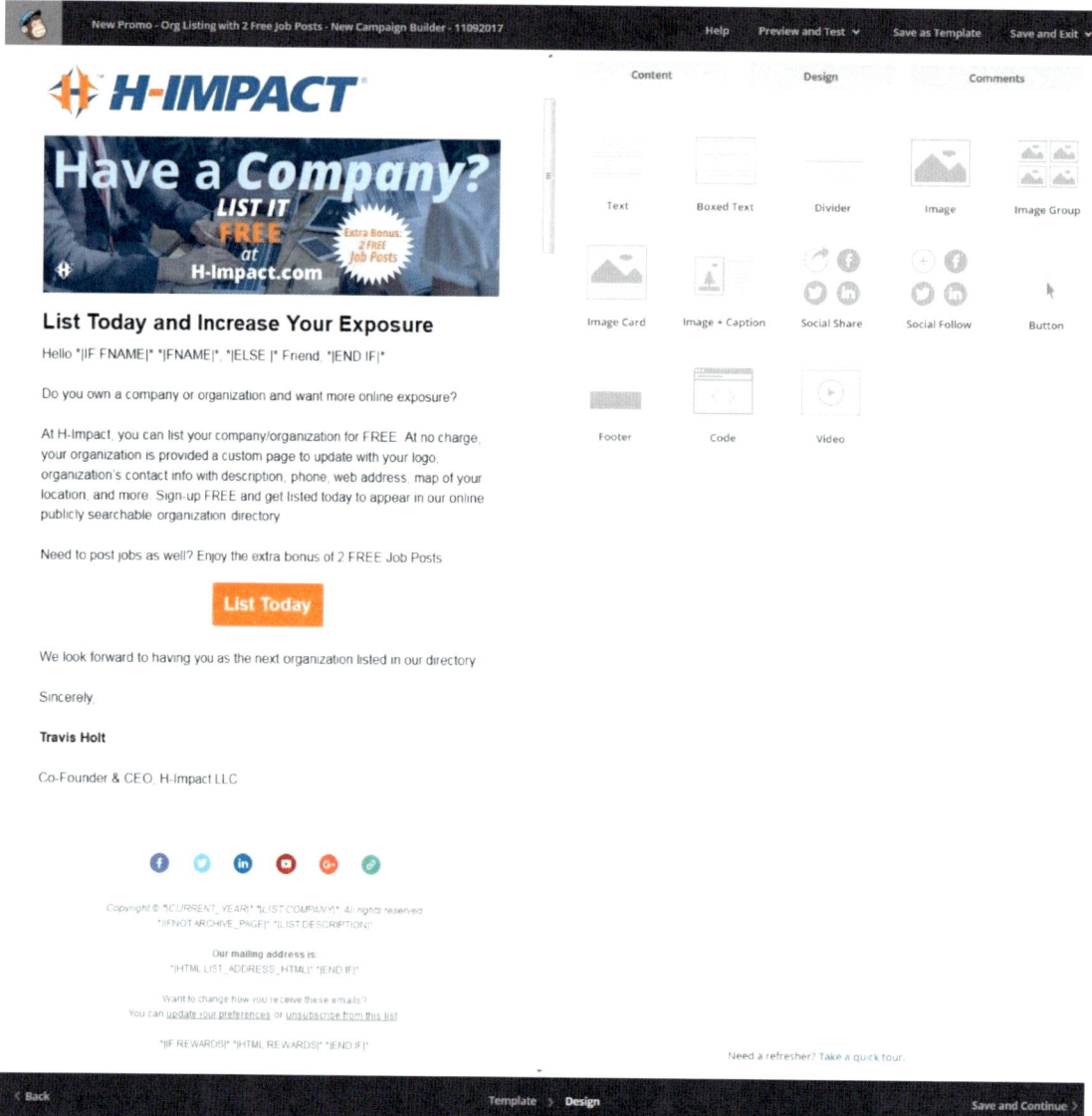

Save and Continue

Click **Save and Continue** at the bottom right corner of the **Template Design** page to complete the **Content** section of the **New Campaign Builder**. Once saved the **Content** data may be edited by clicking **Edit Design**.

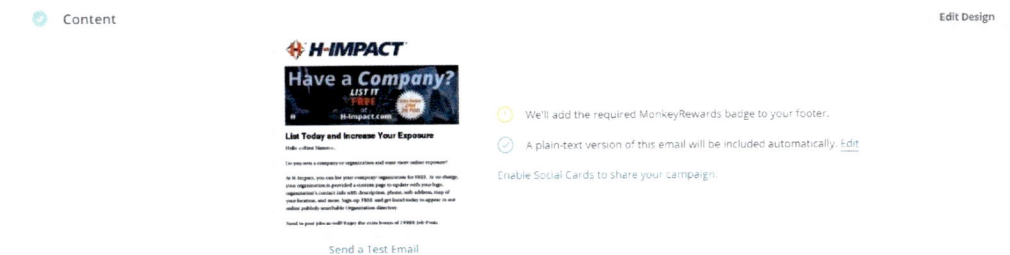

For quick testing at any time while building the **Email Campaign**, **MailChimp** has placed a **Send a Test Email** link within the **Content** section. This link is a convenient way to test the email without sending it to intended recipients. Click **Send a Test Email** to display a dialogue box to configure the **Test Email(s)**. Here is an example of what a test might look like. Notice there is an instructions or personal message text box that is optional and can be sent along with the **Test Email**.

Click **Send Test** to send the test email.

Click **Ok** to return back to the **New Campaign Builder**.

The recipients of the **Test Email** may provide feedback by responding to the test email. The test recipients' comments will also appear in the comments tab. Depending on your business processes, you may then proceed in carrying out the remaining steps for the **Email Campaign Launch**. **Test Emails** are optional but can be handy in catching errors that might otherwise slip through the cracks. Click **Ok** to complete this **Test Email** process.

Now, let's enable **Social Cards**. **MailChimp** created **Social Cards** to allow users the ability to easily integrate **Email Campaigns** into popular social media platforms. **Social Cards** are optional. **Social Cards** are digital representations of the content we include in our **Campaign Emails**. At the time this book was written **Social Cards** were available on **Facebook**, **Twitter** and **Pinterest**. Once configured properly, and the **Campaign** is sent with social media auto post enabled, **Social Cards** will appear in news feeds and on **Social Media** pages and can be easily shared amongst social media networks. Each **Social Card** may include a **Title**, **Description** and **Image**. A **Social Card** by default links back to a **MailChimp** hosted version of the **Campaign Email** being sent. Valid accounts on the respective social media platforms are required in order to take advantage of **Social Cards**.

To enable **Social Cards**, click the link titled **Enable Social Cards to share your campaign.**

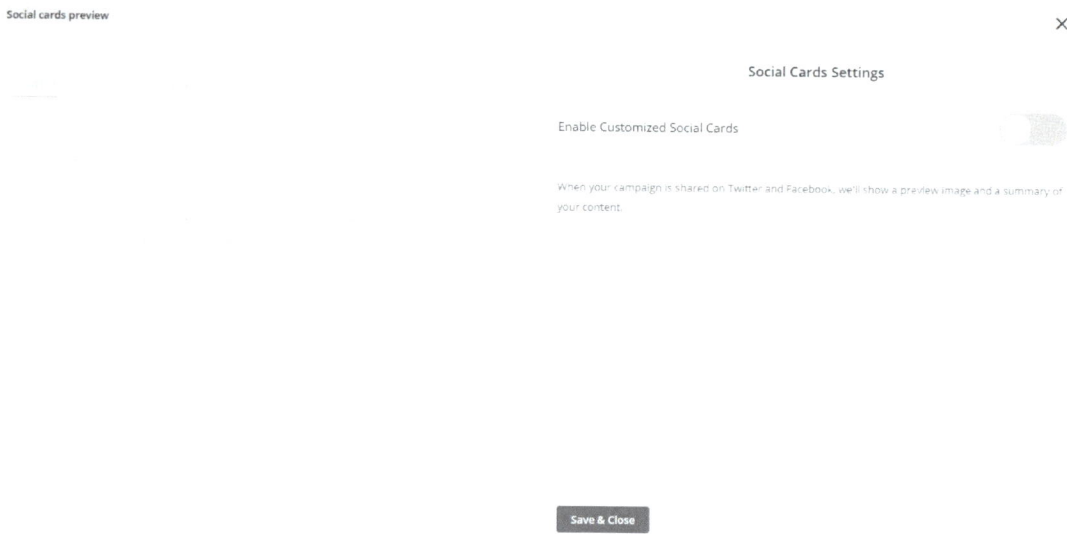

On the **Social cards preview** page **Enable Customized Social Cards** by clicking the toggle slide button under **Social Cards Settings.**

Notice the **Social Card preview** on the left and the configuration panel on the right. Notice the three **Social Media** platform tabs on the left for **Twitter**, **Facebook** and **Pinterest**. For the purposes of this book, we will configure and implement the **Social Cards** for **Twitter** and **Facebook**.

MailChimp approximates what image to include using the **Email Template** associated with the **Campaign. Title** and **Description** text boxes are available to supply the **Title** and **Description** of your **Social Card**.

Neither of the image approximations that have been chosen by **MailChimp** displays properly for **Twitter** or **Facebook**.

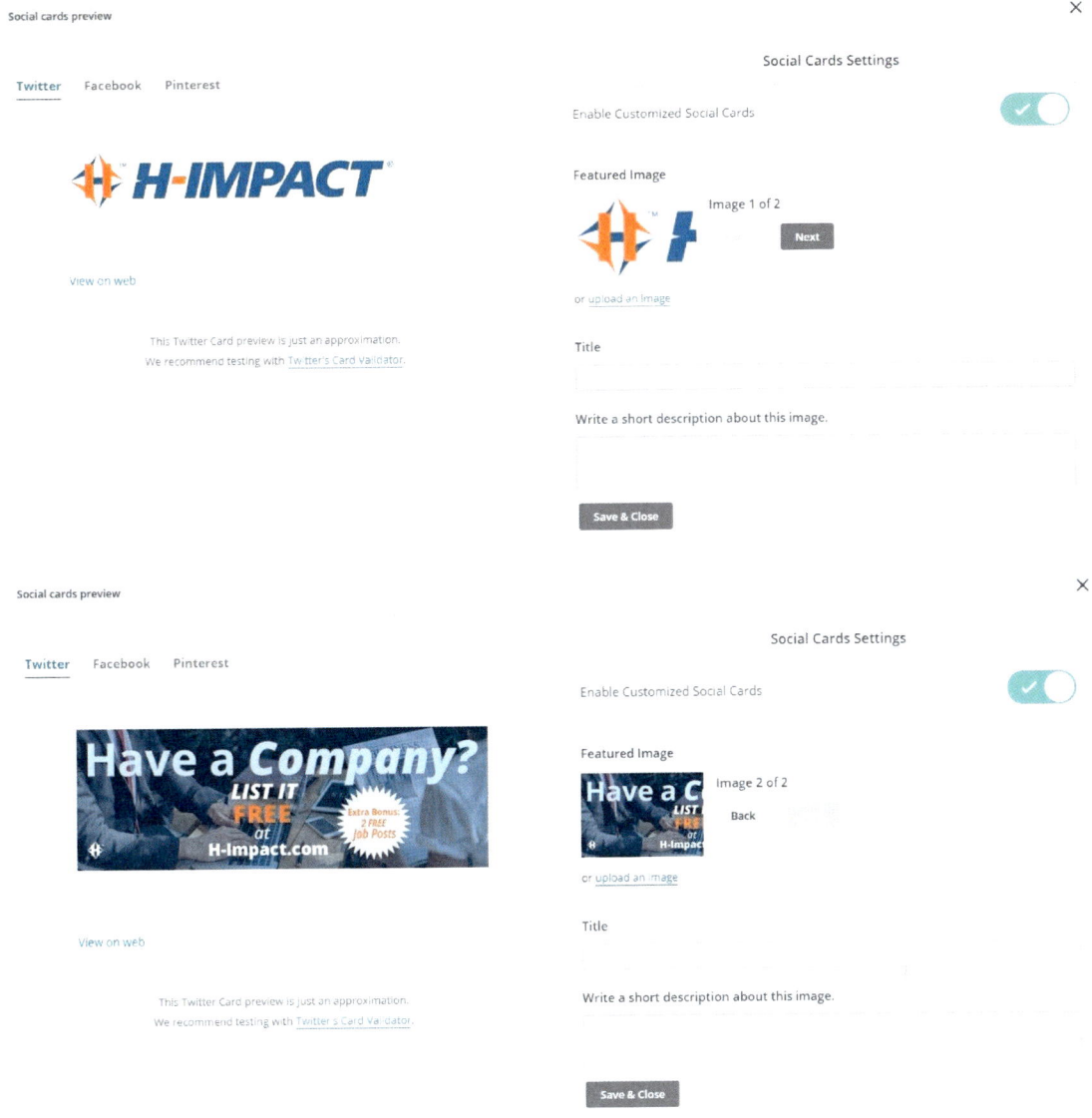

For the best post display of the image, prior to this chapter we prepared and uploaded an image similar to the second image with dimensions of a **477 px width** and a **245 px height**. This image with the desired width and height has been uploaded into the **Content Manager** and is ready to be selected for our **Social Card**.

Note: For each **Social Media platform,** the dimensions that results in the best display for the **Social Card** image may vary.

To select the newly uploaded image with proper dimensions, click the **upload an image** link.

The **Content Manager** displays.

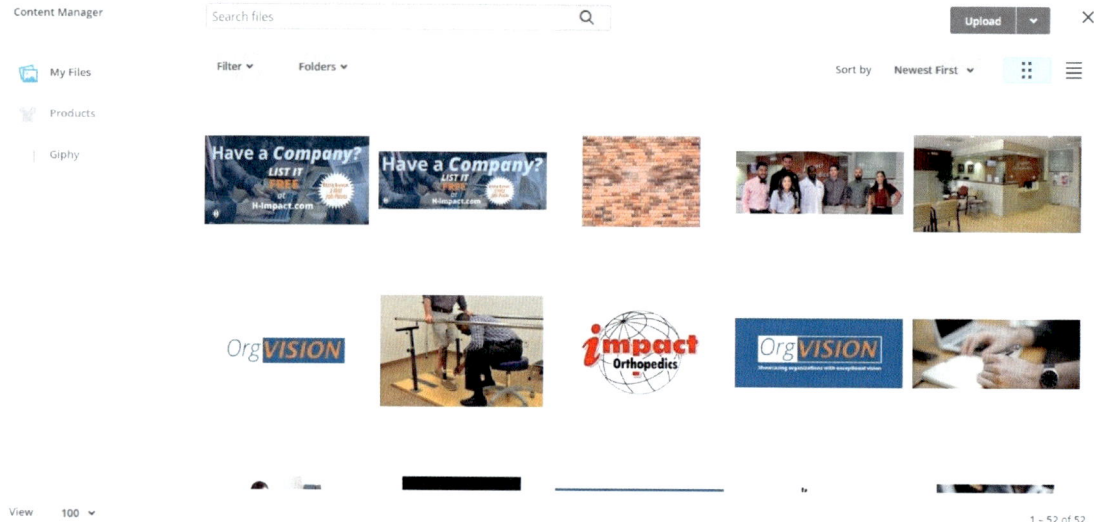

Select the first image with the text **Have a Company?**. This image is very similar to the image we used in our **Email Template**. The first image has the proper dimensions of a **477 px width** and a **245 px height** which will display nicely on **Twitter** and **Facebook** in our **Social Card**. Now click the **Insert** button at the top right corner of the screen.

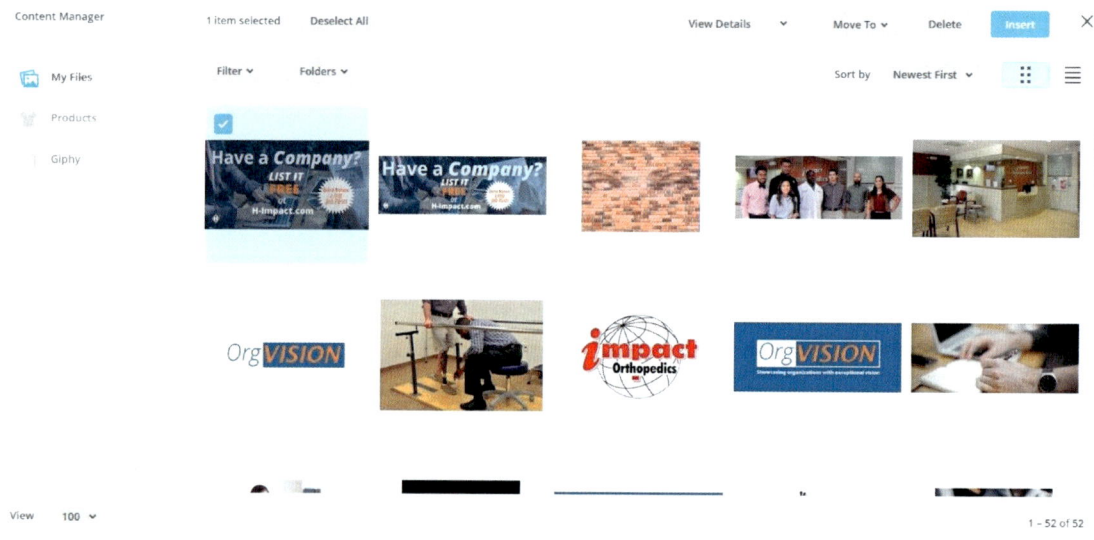

Chapter 4: Creating Campaigns   147

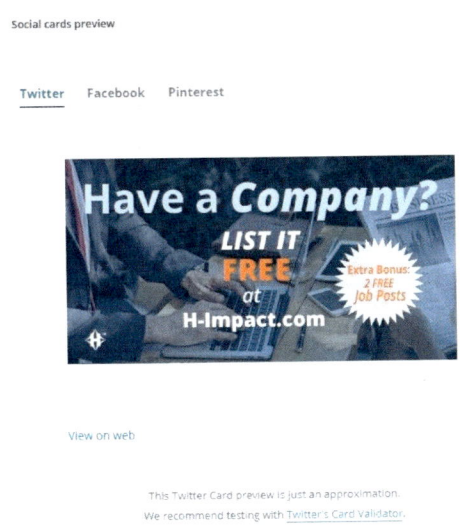
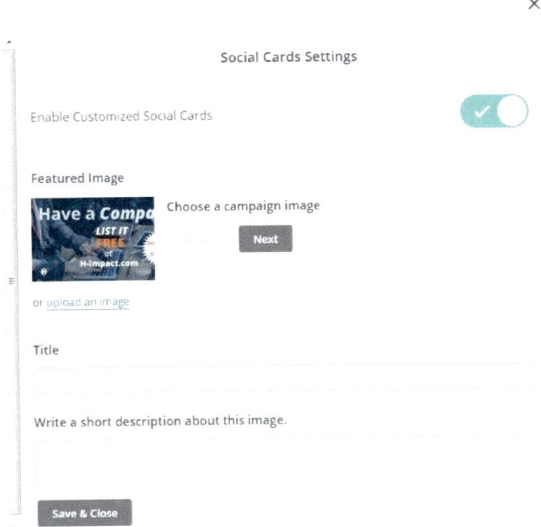

Complete the **Title** and **Description** of the **Social Card**.

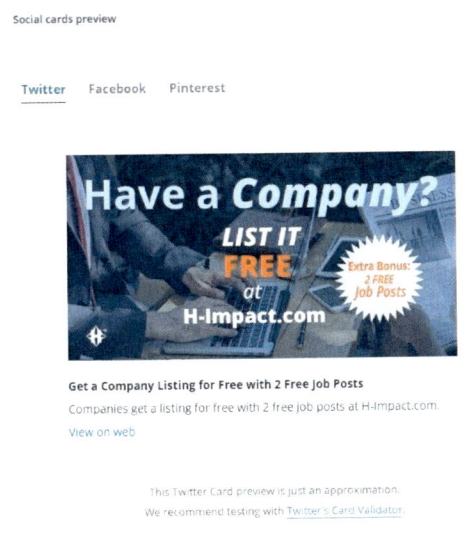
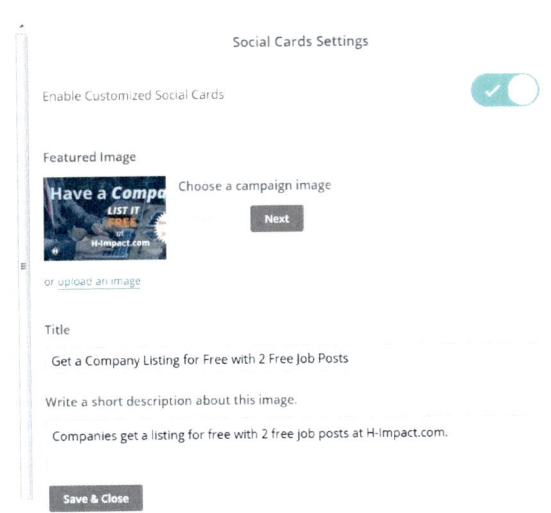

To finish customizing the **Social Cards**, click **Save & Close.**

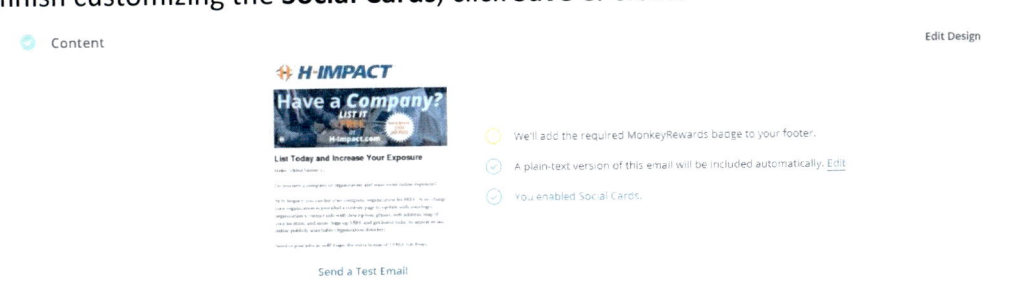

Social Media Connection

Along with **Social Cards, MailChimp** users can send posts out to **Social Media** platforms when **Email Campaigns** are sent.

Campaign URL

Prior to connecting our campaign to the **Social Media** platforms, let's edit the **Campaign URL** identified **URL** next to the **Share your campaign** label to make it more user friendly. The **Campaign URL** is a reference to a web page created and hosted by **MailChimp.** It will be used when **MailChimp** posts users' **Campaign** content to **Social Media** platforms or when a user would like to share the email's content on line with any one regardless if they received the email or not. This **URL** will be redirected to from the **Social Media** platforms and will display a page that contains the same content and similar layout included in the **Campaign** email that is sent to the recipients. **MailChimp** allows you to change the page name part of the **Campaign URL**. From the **Setup** step, to edit the **Campaign URL,** click the **Edit** link.

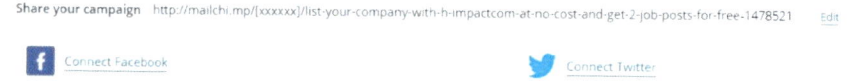

The **Edit Campaign URL** dialogue box appears.

Let's remove the auto number placed at the end of the **Campaign URL**. Click **Save**.

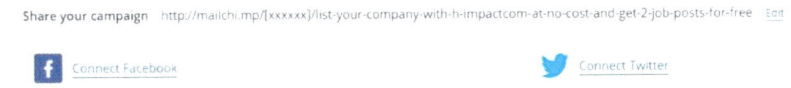

Upon clicking **Save**, the **Campaign URL** identified by the **URL** next to the **Share your campaign** label should now display without the auto number previously at the end of the **URL**.

Now let's connect to the **Social Media** platforms, which will link to the **Campaign URL**. **MailChimp** offers **Social Media Auto post** and **Auto-tweet** options for **Facebook** and **Twitter** that simultaneously post to these **Social Media** platforms upon sending **Email Campaigns**. In order to take advantage of the **Social Media Auto Post** option, you must configure **MailChimp** to use your **Facebook** or **Twitter** accounts by supplying the username and password credentials for the respective **Social Media** platform.

To connect to **Facebook**, click the **Connect Facebook** button.

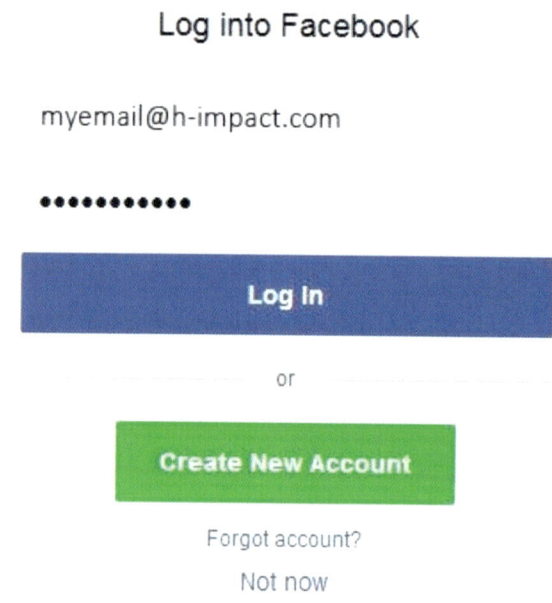

Click **Log In** upon entering **Facebook** credentials.

Choose a **Facebook** personal profile or page to post under.

Click the **link slider** to edit the **publishing profile** or **page** and **post message**.

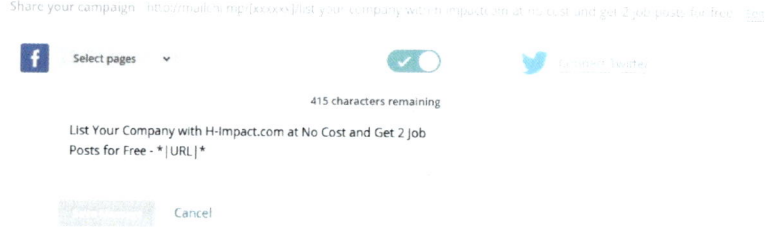

Use the Select pages drop down to choose the personal profile or a page to post from. Select **H-Impact (Facebook Page)** in order to post to and post as the **H-Impact** Page.

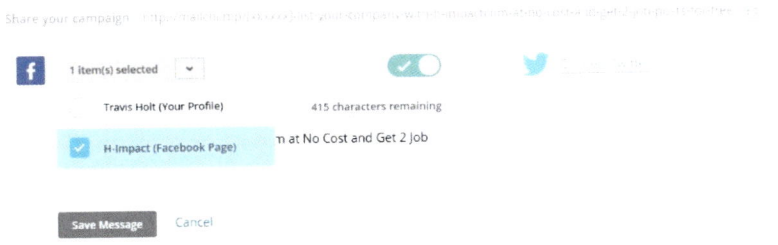

Notice the drowdown list now identifies that there is **1 item(s) selected**. Review the message in the textbox for accuracy and edit the message as needed. Note that the **MERGE field** tag *|URL|* references the Url which is represented by the **Share your campaign** link which links to a **MailChimp** hosted version of the **Campaign Email**.

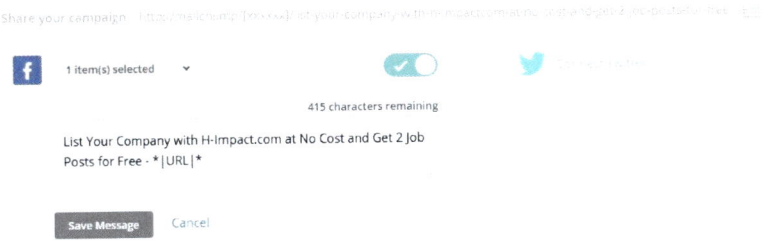

Once you have finished editing your **Facebook** message, click **Save Message** to save the message and confirm the **Company Page** to post to and post as the **Company Page**.

To connect to **Twitter**, click the **Authorize app** button.

Click the **link slider** to edit the **post message**.

Review the message in the textbox for accuracy and edit the message as needed. Note that the **MERGE field** tag ***|URL|*** references the Url which is represented by the **Share your campaign** link which links to a **MailChimp** hosted version of the **Campaign Email**.

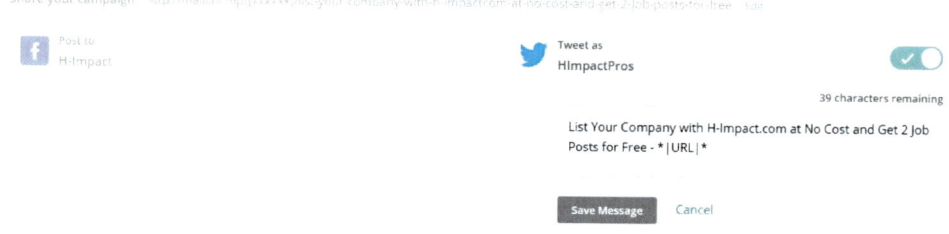

Once you have finished editing your **Twitter** message, click **Save Message** to save the message.

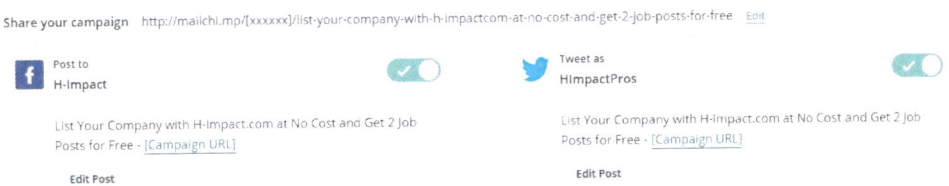

Settings and Tracking

While building **Campaigns** using the **New Campaign Builder**, **MailChimp** provides a **Settings** and **Tracking** area with options that can be configured for each **Campaign** that is created. The current state of these options is displayed in this area with **Edit** links to change these options.

Settings

MailChimp provides a **Settings** area with options that can be configured for each **Campaign** that is created. There are currently 2 settings that you can update with a **Forever Free** account. One allows you to personalize the email's **To** field and the other is designed to minimize errors that may result from improper video display, if videos are included in your email. To update the **Settings** section, click the **Edit** link next to **Settings**.

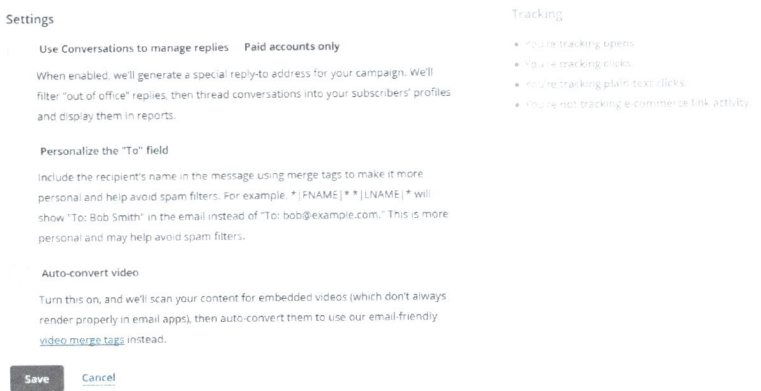

Now check the **Personalize the "To" field** checkbox. Then choose the **MERGE** tag combination with the **First Name** and **Last Name** option. This usually results in higher **Open** and **Click** rates instead of the default email address. Email clients and recipients are less likely to perceive the email you send as spam when there is a personalized **To** line in the emails you send.

 Personalize the "To" field

Include the recipient's name in the message using merge tags to make it more personal and help avoid spam filters. For example, *|FNAME|* *|LNAME|* will show "To: Bob Smith" in the email instead of "To: bob@example.com." This is more personal and may help avoid spam filters.

Specify a merge tag for the recipient's name

|FNAME| *|LNAME|*

We will leave the **Auto-convert video** option unchecked considering a video is not included in our email. This option will scan your email for video tags and will replace them with tags that are more compatible with most email clients to ensure the best display for videos you include. The other option to **Use Conversations to manage replies** is only available for paid accounts and as a result, will not be covered in this book.

Click **Save** to save the **Settings**.

Notice the current status of the **To** field now states the **Your 'To' field is personalized with merge tags**.

Tracking

MailChimp provides a **Tracking** area with options that can be configured for each **Campaign** that is created. There are currently 6 settings that you can update with a **Forever Free** account. To update the **Tracking** section, click the **Edit** link next to **Tracking.**

We'll stick with the defaults for all **Tracking** options. Track options that are currently selected are **Track opens**, **Track clicks** and **Track plain text clicks**. The remaining options require active 3rd party account with an **Ecommerce solution**, **Google**

Analytics, **ClickTale**, **Salesforce**, and **Capsule**. For the purposes of this book we will not cover these integrations. To understand these integrations and more please refer to www.mailchimp.com .

Click **Save** to save the **Tracking** options.

Tracking

☑ **Track opens**

Discover who opens your campaigns by tracking the number of times an invisible web beacon embedded in the campaign is downloaded. Learn more

☑ **Track clicks**   Required on free accounts

Discover which campaign links were clicked, how many times they were clicked, and who did the clicking.

☑ **Track plain-text clicks**   Required on free accounts

Track clicks in the plain-text version of your email by replacing all links with tracking URLs. Learn more

☐ **E-commerce link tracking**

Track visitors to your website from your MailChimp campaigns, capture order information, and pass that information back to MailChimp. Then you can view purchase details, conversions, and total sales on the reports page. You can also set up segments based on your subscribers' purchase activity. Learn more

☐ Google Analytics link tracking

Track clicks from your campaigns all the way to purchases on your website. Requires Google Analytics on your website or Shopify Integration.

☐ ClickTale link tracking

Gain insight to how subscribers interact with your email content. Requires ClickTale on your website.

☐ Track stats in Salesforce

First, enable Salesforce in Account > Integrations.

☐ Track member activity in Capsule

First, enable Capsule in Account > Integrations.

Save Cancel

The current **Tracking** option defaults should still display.

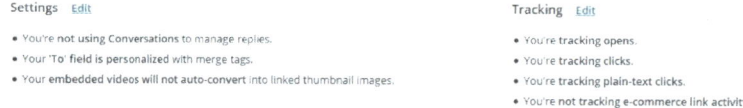

Confirm

The **Confirm** page displays titled **"Your email campaign is ready to send!"** MailChimp provides this page as a means to review the **Campaign** prior to completing it. It summarizes the critical elements of the campaign and allows you to edit them if needed before sending the **eBlast** to the recipients.

Each element appears with their **current value** with an **Edit** button that allows you to edit the value if you wish. There is a **Green Check mark** at the beginning of each row that shows each element has been completed. A **yellow caution Exclamation mark** will show if the element may need your attention.

The elements with their current values include:

- To
- From
- Subject
- Content (with Template Design, Monkey rewards, Plain-text Email option, Social Cards, and Test Email)
- Share your campaign
- Facebook Connection with Auto Post
- Twitter Connection with Auto Post
- Settings
- Tracking

Notice the **Send Later** schedule button next to the **Send Now** button at the top right corner of the page. The **Send Later** schedule button can be used to schedule **Campaigns** which you may prepare in advance but send at another date in time. For the purposes of this book, we will send our **eBlast** manually and in real-time. As a result, the scheduling feature will not be covered. For more information on scheduling **Campaigns** please visit www.mailchimp.com.

For **Resulting Email Example A**,

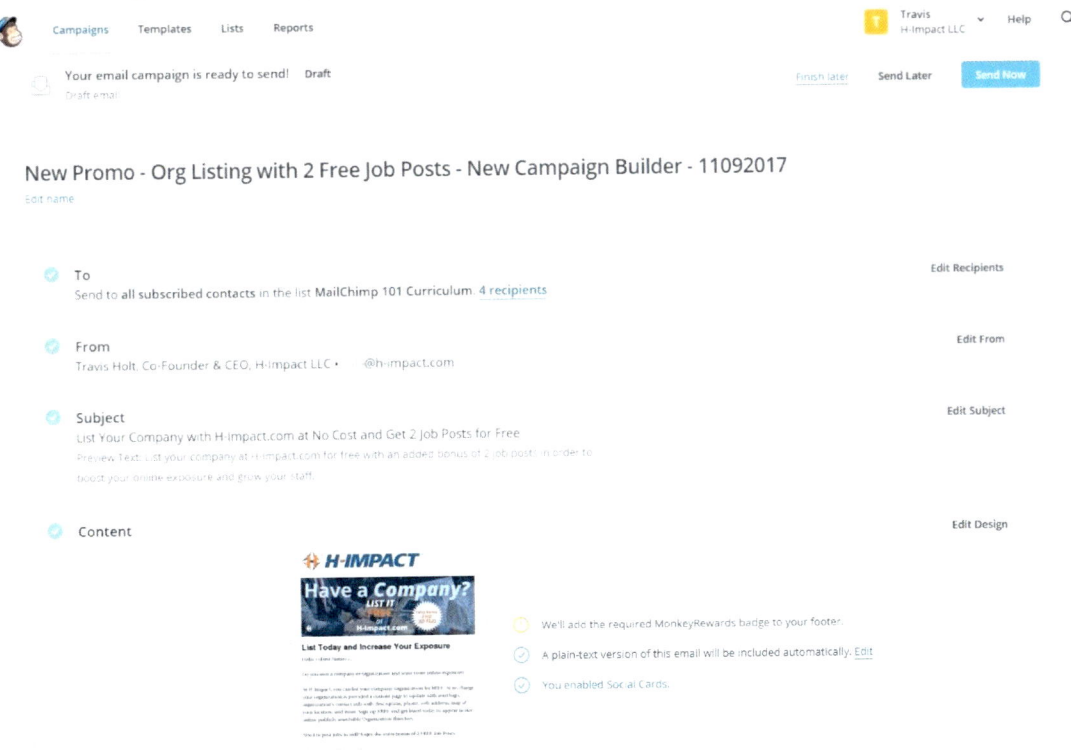

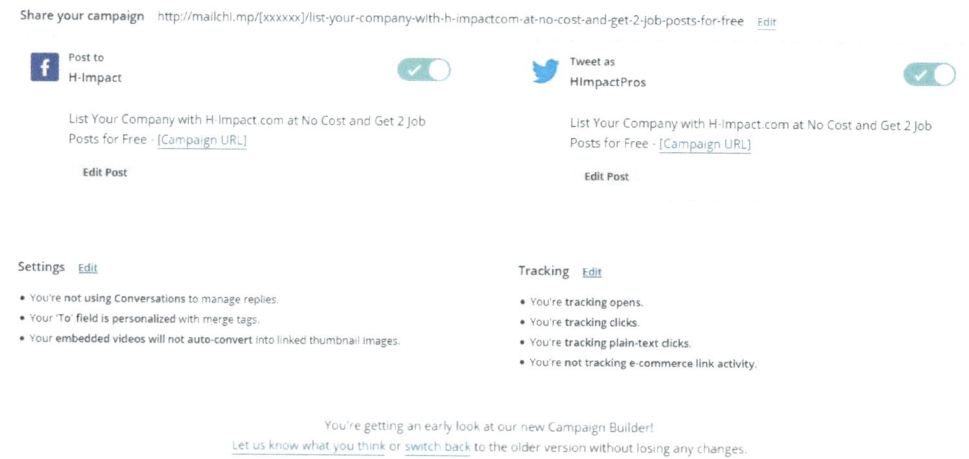

After you've reviewed all the elements of your **Campaign**, you are ready to complete the **Campaign** and send the **eBlast**. To proceed click the **Send Now** button.

Send Campaign

A **Prepare for launch** window displays with an animated graphic including a chimp's hand and forefinger over a red button. The text below the animation reaffirms you are about to send a campaign to the **list name with the number of subscribers.** You are presented a **Send Now** button and a **Cancel** link.

Press **Send Now** to send the campaign.

A confirmation page appears with an animated graphic with a chimp's hand pointing straight up with a green background. Text appears below the animated graphic as follows:

High Fives!

Your campaign is in the send queue and will go out shortly.

- For *Resulting Email Example A,*
  "**New Promo - Org Listing with 2 Free Job Posts - 11072017**" will be sent to [#] subscribers from the list, "**MailChimp 101 Curriculum**".
- For *Resulting Email Example B,*

"New Article Release - The Walls Have Eyes - 08082017" will be sent to [#] subscribers from the list, **"MailChimp 101 Curriculum"**.

This page also allows you to click on:

- A gray button titled **Track Performance in Reports** to the **Report** for this **Campaign**.
- A gray button titled **Track Performance in Mobile App** to **Download** the latest **MailChimp** app for Mobile Devices
- A link to a **web page** displaying your **Campaign's Email** that can be used for the public to view that may not have received your email

For the purposes of this book you may click the **Report** link to begin monitoring the **Campaign's Performance** including **Opens**, **Clicks**, **Subcribers**, **Links**, and **locations opened**. You may also use the link to the web page to view how the **eBlast** appeared in the **Subscribers** inbox. This link is handy if you would like to share it with someone that is not in your original **Subscriber list**. As far as the **Mobile Devices** option, it is totally up to you if you would like to download and install these apps on compatible mobile devices.

Chapter 4: Creating Campaigns

For *Resulting Email Example A,*

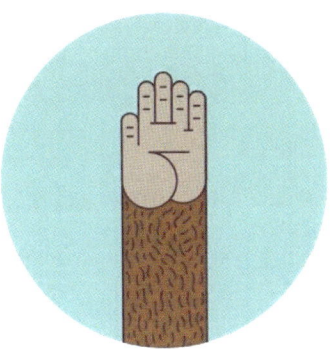

High Fives!

Your campaign is in the
send queue and will go out shortly.

"New Promo - Org Listing with 2 Free Job Posts - 11072017" will be sent to 4 subscribers from the list "MailChimp 101 Curriculum"

Track Performance In Reports

Track Performance In Mobile App

View or share it at: http://mailchi.mp/2f2468060770/list-your-company-with-h-impactcom-at-no-cost-and-get-2-job-posts-for-free

For *Resulting Email Example B,*

Resulting Emails & Posts

Email Example A

This email was generated from the email we built in the **Templates** chapter under the section titled **Create Drag and Drop Template - Step-by-Step.** Here is what the resulting email looks like using this **Template** that was sent out from our **Campaign**.

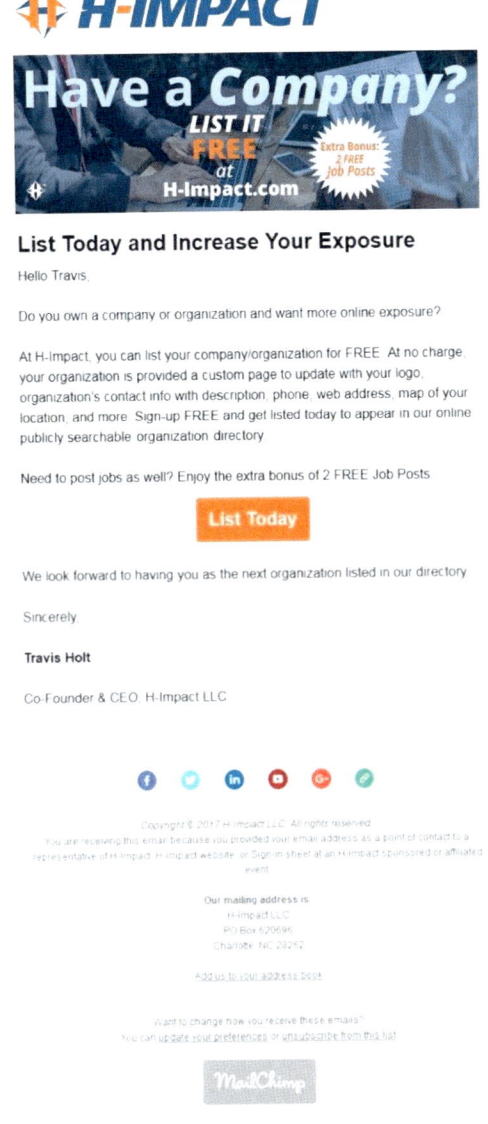

Post Example A

Facebook Post

H-Impact
Published by MailChimp [?] · 57 mins ·

List Your Company with H-Impact.com at No Cost and Get 2 Job Posts for Free

Get a Company Listing for Free with 2 Free Job Posts
Companies get a listing for free with 2 free job posts at H-Impact.com.
US11.CAMPAIGN-ARCHIVE.COM

Twitter Tweet

Email Example B

The email was designed and stored in a similar fashion to the **Template** we created earlier in the section titled **Create Drag and Drop Template - Step by Step**. Here is what the resulting email looks like using this **Template** that was sent out from our **Campaign**.

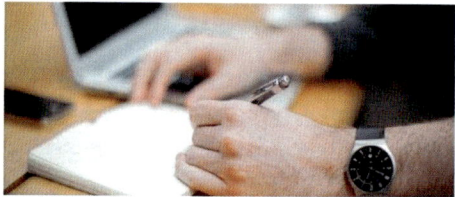

NEW EMPLOYMENT ARTICLE RELEASED

Hello Travis,

H-Impact is pleased to announce the release of a new article from our Employment Articles Section. We've received great feedback from Job Seekers, Employees, and Employers on how helpful our articles have been. Check out the newly released article title and summary below.

NEW RELEASE

The Walls Have Eyes

Have you ever felt like someone was watching you and you were 100% sure there was no one in the room? That eerie feeling that you are being monitored has no boundaries and can sometimes make its way into our work environments. The thing is, at work if you sense someone or something is watching you, proceed with caution because you might just be right? Join us for **"The Walls Have Eyes" by Travis Leonard** as he provides an in-depth look at why employees should mind there P's and Q's inside, and in many cases, outside the office to limit any conflicts of interest with their current or future Employers.

Read More

We hope you continue to find our articles informative and helpful in all aspects of your Employment efforts. Thank you!

Sincerely

Travis Holt

Co-Founder & CEO, H-Impact LLC

Copyright © 2017 H-Impact LLC, All rights reserved.
You are receiving this email because you provided your email address as a point of contact to a representative of H-Impact, H-Impact website, or Sign-in sheet at an H-Impact sponsored or affiliated event.

Our mailing address is:
H-Impact LLC
PO Box 620696
Charlotte, NC 28252

Add us to your address book

Want to change how you receive these emails?
You can update your preferences or unsubscribe from this list.

Chapter 5: **Summary**

As you have seen, if you own a business or are a marketing professional, **MailChimp** can be a powerful tool to have at your disposal.

MailChimp is available right now and doesn't require a cost to get started. New Businesses can get up and running quickly and start sending messages for promotions, event notifications or general updates to their contacts, customers or potential customers. As we have discovered, these messages can further be personalized for the recipient using **MailChimp's** dynamic data driven platform in conjunction with **MERGE Field** tags.

All users can take advantage of **MailChimp's** extensive reporting capabilities. Once a **Campaign** has been launched and emails have been sent, the user can then jump right into an analytics or reporting role. **MailChimp's** reporting platform allows real time and historical analytics to be performed against key metrics like **Opens**, **Clicks**, **Unsubscribes,** or **Bouncebacks,** which can be used as a means of determining how well the **Email Campaigns** are performing. Businesses can use the analytics on these critical metrics and more to determine what adjustments, minor or major, might need to be considered to result in a more effective **Email Marketing** strategy. Adjustments can be made in more obvious areas like the **Email Template** design that may require changes to the layout, images and content, or **Campaign** meta information like **Subject**, **Pretext**, **To** field format and/or **Sender Name**.

MailChimp allows businesses to pick a plan that best fits to their business needs. Ultimately, **MailChimp's** flexible plan structure is set up to grow with the business' needs. As we have discussed, our focus for this book has been around the **New**

Business Forever Free plan. The **New Business** plan is great for many businesses getting off the ground and businesses that need to reach their customers with little to no learning curve and at **no cost**. If a business needs to grow beyond the **New Business Forever Free** plan's 2,000 subscriber limit and 12,000 per month email limit, **MailChimp** provides paid plans compatible with the business growth. The **Growing Business (Starting at $10 a Month)** plan allows businesses to enjoy **MailChimp** with the benefit of a competitive pricing model. This plan is based on the number of subscribers the business has or email credits the business needs. Finally, the more established businesses can choose the **Pro Marketer (Additional $199 a Month)** plan designed for more established businesses with larger subscriber lists, needing to send higher email volumes with the added advantage of more analytics tools at their disposal.

Email Marketing is an essential part of communication for many businesses. Your level of understanding about **MailChimp** and all it has to offer can result in stronger brand awareness for your company or organization resulting in greater profits overall. As you become more familiar with **MailChimp**, we are certain you will become appreciative of the features covered in this book, those you discover on your own, and those that will be available in the future.

About H-Impact

H-Impact LLC, founded November 18, 2004 in Charlotte, NC, strives to serve the greater community, the public, its clients, and students in technical training, employment and consulting services.

We leverage our team of consultants and trainers with years of experience to best serve our clients and students. Check out the exciting things available today at H-Impact.

- Students can register for our **How to Unleash Email Marketing with MailChimp** course taught by the author Travis L. Holt, as well as other courses by creating a Free account and registering on our site. Review our event listings here:
  www.h-impact.com/all-upcoming-events.

- Visit H-Impact today to read articles by this author, Travis L. Holt and more on topics like Employment, Business, and Healthcare. Read articles here: www.h-impact.com/article-search.

- Companies and Organizations can visit H-Impact today to list their Company or Organization at no cost on the Organization Listings page at: www.h-impact.com/organization-search.

- Job Seekers can create employment profiles Free and apply for jobs. See our listings at:
www.h-impact.com/job-listings.

- Companies and Organizations can post jobs (2 Free) or purchase and post more than 2 jobs at our competitive rates listed at:
www.h-impact.com/job-post-pricing.

- All visitors may review our Free computer training videos from certified professionals including this author and more on Microsoft at www.h-impact.com/video-viewer.

- Visitors may also subscribe to more in-depth videos on Microsoft Office by subscribing to one of our affordable plans at:
www.h-impact.com/plans.

Contact H-Impact

You may contact H-Impact about this book or any of our services by mail at

H-Impact LLC
PO Box 620696
Charlotte, NC 28262
www.h-impact.com

Email at: unleashmailchimp@h-impact.com

Web at: www.h-impact.com/contact

Connect On Social Media

Join the discussion on our various Social Media platforms.

- **Linkedin:**
www.linkedin.com/company/h-impact?trk=biz-companies-cym

- **Facebook:**
  www.facebook.com/pages/H-Impact/763388233770079

- **Pinterest:**
  https://www.pinterest.com/HimpactPros/pins/

- **Twitter:**
  www.twitter.com/HImpactPros

- **YouTube:**
  www.youtube.com/channel/UCwR9pelif7dLOzVS4cBGRKA

- **Google Plus:**
  www.plus.google.com/101189913328700271420/about?hl=en

Made in the USA
Middletown, DE
09 February 2024

49362993R00100